REBEL QUEEN

REBEL QUEEN

The Cold War, Misogyny, and the
Making of a Grandmaster

SUSAN POLGAR

With a Foreword by Yasser Seirawan

GRAND
CENTRAL

NEW YORK   BOSTON

Grand Central Publishing
Hachette Book Group
1290 Avenue of the Americas, New York, NY 10104
grandcentralpublishing.com
@grandcentralpub

First edition: March 2025

Grand Central Publishing is a division of Hachette Book Group, Inc. The Grand Central Publishing name and logo is a registered trademark of Hachette Book Group, Inc.

The publisher is not responsible for websites (or their content) that are not owned by the publisher.

Grand Central Publishing books may be purchased in bulk for business, educational, or promotional use. For information, please contact your local bookseller or the Hachette Book Group Special Markets Department at special.markets@hbgusa.com.

Print book interior design by name Timothy Shaner, NightandDayDesign.biz

Library of Congress Control Number: 2024950413

ISBNs: 9781538757291 (hardcover), 9781538757314 (ebook)

Printed in the United States of America

LSC-C

Printing 1, 2024

Dedicated to

My parents, who sacrificed so much to give me an opportunity to succeed

My sisters, for their love and support

My husband, Paul, who has been an amazing partner in the adventure of life

and

My kids, who make my life complete

FOREWORD

It is a great honor for me to be asked to write a foreword for Susan Polgar's memoir. My goodness, what a life Susan has led! In spite of her innumerable challenges, she has had an extraordinary amount of success.

Etta James sang, "This is a man's world...this is a man's world..." Which Rick James famously echoed, "But it wouldn't be nothing, nothing, without a woman or a girl..."

Klara and Laszlo Polgar delivered to the world not one daughter but three. They would form a triumvirate phenomenon, known as the Polgar sisters, that would upend the chess world. They were the outlier in this male-dominated sport where no one believed it was possible for women to rise to its highest ranks.

Susan was the oldest of the three girls and to her fell the harsh, even cruel, duty of being a trailblazer. Trailblazers are the folks who take spears in the back as well as the chest. The world of chess in the 1970s was truly a man's world—in every sense. Susan would blaze a trail not only for herself but also for her siblings. Not only that, but she smoothed the path for every lady playing chess today. Sad to say, many tried to stop her. Happy to say, they failed. Susan's memoir is a testimony to that fact.

It is often said that great artists and athletes have a way of bringing out the best and worst in others. This was the case for Susan. In fact, it started early, very early in her career. Having qualified for the Men's World Championship cycle, the Hungarian chess authorities didn't think *How do we help our Zsuzsa compete against the world?* Rather, their effort started and ended with a vow: *How do we exclude this upstart?* Exclusion the first time around was easy. But they didn't know who they were up against. They didn't count on the indefatigable spirit and the outsized chess skills of Susan Polgar.

Why are the World Championships, the World Cup, the Olympiad, the US Championships now all called "open" championships today? Ask Susan. After her initial exclusion from the Men's Championship, the word *Men's* was dropped from the official world championship cycle competition.

Being a professional lady chess player was one of the most difficult professions in the world at that time. The rewards were not great, but Susan would not have it any other way. Susan became the first woman to earn the title grandmaster, as in "male grandmaster." Better drop the *male* here as well.

I sometimes wondered where Susan got her strength and motivation to keep on fighting. Perhaps it had something to do with her family background. All of Susan's grandparents were Holocaust survivors. Sadly, many members of her family did not survive the Holocaust. It is from her family, a shared history, that Susan gets her iron-willed determination. She is a fighter. A warrior. A great lady. A mother. A wife. And, I'm very proud to also say, my friend.

Susan is now living in her true vintage years, but the accolades keep on coming. In 2019, she was inducted into the US Chess Hall of Fame, and then in 2023, she was inducted into the World Chess Hall of Fame. The following year, the World Chess Federation (FIDE) at the 2024 Budapest Olympiad, recognized her as the

"Best Female Trainer" in history. Considering her students' many championship titles, it was an honor well earned.

I hope you will enjoy Susan's memoir as she takes you through a life of great challenges and great rewards. A person who can look back over her shoulders and say with a wistful smile, "Wow. Did I really do all that?"

GM Yasser Seirawan
St. Louis, October 9, 2024

ONE

My father was obsessed with the idea of genius since long before he was my father. He thought about it more than almost any other subject. The earliest records of Laszlo's passion are from the letters he would send to my mother, Klara, in the 1960s, when they were both still teenagers studying to be teachers. He lived in Budapest, she in the small village of Vilok, just over the border from Hungary in modern-day Ukraine. Even then, my dad truly believed he had unlocked some long-overlooked secret to human achievement, one that he insisted could turn any healthy child into a genius. "Prodigies are not miracles, but natural phenomena," he wrote. For him, the key to fostering genius in young children was to "create the opportunity for them to do what they love." He told her about his plans to have six kids and to raise each of them to be exceptional. My mother fell in love with his ideas before she fell in love with him. "We both thought we would redeem the world, create something wonderful in our own field," she once told me.

My father first began researching the nature of genius sometime after he left his hometown of Gyongyos for Budapest at the age of fourteen. His parents had divorced a couple of years before.

And, in the hopes of starting fresh in a big city, he struck out on his own, moving into a Jewish orphanage for a few years while he finished high school. He spent whatever free time he had at the library, reading all he could about the psychology of high achievement and investigating the lives of his favorite minds.

Out of that work grew a conviction that geniuses—and especially prodigies—are made, not born. One of his favorite quotations was from Aristotle, who remarked that "Excellence is never an accident. It's always the result of high intention, sincere effort, and intelligent execution." He took that passion into college, earning a degree in philosophy and psychopedagogy and ultimately becoming a teacher and counselor in boarding schools for boys.

My parents eventually married in 1967 and settled in Budapest. They borrowed money from their families to buy our first home, a cramped two-room house in a neighborhood called Angyalfold ("Land of Angels"). And they worked multiple jobs so they could pay their debts off as soon as possible.

By the time I arrived on the scene on April 19, 1969, my father had already developed an elaborate method for fostering brilliance in children from an early age. More than that, my parents had officially decided to make me their first experiment. Not only would I be homeschooled, which was practically unheard-of in Hungary at the time, but my education would focus on a single topic—one they intended to choose for me. As it turned out, they wouldn't have to.

I first discovered chess one afternoon just shy of my fourth birthday. I've heard the story so many times I can't say for certain which parts I actually remember and which have been told to me. My mother was in the kitchen preparing dinner when I made my way to the old beat-up cabinet in our entryway. I knew I wasn't allowed in there. But tell a three-year-old she can't have something, and it only makes her want it more.

Rummaging through the folded linens and old clothes, I wasn't quite sure what I was looking for until I saw it. A mysterious wooden rectangle with a strange black-and-white pattern—I had no idea what it was, but I was drawn to it. As I pulled it out, the rectangle hinged open into a square, sending a stream of carved figurines tumbling to the floor in a long crackling crash. I knew I was in trouble.

The noise sent my mother rushing into the entryway. She would have been only twenty-six, but had already grown into the role of the Yiddishe Mame—doting and warm much of the time, but a firm enforcer when she needed to be. She found me on the floor, the board and pieces spread out around me. I held up the small horse-shaped carving I had grasped in my hand, proud of the new plaything I had discovered. "Look, Mommy. More toys!"

"That's not a toy, Zsuzsikam," her favorite term of affection for me (literally "my little Suzie").

"That's a game. But you'll have to wait for Daddy to come home. He'll teach you to play."

Neither of my parents had any real interest in the game before I came along. My mother didn't even know how to play. My father went through a chess phase as a teenager, but he mainly took up the game to impress a girl (a fact I only recently learned from him). During his first week of high school, an attractive young woman approached him and tried to recruit him to the chess team. It didn't matter that he had never played, she explained. They would teach him. He signed up on the spot and ended up losing all but his final game that year. After spending his summer studying and playing chess as much as he could, he gradually improved to the point where he could win most of his high school games. His team even made it to the Budapest final in his last year of high school. But he didn't play much after that.

It just so happened that around the time I dragged that old chess set out of hiding, the game was having a cultural resurgence. It was 1973, less than a year after a young grandmaster from Brooklyn named Bobby Fischer had become a global celebrity with his historic World Championship victory over the Soviet Boris Spassky. He was the first American in the modern era to win the title. And he was cast in the press as a Cold Warrior, a lone Western genius who had single-handedly defeated a Soviet chess machine that many considered unbeatable. Maybe this was on my father's mind when he decided to teach me the game, or maybe it was just a coincidence.

At the very least, my parents saw chess as an opportunity. I was genuinely interested in learning how to play. So instead of choosing an area for me to excel in—chemistry, say, or the violin—they figured they could put this natural curiosity to use.

The day after my run-in with that chess set, my father sat me down in the kitchen for our first lesson. I'm sure it seemed like just another day for me. But for my parents, it was their first chance to put their plans for me into action. I could tell something special was about to happen just by the excitement in their voice when they called me to the table.

"You want to play a fun game, Zsuzsi?!" my father asked me.

"Is it the game with the horsey?"

"Great guess! How'd you know?!"

By then, my father had already figured out the fundamentals of his teaching philosophy, an approach he would summarize as "genius = labor + luck + favorable circumstances." He also believed that with each passing year, a child's potential to "reach the summit," as he sometimes put it, diminishes. So there was no time to waste. Chess was an ideal test case in many ways. If his methods worked, the results would be apparent almost immediately. And any improvements after that would be relatively easy to measure. Before any of that could happen, though, I'd need to learn to play.

But how does one teach a young child such a complicated game? I don't know when he found time to plan his first lesson—he often worked nights in those years—but my father seemed to know exactly what to do. Instead of teaching me chess in one sitting, he would teach me a much simpler game he called "king against king." In this game, each side has a king and nothing else. The purpose of the game was to move your one piece from your first rank (the row of squares closest to you) to the other side of the board before your opponent. As in traditional chess, each king could only move one square in each direction and could never come within one square of the other side's king.

It's a simple idea. But it was just complicated enough to keep me focused. And it definitely didn't seem like work, not to me at least. I was just playing a game with my dad—something I would have wanted to do anyway. I would have spent all day with him at the chess board, if my father only had the time to give.

When he was satisfied with that game, he introduced a new one: pawn wars. The rules were very similar to king against king. The goal was to be the first player to advance a single pawn to the other side of the board. Once my interest started to fall off, he'd introduce the rook; then the bishop; then the queen. The horse-shaped knight that first caught my attention he saved for last—not only because it's the trickiest piece to master, but also as a reward. "Daddy, are we going to learn how the horsey moves today?" I remember asking at one of those first lessons. "You mean the knight? Why, are you afraid it's going to gallop away? I promise we'll get to it soon, Zsuzsi. But first we need to meet the knight's good friend, the bishop." Within a month or so, I had learned how each piece moves. More important, though, I had gotten weeks of practice making decisions about how to move those pieces and watching the consequences of those decisions play out.

Once I had internalized the basic rules, we started on simple checkmate patterns. My favorite was the "smothered mate," which is when one side delivers checkmate to an opposing king that is blocked on all sides, or "smothered," by its own pieces. Finding those winning moves over the board felt uniquely satisfying. I also liked that this particular checkmate only worked with my favorite piece, the knight. "Please show me more smothers. Please!" I'd beg my father. "More smothers?!" he'd say, with an exaggerated look of astonishment. "Well, alright. But just one more."

It wasn't long before he had taught me all of the rules. I learned that in addition to winning and losing, there are also draws—which means that neither side wins. Sometimes this occurs because a position is a stalemate, or there isn't sufficient material to checkmate. Sometimes a player can offer a draw and give the opponent the option to accept or decline.

At the end of each session, my father would always remind me that "Every day you should know more than you did the day before." The only times our lessons felt serious were when my father could tell I wasn't trying. If he saw my mind wandering, he would pull me back to the chess board with a single curt "Focus!" or "Concentrate!" He never scolded me for making mistakes or losing a game. It went against his views. But any lack of discipline he simply wouldn't tolerate.

On the other hand, when I showed even small signs of improvement—by finding a creative move or solving a difficult puzzle—he'd gush with praise. "Fantastic!" or "Amazing!" he'd shout. This was more than just fatherly pride, although I'm sure that was part of it. Positive reinforcement was instrumental to his approach to teaching. "If the parents and tutors tell the child that they are foolish and bad," he would later explain, "the child will probably truly believe this. But the opposite also applies: if we say that they are clever and skillful, they will believe that as well."

My mother still remembers the day my father and I played our first game. She arrived back from work to see her three-year-old, kneeling on a kitchen chair, carefully considering her moves in a game that, weeks earlier, that same child had mistaken for a toy. This was a little girl who couldn't sit still long enough to hear the end of a children's story. Yet by the time I had mastered the rules of chess, it was my favorite thing to do.

The fact is, much of who I would become—not just as a chess player, but as a teacher, a parent, and an individual—can be traced back to my time with my father at those living-room chess sessions in Budapest. I wasn't just mastering the rules of chess. I was learning lessons and skills that I would draw on for the rest of my life. My parents were showing me, in a very deliberate way, how to remain motivated in the face of despair and frustration. How to embrace setbacks and mistakes as opportunities. And how seemingly lost positions could, through small, incremental improvements, give way to success. Most people learn these lessons at some point in life. I just learned them earlier.

TWO

I don't have many memories from those first few years. If I try, I can flash on the sandbox at the Russian-language daycare I attended as a three-year-old, or a sunny day in my garden playing with my dog, or riding a four-person bicycle with my parents in the park on Margaret Island. My first visit to the Voros Meteor chess club at the age of four is one of those memories.

I had been playing chess for less than a year, and it had already become my favorite thing to do.

By then, my daily chess lessons with my father took up hours each day as we tackled increasingly complicated aspects of the game. I would work on reading and writing a little each day, and math lessons were still a major part of my father's instruction, but chess kept consuming more and more of my attention. My father had this gift for presenting each new idea as if it were some exciting discovery, a kind of arcane knowledge instilling magical powers, like in the fairy tales he and my mother would read to me. "Zsuzsi, wait until you see this! It's amazing! You're going to love it!" he'd say when introducing a new lesson. Sometimes, he'd deliberately withhold some idea or principle or instructional game, just to sharpen my appetite. "I'm not sure you're ready for this next part. I think

we'd better wait." It got me every time. "I'm ready, Daddy! I promise! Please! I need to know!"

Pretty soon, my parents were using whatever money they
could spare on chess books. My dad and I would spend weeks
poring over classic Hungarian books like Laszlo Alfoldy's *33 Chess
Lessons*, or *200 Opening Traps* by Emil Gelenczei, extracting every
last insight and bit of wisdom we could from each page. My father
would usually read through the text himself before translating
the ideas to me over the board in a manner a four-year-old could
grasp. By the time we were through with a book, it was dog-eared
and creased within an inch of its life.

My father used these materials to create lessons tailored to my
specific strengths and weaknesses. His idea was that if I felt like I
was improving each day, I would remain motivated to keep learning more. This, in turn, would lead to more improvement, which
would lead to more motivation, and so on. It worked beautifully.

Finding mates in four, or winning material with pins, skew-
ers, and forks—these tasks quickly became second nature to me.
He'd make whole lessons out of famous "miniatures" (short games
where each player makes only ten or twenty moves), some of which
I would commit to memory and recite to him without the board
in front of me. The best miniatures tend to be beautiful in their
ingenuity and elegance while also illustrating some larger principle. And for me in those years, memorizing miniatures was like
learning a great poem by heart. Through repetition—by replaying
the game, first on the board and then over and over in my head—I
came to understand on a very intuitive level how certain combinations of moves, played in exactly the right order, can build to a
satisfying conclusion in which checkmate is inevitable.

Sometimes, when my father would head off to work, he'd leave
me a miniature to memorize while he was gone. Technically, he
was giving me homework. But it never felt that way. It was more
like a present from him to me, a treat he had hand-picked for my

enjoyment. When I was confident I had committed it to memory, I'd ask my mother to quiz me, which she gladly did, even though she still didn't know how to play.

And then there were the actual games—my favorite part. As precocious as I was, my father was still the stronger player in those years. So he would carefully calibrate his moves to make the games just challenging enough to keep me engaged. He'd never go so far as to take one of his pieces off the board to give me an advantage, as some parents do. He believed that this altered the dynamics of the game too much. He would, however, deliberately insert the occasional mistake into his play to keep things competitive. I didn't always win, but our games were never boring—even the ones that stretched on for an hour or two. Soon I was counting the seconds until my next chess lesson each day. I was falling in love with the game. Still, it remained an open question what would happen when I sat down with a player who wasn't my father or my teacher, but an actual opponent. It was only when he finally thought I was ready that my dad brought me to the chess club.

My father had spotted a sign for the Voros Meteor club on his way home from work one evening that summer on what was then Lenin Boulevard. When he took me there for the first time a few weeks later, he didn't tell me where we were going. It was a surprise, he said.

Getting there was somewhat of a hassle, I remember—a walk to the bus, an even longer walk to the metro, and then more walking after that. "Is this where we're going?" I'd ask him at nearly every stop and station, pointing out of the window at whatever caught my eye. "No, not here. You'll have to wait a little longer, Zsuzsi." I usually hated waiting, but this was different. My dad and I were on an adventure. I was just hoping we'd end up at a sweet shop, or maybe someplace with rides.

Lenin Boulevard was a carnival compared to our quiet street in Angyalfold, crowded with grown people hurrying in all directions around me and lined on both sides with shops and restaurants and theaters. It was always a special thrill for me to visit new parts of the city and see new faces. I'd make up my own story about where some stranger I had just spotted might be going, or what they did for a living. This woman in the colorful dress was on her way to act in a play in that theater over there; that man is a very important businessperson with a beautiful wife and three kids and a big house and a dog.

That heady feeling of anticipation completely went away the instant I saw our destination—a colorless stone building in the middle of an otherwise lively street. I didn't know what went on inside there, but there surely weren't going to be rides. I still remember holding my father's hand as we went up the building's stairwell, the glossy mustard paint on the walls, and the stale smell of tobacco smoke that grew stronger as we approached the club on the second floor.

Up until that point, chess was something that existed solely within the walls of our home, just a fun thing my dad and I did together. My father would tell me stories about Bobby Fischer sometimes, and I'd see pictures of players on the covers of the books and magazines we were studying from (all of them men).

What I saw as we entered the chess club didn't seem real. The playing area was just a single room populated entirely by adult men, most of whom were quite old. It had distinctive herringbone wood floors, and trophy cases along one wall. Scattered around the room were dozens of chess tables with players on either side hunched over in deep contemplation.

I was thunderstruck when it finally occurred to me what was happening—these men were all playing my favorite game. *How can this be? How long has this been going on without me? And where are the other children?* That all of these grown-ups would gather to play games and leave their kids at home—it was too much for my four-year-old mind to comprehend.

Just imagining the place now, I can hear the click-clacking of pieces against chess boards, the sound of old mechanical chess clocks being punched after each move, the din of hushed-tone conversations, the intermittent coughs and throat-clearings that would echo through the room, the occasional squeak of a chair against the floor. It was a combination of sounds that would become familiar to me in the years ahead, but it reached my ears for the first time that afternoon.

"Are you looking for a game?" one of the players asked my father.

"Not for me, no. For her," he said, looking down at me.

The men exploded with laughter, which surprised me. *What did my dad say that was so funny?*

"Yes, really, my daughter wants to play. Can anybody give her a game?"

Most of the men just went back to what they were doing. I imagine they thought my father was just a crazy person, but he didn't give up. He did a lap around the room, never letting go of my hand, politely asking each player if they wouldn't mind playing some chess with his little girl.

"I think she'll surprise you," he said to one of them. "I know she will."

Eventually one older man agreed to sit down with me, probably so that my dad would stop asking. This got yet another round of laughter and taunts from the other men. "Oh, you're going to play the little girl?" one of them remarked to my opponent. "Why, tired of losing to men?"

Within seconds, somebody was setting up a board for me and my opponent and stacking a couple of phone books on a chair for me to sit on so that I could reach the far side of the board. The other club members started pushing past each other to get a spot to watch from, like spectators at a prizefight. Before I knew it, there was a crowd of full-grown men gathered around the board, smoking and murmuring to one another, curious to see what I could do. At first I felt nervous, like I wasn't supposed to be there, although I wasn't sure why, exactly. The strange mix of laughter and hostility confused me and put me on edge. I didn't want to let go of my dad's hand. But I could see in his face that he wasn't concerned.

"Don't worry," he told me. "Just go show them what you can do."

Once I had a chess board in front of me, everything made sense again. This might have been a stuffy smoke-filled room full of old men I didn't know, but I felt at home. My parents had already explained to me that in chess, it doesn't matter who, exactly, is sitting on the other side of the board, or how old they are, or their size or gender or skin color. All that mattered was how well each player moved the pieces. I didn't really understand what they meant until that day.

I played several games that afternoon from my perch atop two phone books, the details of which I can't really remember. I know I won a few of them. The thing that stays with me, though, is the reaction I got from the old-timers. Every time I made a good move or avoided some beginner's trap my opponent had set for me, the crowd would give a little chuckle—not in the dismissive way they had laughed at my father, but out of surprise and approval, like a pat on the back. In those moments, I just felt special and powerful, like a fairy tale queen ready to conquer the world.

Sometimes, I'd look over to my father, who was just standing in the crowd silently with a smile on his face. I knew that look—it was the one he'd give me during our own games, when I surprised him with a good move. I knew I was doing something right.

When I'd actually beat one of the older players, the whole place would erupt with whoops and taunts and trash talk for my opponent. "How can you go home to your wife after losing to a little girl?!" one of the men shouted. Again, I didn't quite see what the big deal was. It wasn't like we were arm-wrestling, after all. This was chess! Why can't this man go home to his wife?

However confused I might have been, I was also having a whole lot of fun. I loved playing chess, especially when I won. And I loved taking the things my father had taught me and using them properly and in a way that made him proud. But I also loved getting these abrasive old men to change their minds about me—to actually root for me! These men weren't reacting in the goofy, exaggerated way that a parent applauds a young child—which is the only kind of praise I had experienced at that point, really. No, they were expressing themselves like grown-ups who were actually impressed—who couldn't believe what they were seeing. It was a kind of satisfaction I'd never felt before, a sense that I had earned all of this attention by doing something right. I wanted more of this feeling.

For my father, our little chess-club outing had its own significance. He had finally seen his theory put into practice, and not just in the laboratory setting of our kitchen. These were experienced club players trying their best to beat me, and some of them still couldn't. It wasn't conclusive proof that his methods worked, but it was enough for him to keep going.

THREE

M y visit to the chess club convinced my parents that I was
ready for a real competition, which was always part of
my father's plan. Both my mom and my dad had been
cautious about entering me in tournaments before then. I was
still only four and a half. And they feared that a bad tournament
experience—a string of losses, say, or even just a bad game—might
spoil whatever natural enthusiasm I was developing for the game.
Now that I had proven I could hold my own against strangers and
take defeats in stride, they saw no reason not to enter me in the
elementary school girls district championship that fall.

My father started talking about it with me weeks before to help
get me excited and to prepare me. Tournament chess is a completely
different experience from casual club games—and not at all like
the games I'd play with my father. For starters, there are a lot more
rules, none of which I really knew about yet. I needed to learn that
if you touch a piece, you must move it, and that speaking to your
opponent during a game isn't permitted. I needed to learn to shake
hands with my opponents before each game started and right after
it finished, and how to consult one of the tournament officials if I
thought the other player had made an illegal move—all of which
my father taught me.

One night, he came home from work with our very first chess clock. It was a classic Hungarian model, with a curved base made of stained wood and two big round off-white clock faces on the front. Right away I wanted to play with it. I liked winding it up in the back and pressing the levers on either side, which turned off one clock and started the other. But my parents put a stop to that pretty quickly. It's not a toy, my father said. It's something serious. In fact, it's an entirely new way of winning at chess—or losing.

He explained that if time runs out on your clock and the little red flag at twelve o'clock falls over, you lose, even if you have a winning position and even if the other player doesn't checkmate you. At first I thought he was teasing. I thought I had learned all of the rules of chess. And I definitely thought I knew all the ways to win or lose. Now this? What else didn't I know?! It was the same "a ha!" feeling I got when my father would introduce a new piece during our early lessons—a recognition that this thing I already adored was even richer and deeper than I had thought.

It took a few days for me to get in the habit of punching the clock after every move—and with the same hand (which was the official rule back then, as it is today). Pretty soon, I only wanted to play games with the clock. Time, my father explained, is almost like another piece on the board, something to treat carefully and to never throw away if you can avoid it. Sometimes, to illustrate how valuable time can be, he'd give me an advantage on my clock, so that I had more time to make my moves than he did. I often won those games, which I liked, but I also came to understand that it wasn't a fair fight.

My mother also did her part to get me ready for the big day. One afternoon when my father was at work, she and I had a long talk at our kitchen table about how I should behave myself when I played. I thought she was going to remind me not to talk during the game, which I already knew. Instead, she explained how important it was to treat my opponents nicely and to be a good sport. She told me not to brag or cheer if I won a game, even if I felt really happy. "Remember that when you win, the other player will be sad and maybe even angry. Nobody likes losing, Zsuzsi. So remember to be nice." If I lost, she told me, I should always make sure to shake my opponent's hand and look them in the eye and tell them "good game," even when I didn't feel like it. I promised I would.

Those few weeks leading up to the tournament felt like decades to me. At night, I'd lie awake imagining what the playing hall would be like, picturing an elaborately decorated room with chandeliers and heavy wooden tables and beautifully carved chess pieces. Of course, the reality was nothing close to this. The tournament was held in a pretty ordinary room at a local cultural center, and we played with worn-down wooden pieces on roll-up vinyl chess boards. I didn't care, though. From the moment I walked into that room, I knew this was going to be fun.

Most of the other girls playing that day were at least twice as old as me, and some were nearly three times as old. The age difference didn't bother me—I had only played adults at that point, after all. But it didn't seem to sit well with the other parents at the tournament. Some of them just couldn't believe that a four-year-old girl would even want to compete in a chess tournament. I remember a few of the parents leaning down to me in between rounds asking me condescending questions about whether I really liked chess, or whether I'd rather be playing with toys. I didn't think much of it. I really did like chess, I told them. I also liked toys, especially my stuffed bear. Why did I have to choose? And why did they care so much?

Their assumption was that my father was forcing me to be there, which, of course, he wasn't. Even now, I don't blame people for being concerned for my well-being in those years. Most of them weren't malicious; they were just narrow-minded or, at best, uninformed. But I do still smile when I think about what must have gone through all their heads when I actually won that tournament.

I tried not to celebrate, just like my mother had told me. But I couldn't control myself. I jumped out of my chair after that last game and ran to my father, giggling uncontrollably. He scooped me right up and spun me around, while my mother looked on, smiling. I knew I had broken her rule, but at that moment it didn't seem to matter to her. The next day, my grandma on my mom's side arrived with a homemade apple tart—one of her specialties that she knew I loved—and we all celebrated in our house. I had already fallen in love with chess. Now I was falling in love with winning.

Unfortunately, the side-eyed glances and disapproving comments we heard at that first tournament were just a taste of what would come. Not long after that, my father secured an audience with a higher-up at the Hungarian Chess Federation, hoping to get some advice about my instruction. The meeting didn't last long. The official was appalled that my father would subject a four-year-old to such a training regimen and insisted that he stop before he did any lasting damage to his daughter.

The real pushback wouldn't erupt until my next tournament. As the winner of the district event, I qualified to compete in the 1973 Budapest Elementary School Chess Championship, or the "Pioneer's Olympics," as it was then called in classic Soviet fashion. The competition was divided into girls' and boys' sections, which was standard practice in Eastern Europe back then. As with the previous tournament, almost every other girl playing was at least twice my age—and noticeably larger. As usual, I had to sit on my knees in order to reach certain parts of the board, and writing down my moves (as players are required to do in official tournaments) was still a clumsy affair for my little four-year-old fingers. After one game, someone asked me why I had chosen to checkmate my opponent in the manner I had. "There were two ways to give a checkmate in that position," I explained. "I picked the one that was easier for me to reach." I wasn't kidding.

It's fair to say that the results of that tournament changed my life forever. Not only did I take first place, but I did so with a perfect score—winning all ten of my games. To commemorate the victory, the tournament organizers awarded me a certificate, which my parents have saved to this day. It was the first time I had any real sense that I might be exceptional. Up until then, I had considered myself a normal Hungarian girl. I liked running around in the park and playing hide-and-seek with my friends in the neighborhood, just like any kid would. That my father spent hours a day with me studying and playing chess seemed like the most natural thing in the world. But the world was about to remind me just how unusual my life really was.

News of my victory traveled fast. I'm not exaggerating when I say I became a minor national celebrity. Journalists visited my home to interview my parents about their little girl, a four-year-old chess prodigy who wiped away her competition. And I'd sit on our living room sofa as some reporter asked me questions and made silly jokes trying to get me to laugh. Early on, my parents would prepare me for each interview, asking me questions and helping me with my answers. But I got the hang of it pretty soon. It helped that most of the journalists asked a lot of the same questions. Did I like playing chess? Did I have a favorite piece? A favorite player? A favorite toy? A favorite food?

I enjoyed the attention, at least at first. What four-year-old doesn't like positive attention? It made me happy when strangers came up to my parents and me on the street to say something nice, or when my picture was in the paper. But even at that age, I could sense how strange it all was. I knew plenty of kids my age, and none of them got featured on the evening news when they won a game against another kid.

When I asked my parents what all the fuss was about, they explained it to me as simply as they could: "All of these people can't believe that a girl your age can be so good at chess. They just want to hear how you got so good."

"Why am I so good?" I asked my father.

"Because that's what happens when you work hard at something you love."

It made perfect sense to me.

The media frenzy got so intense that sometime around my fifth birthday, I was asked to give two separate simultaneous exhibitions, which of course the papers loved. In each of those events, I played against more than a dozen school-aged students at once (thirty-five games in all), and ended up winning all but three.

Of course, chess had been a major cultural force in Hungary since long before Bobby Fischer's rise to prominence. Fans followed the game in the newspapers the way some follow soccer, and great Hungarian grandmasters like Laszlo Szabo and Lajos Portisch were household names in many quarters. I was the country's latest young talent. That I was a girl just made for good newspaper copy.

I followed my convincing victory in the Pioneer's Olympics with a strong fourth-place showing in the same section at the Hungarian nationals. After that, tournaments became a regular part of life, the one activity I never tired of. My lessons continued to take up several hours a day. And on the weekends and sometimes weeknights, my parents would bring me to whatever tournament was nearby. It was a perfectly lovely existence, as far as I was concerned.

Before long, I wasn't beating just girls, but also much older boys and even men, although mostly in casual games. The boys really didn't like losing to me, and a lot of them weren't afraid to show it. They would refuse to shake my hand after a game and stomp off in a huff. Or they would run to their parents with some made-up excuse for why I had beaten them. The girls I played with didn't like losing, either. But they rarely seemed too upset about it, and they never made excuses. It was my first inkling that a chess player's

gender really mattered to some people—and particularly to boys—
even if it didn't matter to me.

Unfortunately, not all of the media coverage I was getting in
those days was flattering. A lot of it was downright mean. One journalist openly accused my father of child abuse, claiming that our
intensive chess training would leave me "spiritually handicapped"
for life. When my paternal grandmother, Szeren, read that, she was
beside herself with grief. She passed away not long after that. And
to this day, my father still blames the article, at least in part, for
her untimely death.

Several of my family members were also concerned about me
and weren't shy about saying so. Occasionally, when one of these
relatives was visiting and I had gone off to bed, I'd listen through
the thin walls of my bedroom. Things would always get tense when
the subject turned to me and my chess. I'd hear things like "You
know this can't be good for her. She's just a little girl. She should be
playing with dolls. I'm not going to sit by and not say anything." All
I could think was *Please don't take chess away—anything but that.*

For a while, everyone seemed to have an opinion about how
Laszlo and Klara Polgar were raising their little girl. And that opinion was *Stop what you're doing.* I imagine that many parents would
have succumbed to this sort of pressure, issued a public apology,
abandoned their principles—anything to make it all go away. But
my parents remained determined, even though they must have felt
like the entire country was questioning their ability to raise a child.

If anything, they seemed to be growing more confident in
the path they had chosen for me. Before those early successes, my
mother still wasn't convinced that an education that prioritized
chess was the best path for me. She was mainly just grateful that I
could finally sit still for something. And as long as I kept progressing and was actually enjoying the game, she was willing to support
it. My father was a whole lot more optimistic, of course, but even
he was willing to walk away from the project if I lost interest or

didn't show any promise. As he saw it, if chess didn't pan out, he could refocus his efforts on teaching me mathematics, our other main area of study in those years. Now that my chess abilities were beyond doubt and my father's pedagogical techniques were bearing fruit, we would move full-steam ahead, and no amount of slanderous media coverage would discourage him.

It was around that time that the family visited my mother's hometown of Vilok, then part of the Soviet Union. One day, walking through the park in the nearby city Uzhhorod, along the Uzh River, I spotted a group of men playing chess. To me, it just seemed like an outdoor version of our chess club on Lenin Boulevard. No, my parents said, these weren't hobbyists, they were gamblers, and we shouldn't get in their way. But I wasn't going to leave without at least one game. They might as well have taken me to an amusement park and told me I couldn't get on any rides. Most of the men they approached weren't interested, but eventually my dad talked one of them into playing me—a stubble-faced gentleman of around fifty or so in a short-sleeve button-up shirt and a fedora. He explained to me in a mock-serious tone that, to play at these tables, I'd need to bet something. We agreed to wager a chocolate bar, which sounded just fine to me.

I don't know if he went easy on me or if I just outplayed him. At the very least I took him by surprise, winning the game in twenty moves or so. Then, at the moment checkmate was on the board, the man got up and ran out of the park, apparently welching on his bet. My parents burst into laughter. I, however, wasn't amused. There was chocolate at stake, after all. And I wasn't leaving without it. I took off after him immediately, chasing him through the park, yelling in Russian "Thief! Thief!" as loud as I could. By the time I caught up to him, he was coming out of a store nearby. He had dashed off to buy me a chocolate bar.

It was on that same visit to Vilok that I first asked my mother's mother about the numbers tattooed on her arm. "Why is that there,

Grandma?" I said one morning while sitting at her kitchen table. The visible shift in her demeanor frightened me. She was never anything but fawning and affectionate toward me. So to see the joy drain from her face so suddenly, I could tell I had said something wrong. "Oh, you're too young to hear about any of that," she said, trying to change the subject. "I'll explain it to you when you're a little older." She sat for a moment, composing herself in silence. "I hope you never have to learn how much a human can endure." All I knew was that it sounded serious and that I shouldn't ask again.

My mom must have overheard all of this, because she sat me down later that day to tell me what my grandma was talking about—that something terrible had happened not too long ago, and that many of our family members had died. It was the first time I ever heard the word Auschwitz. She told me that Grandma had been there, and that she was still very sad about it.

"Were you and Daddy there?" I asked.

"No, we weren't born yet."

"Were my other grandparents there?" I asked.

"All of them."

———•◦•———

My first real encounter with chess's gender problem came in 1974, when I was just five years old. My parents had entered me in the district qualifier for the Budapest Elementary School Championship, just as they had the year before. Only this time, they signed me up for the boys' section. Their reasoning was pretty straightforward: For me to keep improving, I needed to play against better opponents. And, for whatever reason, the stronger players in that age group happened to be boys. Fortunately for us, the event's organizers didn't seem to mind.

By then, I was already a known quantity in our local chess community. So it came as no great surprise to anyone when I won the tournament, or that I did so without losing a single game. Now, ordinarily, winning that event automatically qualifies a player for the Budapest Elementary School Championship—that's the tournament's entire purpose. But the Budapest Chess Federation had other ideas. The organization's president was a strict believer in the game's gender line. And he didn't like that a five-year-old girl had even entered the boys' district qualifier, much less that I had swept the field. As far as he was concerned, it didn't matter how convincingly I had earned my spot at the championship. The event was for boys only, and he saw to it that my name was withdrawn from the pairings weeks before the competition took place. Nobody bothered to inform me or my parents of this decision, of course. So we spent the run-up to the event training intensely. It wasn't until we arrived in the playing hall that we learned that I'd been disqualified.

My father assured me this was a mistake and went off to have a word with the president, who he found in the venue's stairwell. The conversation didn't go well. According to my dad, the federation president was adamant that girls not play in the event, and there was no talking him out of it. He also didn't like that I was not yet enrolled in school—even though that hadn't been a problem at the previous year's tournament. Fine then, my father said. He would just have to file a formal complaint. That's when the exchange got heated. At one point, the president threatened to throw my father down the staircase in a tone of voice that suggested he wasn't bluffing. I spent the bus ride home crying to my father uncontrollably, begging him to go back and fix it. But there was nothing he could do. The tournament had started, and I wasn't going to be playing in it.

This was all incomprehensible to me at that age, and it still is today. I was just a little girl who wanted to play chess. And almost from the moment I started playing, people kept finding a reason why I couldn't. First, I was too young. Then, I was the wrong gender. Why did this have to be so complicated?

But the dustup over the Budapest Championship was just a prelude to a much larger battle that would consume my family and me for the next year, one with far higher stakes. I was about to turn six, which meant, by law, my parents would have to enroll me in school the following September. This was a frightening prospect for them. They had already been homeschooling me for years, and by any reasonable standard, the one-on-one education they were providing was far superior to anything I would get in the normal education system. That was the whole point. I wasn't even school age yet, and I was already doing math at a fourth-grade level, and in some areas well above it. I could read and write Hungarian well above my grade level. I was on my way to being fluent in Russian and was starting to pick up German, too.

More than that, I really liked being taught by my parents. I had friends my own age in the neighborhood, and I enjoyed being social. But I also knew that the work I was doing each day with my parents was special. I didn't want to trade them for a teacher I had never met in a school I'd never visited.

None of this mattered to the government, though. In Hungary, withholding your child from school simply wasn't done. So unless my parents wanted to end up in jail, they needed a way around the law.

Our best hope was to apply for a waiver from the Ministry of Education. It was the kind of permission usually reserved for children who were physically unable to attend school. But in my case, my parents argued, school would hold me back. To help make their case, my parents called in a favor from Comrade Gabor, the vice president of the Hungarian Chess Federation and one of the few people in our orbit who had any pull with the government. Gabor seemed happy to help. He promised to put in a good word for us with the Ministry of Education the very next day. It did no good. Within a week, we had received an official rejection.

My father wasn't ready to give up just yet, though. He headed down to the ministry office the next day, confident he could turn this around. When he dropped Gabor's name, the official there laughed. "Of course we know who he is," the man said. "Gabor was the one who told us to reject you!" It was an eye-opening moment for my dad. He considered himself a savvy person and was never quick to trust people. That one of our few allies was actively conspiring against us was difficult for him to accept. He refiled the application right then and there and asked that we be considered on the merits.

This time, the government wasn't in a rush. Months went by before we got an official decision. In the meantime, the authorities seized their opportunity to make an example out of me and my family. Hungary was still a communist dictatorship, after all, a regime in which being exceptional wasn't just frowned upon—it went against basic principles. We were supposed to be a nation of equals, or so the official ideology told us. And that meant nobody got special treatment, especially not a young Jewish girl like me.

It wasn't uncommon to hear critics refer to our family as somehow less than "real" Hungarians. Of course, this was a not-so-subtle way of saying "Jewish." Nobody would ever express such antisemitism to us directly. But we knew from friends and allies that such attitudes were in the air. And we weren't surprised.

The war may have ended decades before I was born, but in some forms, antisemitism was still alive throughout Europe in those years, and in Hungary more than most places. Whereas a lot of Europeans involved in the Holocaust only reluctantly complied with the Nazis, some Hungarians did so by choice. They were more than happy to rid their nation of Jews, even if it meant collaborating in the most heinous acts of genocide. Those same bigotries still had roots in Hungary's culture and likely played a role in the campaign against me and my family.

As we sat in limbo, waiting for permission to keep homeschooling, the authorities did their best to intimidate us. They accused my father of child abuse and threatened to throw him in a mental institution. I remember one occasion when an armed police officer came to our home intending to arrest my parents and take me into custody.

After the officer left, my dad calmly explained that some people in the government didn't want me playing chess. They wanted me to go to school like everybody else.

"They're just trying to scare us," my mother told me. "But we aren't afraid of them, are we Zsuzsi? We're going to fight."

"I'm not scared," I told her. I really wasn't.

Through some miracle of bureaucracy, the government ended up approving our petition. But I'm still not exactly sure why. We had called in some favors from a few other friends in the chess world, which I'm sure helped a little. But it was still a long shot. The authorities clearly had it out for us, and there was nothing stopping them from following through on their threats. All I can think is that it wasn't worth the bad press. For all the negative publicity I received, I also had a lot of admirers in Hungary. Continuing to punish such a high-profile family could have caused a stir.

Nevertheless, when the media circus finally left town, my family and I were happy to see it go. We had gotten all the attention we could handle for a while. Even though our critics liked to depict my parents as egomaniacs selfishly chasing the limelight, fame was never what we were after. In fact, fame actually got in the way of the real goal, which was for me to keep getting better at chess. I, for one, couldn't wait to return to my regular life and get back to work.

FOUR

One of the most common questions you hear as a chess player is "How many moves do you see in advance?" An early chess hero of mine, the legendary Cuban world champion Jose Raul Capablanca, is said to have remarked, "I only see one move ahead, but it is always the correct one." He was being facetious, of course. But he was also getting at something very true about the experience of playing chess. It's often assumed that chess is mostly about calculation, about anticipating the precise consequences of each potential move. But while calculation is without doubt an important part of the game, many situations are just too complicated to plan out move by move. And that's when intuition comes into play. Intuition is by far the most mysterious skill in chess. It's a kind of internal sense that points you toward a particular decision, even though you don't know why or have no clear idea of where it will lead. This is sometimes how I think about the first major decision I made in my life.

I was only around six at the time. Up until then, my homeschool education was focused on two main areas: chess and math. Hungary is known for producing brilliant mathematicians. And I suppose my father hoped I might follow in that tradition. My affinity for chess complicated that plan. Early on my parents realized that if I was to be great at either math or chess, I would need to choose.

"If you don't pick just one," my father said, "you'll never be great at either. But only you can decide."

I didn't think twice about the fact that they were letting their six-year-old make such a significant decision. By then, my parents had already started speaking to me as an adult, telling me exactly what they thought and why. And this time was no different.

It wasn't a difficult choice. I may have had an aptitude for math. But I had no great love for the subject. I didn't like that math was so concrete, that it was purely about calculation. Chess was so much more fun to me. It was creative and challenging and surprising. I had only just glimpsed what this beautiful game had to offer. And the prospect of walking away was unimaginable to me. It just felt like the right choice. I saw only one move ahead, and it turned out to be the correct one.

My parents weren't surprised that I chose chess. In Hungary at the time, it was not unheard of for chess players to make a decent living, at least by the standards of Cold War Eastern Europe. Some even had financial support from the government, which they could supplement by winning the occasional tournament prize. So the possibility that I could make my way in the world as a professional chess player was by no means outlandish. Regardless, at that time, money wasn't a major consideration for them when it came to my future. What mattered was that I loved what I was doing and that I had a chance to succeed.

The next few years were easily the most formative for me as a player. Before then, chess was just something I did a lot. Now that I had decided to make this game my life's work, it became something more—not just a career but a calling.

The more I learned about the game, the more entranced I became with its secrets and possibilities. I loved how minor subtleties and seemingly quiet moves could turn a losing position into a powerful attack. I loved that the game rewarded patience and finesse just as much as big bold combinations—and sometimes even more so. There's an Indian proverb that says "Chess is a lake in which a mosquito can bathe and an elephant can drown." In other words, it's a game that can be engaged with in a shallow, superficial way but also has a bottomless depth to it. What I found so captivating was that the deeper I would go—the more I would analyze and study and educate my intuition—the more I would realize that I'd never find a bottom, that there is always something new to discover.

At first my father remained my main teacher. He was still working at a boys' boarding school in the afternoons and would usually pick up the overnight shift as well, in addition to holding down one or two part-time jobs. This meant he had just a few hours early each day to work with me on chess and a few other subjects.

At the end of our lessons, my dad would leave me with some assignments for me to do on my own in the afternoon. I might have to solve twenty puzzles, or memorize an important game, or something of that sort. My mom would come back from her job as a high school foreign language teacher just after lunchtime, my father would head off to work, and I'd spend a good part of the afternoon in my bedroom with a chess board in front of me.

This routine worked pretty well for a little while. Soon, though, it became obvious to my parents that I needed more and better instruction than my father could offer. They kept a lookout for teachers who could help me improve, usually hiring them to come by the house once a week for an hour or two. They had a good eye for skilled educators.

The first coach I remember working with regularly was Eva Karakas, a lovely woman in her mid-fifties with short curly blond hair and a warm smile. We first met at the Voros Meteor chess club, where we both played. And she was known throughout Hungary for hosting several television shows about chess, including *Attack the King* and *Check-Mate*, neither of which I had seen when we began working with her. She also happened to be a multiple-time Hungarian women's champion and was still among the strongest female players in the country.

From our first lesson together, her enthusiasm for the beauty of chess was absolutely infectious. She had this way of finding puzzles or concepts or instructional games that presented chess as a creative pursuit, full of counterintuitive ideas and elegant solutions. Like my father, she understood the value of igniting my imagination. And her choice of material—things like underpromotion and daring sacrifices that lead to checkmate—did exactly that.

Another important early influence was a local master named Bela Papp. A tall balding man of around sixty or so, Bela was more of a friend than a teacher. We first met at one of my early tournaments, when he took an interest in one of my games. Even though he worked as a coach for a rival club team, he saw something in me and did what he could to encourage my talent. I'd see him at tournaments, and he even visited the house once or twice. Bela could always make me laugh with some crazy story or funny joke. But what inspired me most about him was his deep love of chess and its magic. We'd sit at the board and work through interesting ideas, or go over a particularly beautiful game. Like Eva, he helped awaken in me a sensitivity to the artistic dimensions of chess that never really left.

Not all of my teachers had this effect on me. The sessions I had with the legendary Hungarian grandmaster Laszlo Szabo brought me little joy. Although undoubtedly a world-class player, his teaching style was strict and formulaic, which spoiled a lot of the fun. My father could tell early on that Szabo's approach to teaching wasn't working for me, and we ended that relationship after just a few lessons.

My time with another teacher, Gyula Zentai, marked a big turning point in my approach to chess during those years. He was around sixty when we first met, with a full head of white hair he wore combed back over his head. Once a week he'd come to my home to work with me specifically on endgames. I remember he had his own system of points that he'd use to keep me motivated. If I solved a puzzle or found a strong move—or even if I just behaved well during the lesson, which is no small task for a six-year-old—he'd award me points, which he'd keep track of in this notebook he carried. After about a month or so, when I reached 100 points, he'd reach into his bag and produce a reward. Sometimes it was a chocolate bar or a lollipop. Other times it was a special pen or a little notebook or some stickers.

What really set him apart from my other teachers, though, was his laser focus on endgames. Many young players have very little patience for endgames, and early on I was no different. Since most of the major pieces (rooks and queens) and minor pieces (knights and bishops) have usually been traded off the board, this final stage of the game can seem dry and tedious to the untrained eye—especially compared to the opening or middlegame, when it's still possible to find dramatic combinations of moves to stun your opponent. But this is really just a myth, as Zentai helped me to see.

I came to understand that for all its seeming simplicity, the endgame can contain extraordinary richness. Sure, there might be only five or ten pieces left on the board. But there are still so many delicate moves, unexpected resources—and even tactics and combinations—to discover. The stakes are also far higher than at any other stage in the game, since the cost of even a slight inaccuracy can be devastating. It's almost as if once the queens are traded and the position simplifies, chess transforms into a completely different game, with its own unique rules, principles, and subtleties. The pawns and the king—which are by far the weakest pieces early in the game—become dominant. And concepts like zugzwang—a situation in which any move worsens your position—take on new relevance.

For those who master the unforgiving logic of endgames, this ability becomes like a superpower—one I desperately wanted to have. Zentai and I must have worked through Vasily Smyslov and Grigory Levenfish's classic treatise on rook endgames at least half a dozen times—as we did with Jeno Ban's book *The Tactics of End-Games*, which focused on what I found to be the more exciting parts of endgame theory. Ban's book holds a special place in my heart to this day, in no small part because of Zentai.

Once I began to internalize the endgame principles he was teaching me and put them to work in my games, my chess took a huge leap forward. It no longer mattered as much if I found myself in a difficult middlegame position or under a dangerous attack. If I could defend well enough and trade off enough pieces, I could lead my opponent into a different kind of game, one in which my growing body of endgame knowledge could prove decisive. Not only did this strategy help me to win games, but it instilled in me a new kind of confidence. When I stopped seeing early mistakes as death sentences and realized that nothing is truly over if you can find your way to an endgame, I began to have more composure at the board. My calculations became more sure-handed and precise, and I started trusting my intuition more—all of which led to more wins, as well as more draws from seemingly lost positions.

There are many ways to win a chess game. For less-skilled players, games can often be decided by a catastrophic blunder. One side might hang a queen or inadvertently hand their opponent mate in two. But this tends not to happen beyond the beginner level. Regardless, this is among the least satisfying ways to win. On the other hand, clawing your way back from a deficit and winning in an endgame position that appears dead even is one of the great pleasures the game has to offer. You've overcome a seemingly insurmountable adversity through careful, disciplined play, and now you can slowly squeeze your opponent by accumulating tiny advantages that eventually lead to victory. When done properly, your opponent is left without any idea of where they went wrong. Sometimes, you can feel the whole energy in the room change as the person across the board from you realizes that this once equal position has turned dangerous, that they are no longer in control—that they are actually in trouble. It's an immensely satisfying feeling that, for me, was almost addictive.

One challenge I faced in those years between six and ten was finding opportunities to play. In the last decade or so, the internet has made it astoundingly easy for any player to find an equally skilled opponent in seconds at any moment of the day. It's one of the reasons why today's young players improve as quickly as they do. But back in the 1970s I usually had just a few chances a week at most to play against someone who could give me a decent game. And finding those chances always required a lot of planning.

My father and I continued to play regularly, and until I was nine or ten years old, he could still give me a run for my money. But to find new opponents sometimes took creativity. It definitely helped that we lived in a place like Budapest, where chess was such a big part of the culture. A few times a week we'd visit the Voros Meteor chess club—which by then had merged with another local club to become MTK-VM. And we'd invite local players to our home to spar with me. Even though they were almost all adult men, it didn't seem to matter. Our shared love of chess always gave us something to talk about. My mother might cook us lunch. And sometimes they'd stick around after our games and have long chats with my parents about politics or current events, which was always educational for me. Once in a while I'd chime in, trying hard to talk like a grown-up, even though I was still a kid.

One player in particular, the international master Gyula Kluger, was a fixture at these living-room blitz sessions, and he would eventually become a close family friend. A strong kinship developed between him and my family, which probably had something to do with the fact that, like my grandparents, he had survived the Holocaust. You could tell he had a stake in my success from very early on. I still think about him fondly.

In the warmer months, I'd play on the stone chess tables at City Park—or Liget, as the locals call it—a sprawling public park at the center of Budapest similar to New York's Central Park. This is where I really fell in love with blitz chess—short, timed games in which each player gets anywhere from one to five minutes to make all of their moves. The first player to run out of time on their chess clock loses, even if they haven't been checkmated. This means that quick calculation and fast intuitive moves are far more important than perfect play. It's like the 100-meter dash of chess formats. The games tend to be more wild and unpredictable compared to the longer classical format—all of which is part of the thrill. I'd usually end up playing one of the older men who came to the park to gamble. We'd bet one forint per game, which was equivalent to a few pennies in those days. The money didn't really matter, though. It was just a way to keep things interesting. There would be plenty of trash-talking and lively banter during the games, which I also came to enjoy.

The thermal baths that Budapest is famous for were another place my dad and I would look for games, particularly at the Szechenyi bath. The pools there had long stone chess tables that extended over the water like low diving boards. It's one of the few places I know of where you can play chess all day while wading chest-deep in water. In cold-weather months, the Belvarosi coffeehouse—a well-known chess hangout in those days—was one of my favorite spots to play in. It was a majestic place with impossibly high ceilings, dripping with ornate details and elaborately carved wood moldings, like something out of Belle Époque Vienna. We'd try to spend as little money as possible at the coffeehouse. Afterward, though, on very special nights, as my dad and I walked home through the Eastern railway station, he would treat me to my favorite sandwich from one of the bistros there.

When I was new to these places, my father would almost always have to talk people into a game with me. Men in particular were often reluctant to take me on. I suppose the thought of losing to a young girl was too much for their egos to bear. It's also a lot harder to insist that women are inferior at chess if you're consistently getting beat by an eight-year-old girl. As I became a regular at these spots, the atmosphere got a little more welcoming.

I would play at least once a week in the city's club league tournaments, traveling to different places in Budapest to compete for MTK-VM. Even in this environment—my "home field," as it were—a few of the men didn't like having me there. Nobody was openly hostile. The worst anyone would do is use foul language around me, as a reminder to my father and me that this was no place for children. But most of the other members were happy to have me, especially people like Gabor Kallai and Gyula Forgacs.

I learned a lot in those years, and not just about chess. It's one of the benefits of spending so much time around adults at such a young age. I was probably around seven or eight when it really sunk in that grown-ups could be fundamentally wrong about things that even a child could understand. This came as a real shock. I knew already that I was years ahead of most kids my age academically. As part of my homeschooling arrangement with the state, I would have to take grade-level exams at the end of each school year, most of which I could pass without studying very much. Adults, however, were supposed to be much smarter, or at least more knowledgeable. So how could a man five times my age not grasp something as basic as king opposition in the endgame, or the importance of keeping the bishop pair, or the dangers of doubling your pawns? What's more, if they could be wrong about these elementary things, then what else might they be wrong about? These experiences made me much less comfortable bowing down to authority or getting bossed around by adults simply because they were older than me. But it also helped me understand chess as a great equalizer, a game that was blind to categories like gender or age.

———•◦•———

Our home life got a lot more lively in 1974 with the birth of my sister Sofia, and even more so in 1976 when my youngest sister, Judit, came along. I can still remember my mother arriving home from the hospital in her yellow-and-brown-checkered dress, carrying Judit in her arms. Judit had a full head of red hair even then. I couldn't wait to hold her. You would think that homeschooling with a crying infant in the house would be difficult, but really it wasn't. Even in our little home, my parents were incredibly good at setting boundaries—and I loved having both of my sisters around to play with and look after. I didn't mind at all that my parents' attention was now divided between the three of us. In fact, I was happy not to be an only child any more. I would work in the room at the very back of our house with the door closed most of the day, while my mother cared for the babies near the front. I'd occasionally help out by changing diapers or doing chores around the house. But my studies were treated as sacrosanct and not to be interrupted unless absolutely necessary.

Some days, my maternal grandmother would come over after work to help out. She'd almost always arrive with something sweet she had just baked—cherry squares or sometimes a chocolate babka—which was usually still warm from her oven. Those afternoons we'd sit and eat and talk for an hour or so while my mother tended to my sisters. My grandmother would ask about my latest chess accomplishment or tell me stories about my mother growing up. If something was bothering me, she could always tell right away. And whatever it was, she would find exactly the right thing to say to put it all in perspective.

On weekends when I wasn't playing in chess tournaments, my dad and I would travel to his hometown of Gyongyos to visit his family. My grandfather would sometimes tell stories about his time as a horseman in the First World War, or even the degradation he suffered as a forced laborer during the Holocaust, when he was sent to the front lines to collect stray bullets for the Nazis. But mostly, he and my father would discuss politics or some other topic.

It was in this period, when I was nine or so, that my father started teaching me Esperanto, a language invented in the nineteenth century by a Polish doctor as a kind of universal tongue that privileged no particular culture or country or people. Neither he nor my mother spoke the language when we first started, so really we were learning it together. They were young and idealistic, and they both really believed that this new language could foster better communication between cultures and get us past the kind of geopolitical conflicts that defined so much of our lives in those years. That dream never quite materialized, sadly. But I admire them for trying.

I also cherish the people I got to meet as a result of Esperanto. It has been an incredibly tight-knit community, so much so that the movement published a directory featuring the names and addresses of Esperantists all over the world. My very first tournament outside of Hungary was an Esperantist event in what was then Czechoslovakia. And for years after that, whenever we traveled abroad, we'd often look up local Esperantists in our directory and ask them to show us around or occasionally even to host us. When fellow Esperantists came to Budapest, we'd always do our best to return the favor.

It was a truly happy time, when I look back on it. Not only did I have two little sisters to play with and take care of, but I got to spend more time with Mom while she was on maternity leave. In addition to our dog Bogi, we now had six rabbits, twenty pigeons, and several chickens, which I would tend to every day. Waking up at six a.m. to feed the animals wasn't exactly a joy for me. But I did take pleasure in no longer being treated as a child, in playing a more meaningful role, in learning to be responsible and disciplined.

When it was time to work, whether on my own or with one of my chess coaches, I could retreat to my room at the back of the house and close the door.

As Sofia and Judit got older, though, they started to wonder what their big sister was up to back there. So it's really no surprise that they would eventually take up chess themselves. They must have gotten the impression early on that the game I was studying was important and interesting. And the fact that they weren't allowed to join in only made it more attractive.

When we moved to a new apartment in 1979, which was about half the size of our house, it became a lot harder to keep them away. It was technically a step up. The old house had so many problems that my parents gave up trying to fix it. But the apartment was brand-new—and even had reliable hot water, which the house never did. In fact, my mother would occasionally have to boil water for us to bathe in.

Sofia had taken up the game a year earlier. My dad was an experienced chess teacher by that point, having honed his techniques through trial and error during our own lessons together. She picked the game up quickly and even worked with my old coach Eva early on. It wouldn't be long before she was competing in tournaments herself, sometimes right alongside me.

The first of those tournaments was the 1979 Kids at the Chess Board event, which was held as part of the Children's Day Festival in Budapest. Few were surprised when I won the middle school boys and girls open section. Sofia's third-place finish in the elementary school section was what really got people's attention. That was when the "Polgar sisters" narrative began to take shape. For me personally, though, 1979 was the year I started to come into my own as a mature player.

I was finally growing into the playing style that I would continue to rely on in some form for the rest of my life, a kind of solid positional play modeled off of the games of Jose Raul

Capablanca and Anatoly Karpov, who was then the world champion. My goal in every game was to foresee my opponent's potential plans as early as possible and to neutralize them as best I could before they developed into threats. Then, when the moment was right, I could launch an attack that could turn the momentum of the game decisively in my favor. This last part was what I struggled with the most. Knowing exactly when to capitalize on your positional advantages is more art than science. Attack too early, and your entire position can fall to pieces. Wait too long, and your positional edge can dissipate into nothing.

It's an approach to the game that lacks some of the astonishing turns and flashy moves that attacking players like Mikhail Tal, a former world champion, was famous for. But it suited my personal strengths and temperament quite well. So much so that when I really found my stride, I became very difficult to beat, as I made clear that summer at the semifinal qualifier for the Hungarian Women's Championship. At just age ten, I won the tournament without a single loss, giving perhaps my best performance up to that point—despite being the only child in the competition that year. Still, I struggled with consistency and finished only in the middle of the field at the final that November (although I did manage to beat the tournament winner Tunde Csonkics, which was some small consolation).

That event might not have been my strongest showing, but it did put me on the international stage for the first time. I performed well enough to qualify for an official rating through the International Chess Federation, or FIDE, as it's known, becoming the youngest person in history to accomplish that feat. I also walked away from the tournament with the title of national woman master.

During the final round, the Hungarian premier, Comrade Janos Kadar, a serious chess fan, showed up to personally congratulate me. He even posed for a photo. It was an important vote of confidence for me, especially after the battles I had fought with the authorities before then. The photo op led to a fresh wave of press attention, including a spot on the evening news that night. Only this time was different. The story emerging in the media wasn't about the novelty of a four-year-old girl excelling at chess. It was about a promising talent who was fast becoming one of the strongest young players in the world of either gender. For the first time, I had the distinct feeling that there was no real limit to how far I could go in this game. Now I just had to prove it.

FIVE

Before the age of twelve, most of the world outside of the East-ern Bloc was just an idea in my mind—something I had only seen in films and read about. In fact, almost all my days until then had been spent in my home country. It turned out that 1981 would be the year I saw the world, or at least little more of it. My rapid ascent up the chess rankings gave me access to a wide range of tournaments outside of Hungary, beginning with the European Girls Under-21 Championship, which took place that spring in Panonija, a small town in what was then Yugoslavia.

My main coach at that time, Gyula Forgacs, would help me prepare for the event. I had become friends with Forgacs years earlier at the chess club, and he was one of my favorite people to be around. He could respond to any situation with a perfectly timed joke that would send me into a fit of laughter. He was also a master of trash talk, naturally only during our casual blitz games, a skill I was gradually improving at myself.

"Are you kidding me with that move!" he'd say.

I'd usually shoot back something like " Nice try, Gyula. But it's over for you. Just resign now and save yourself the humiliation."

As our training for the Yugoslavia event got going, I could feel my excitement for the trip giving way to what can only be described as a crisis of confidence. It had to do with a major shift in my approach to chess openings—that is, the series of moves a player uses to begin a game of chess.

Having a sound and well-researched opening repertoire is absolutely critical for any top player. And for much of my career up until that point, I had relied on the move 1. e4—a move in which the pawn in front of white's king moves forward two squares—as my main strategy when playing with the white pieces. Starting around 1980, though, I decided to deviate from this idea, opening instead with 1. d4—that is, with the queen's pawn moving two squares forward. As a more solid, positional player, queen's pawn openings fit my personality far better than the more aggressive lines one often sees in king's pawn games.

Nevertheless, this was a pretty dramatic change in my chess—the equivalent of a right-handed boxer deciding suddenly to fight left-handed. In other words, it required me to relearn a lot of things. And in preparing for the event in Yugoslavia, I had discovered a major weakness when faced with a specific reply from black: the Stonewall variation of the Dutch Defense.

Again, to succeed at the highest levels of chess, you have to feel comfortable playing against any opening your opponent might choose. There's simply no getting around this. And for me, the Stonewall Dutch—an opening with the black pieces that happened to be growing in popularity—caused me immense anxiety when my opponent used it against me.

Objectively, the Stonewall isn't that great of a defense for black. And yet, my intuition seemed to malfunction every time I played against it. I would make a series of moves that each seemed reasonable, only to find myself in a deeply unpleasant position in the middlegame. Black's strategy with this opening is to know-ingly create weaknesses in the position in order to develop a very dangerous attack on white's king. The goal for white is to capitalize on black's weaknesses, while still being careful to defend against the kingside onslaught. It was a balance that I just couldn't seem to manage with any consistency. And this one shortcoming—despite being highly specific to this one opening—was enough to shake my confidence.

It's at times like these that a good coach has a chance to really shine. And in this case, Forgacs rose to the occasion. He asked me to block off an entire day on my calendar for a very special training session. What followed was a twenty-four-hour chess marathon during which we played what must have been a hundred blitz games in my chess room in my parents' apartment. In all of them, I played with the white pieces, opening with 1. d4. And in all of them Forgacs replied with the Stonewall Dutch. His idea was ingeniously simple: By drilling me in this one variation, he could cure me of my butterflies. It worked brilliantly. By the end of the session, I was physically exhausted and a little delirious. But I was no longer intimidated by the Stonewall. In fact, I was actually hoping to see it on the board in Yugoslavia.

Chess had already become my main social outlet in those years. So the prospect of exploring a different culture and making friends from distant places genuinely thrilled me. And the first few days of our visit were actually quite pleasant. My twelfth birthday fell in the middle of the tournament, which made it just a little more special for me. And when I wasn't playing chess, my father and I would take long walks around the village, meandering through shops and experimenting with new foods. On one of my days off, Janos Kubat—a Hungarian friend who lived in Yugoslavia—took us to the neighboring town of Novi Sad, where it just so happened that the World Table Tennis Championships were underway. We were all big fans of the sport, although neither my father nor I had ever played in any serious way. We also knew that the Hungarian team was in the running for the championship, so we seized the chance to watch a few rounds and cheer on our compatriots, particularly Istvan Jonyer and Tibor Klampar, who were two of Hungary's top players at the time. Sitting there in the stands, I just couldn't believe how far away from the table the players would stand and the speed and precision in which they hit the ball.

My first encounter with genuine danger came during that event. I was walking back to our accommodations with my father and Forgacs sometime in the middle of the event. "I'm going to run ahead. I really need to use the bathroom," I told them, leaving them behind. I was alone when I finally reached the building. But as I made my way up the stairs to our room, I noticed a young man in his late teens close behind me in the stairwell. He had dark hair and stubble and was at least six feet tall. I didn't know him, but I had seen him before, wandering around the tournament. I was only twelve, but well-developed for my age and often mistaken for a sixteen-year-old. And I had just started to notice that boys looked at me differently from how they once had. The expression on this boy's face was something new. He didn't smile or wave. He just looked at me with a kind of intensity that suggested he was on some sort of mission, that our run-in was no accident. *I wish I hadn't run ahead* was all I could think. *I wish I wasn't alone right now.*

"Polgar!" he shouted in a barking, belligerent tone.

I didn't know what he wanted, but I felt it wasn't good. Without thinking, I took off, running up the stairs as fast as I could, trying to get to my room. But he caught up to me in just a few strides and tackled me on the landing. Everything after that was pure panic. He was trying to force his hands inside my clothes and kiss me, and there was a lot of pushing and slapping and struggling. I felt like I was fighting for my life, but he was overpowering me. And the more I resisted, the angrier he got. He threw me up against the railing.

"Stop fighting me, or I'll throw you off this balcony!" he said.

I knew he meant it. This was not how I wanted to die. And I may have, had my father and Forgacs not entered the stairwell. The man let go of me when he heard them coming and ran up the stairs. When my father and Forgacs saw me, lying there on the ground out of breath and disoriented, they thought I had tripped. "No," I said. "A man pushed me over and ran away. But I'm okay now."

I told them not to worry, that this was just an overzealous spectator from the tournament trying to get inside my head. And I stuck to that story. I knew that if I told my dad and Forgacs what really happened, they may want me to withdraw from the tournament. My parents were very protective of me in those years, and part of me didn't want them to worry even more. I still wanted to win a championship, and I was going to play all of my games, whether I felt like it or not. It was my mistake for running ahead, I thought. I should have known I could be in danger. If I wanted my independence, I needed to be more careful. Lesson learned.

I really thought I could walk it off, but it wasn't so easy. I cried that night, after my father had gone to sleep. I kept going over the attack in my mind, with a combination of anxiety and sheer exhaustion. My first real encounter with physical violence had shocked my entire system and reminded me just how hostile the outside world could be. It took me more than an hour to calm myself down and get to sleep.

I was still a little shaken up before my game the next morning, mostly because I wasn't sure if my attacker would be there waiting for me. He never showed his face again, although I was still shaken up and never stopped scanning the crowds to look for him. I knew that if I stayed around other people during the tournament and kept close to my father the rest of the time, this man wouldn't dare come after me again. I just didn't know how I would react if I saw his face again. And I still had chess to play.

I can't remember who I played that next round. But once my game started, everything felt different. This was my own private world, where I knew all the rules, and all I had to do was find the best moves. I had recognized by then that I was good at blocking distractions out and focusing on the task at hand. I just didn't know how good until that day.

I finished the tournament undefeated, although with only two actual wins (the rest were draws). It was a respectable result, considering the circumstances (and that the rest of the players were far older than I was). But it didn't bring me much joy. I was just happy to have gotten through it. I wanted to put the whole thing behind me, get back home, and forget that it had ever happened.

I had gotten pretty used to absorbing personal attacks from the media or the authorities without losing my calm or taking it to heart. I tried to treat what happened in Yugoslavia as just an extension of the vindictiveness I'd experienced at home. But the attack and trauma stayed with me for a long time. I now understood that there were people in the world who wouldn't hesitate to harm me in the worst way if I let my guard down even for a second. So, I always did my best not to.

For years after, I tried my best never to be alone in public, especially when traveling. In fact, I wouldn't travel by myself until my early twenties. On my family's next big trip later that year—to the Bulgarian resort town of Varna—I almost never left my parents' sight. It's a rule I would follow for at least the next few trips, and especially that summer, in England.

I had been nominated to represent Hungary at the World Girls' Under-16 Championship in Westergate, England. Our conflict with the state seemed to have died down after the education ministry agreed to let my parents homeschool me, but we couldn't be sure it would stay that way. Fortunately for us, the sports ministry wasn't going to deny me a chance to bring home a world championship for Hungary. My parents, Forgacs, and I all got the official go-ahead to travel. But even then, they didn't make things easy.

For starters, all trips outside the Eastern Bloc required a special blue passport. That document would remain in the sport ministry's possession until hours before you were scheduled to leave, at which point some government officer would issue it to you. Once back in Hungary, you'd have to give your blue passport to the government for "safekeeping." It was one of many ways the Communists had devised for controlling when and where people traveled.

Forgacs didn't get hold of his blue passport until the morning we were scheduled to fly to England. He was already driving us to the airport when he noticed he had received the wrong document. By coincidence, a different Gyula Forgacs had also requested a passport, and the sports ministry had mixed the two up.

"That doesn't look like me, does it?" he asked, handing me his passport.

"Not even close, Gyula," I told him.

"That's what I thought."

I was halfway convinced the trip was over. Traveling to the West with another person's passport was the kind of thing that could get you thrown in prison. So there was no question that we would need to head back to the sports ministry. Whether we could get all this sorted out in time to make our flight, however, was far from certain. The entire ride to the sports ministry, we sat in silence, as my coach drove as fast as he could without getting pulled over.

While Forgacs rushed inside to explain his situation, my parents and I waited in the car, trying not to think what would happen if he didn't come back in time. We still had to drive to the airport, park the car, check our luggage, and board the plane— which was scheduled to leave in about two hours. My father must have checked his pocket watch half a dozen times in the fifteen minutes we were there. When I saw the smile on Forgacs's face as we walked back to the car, I knew he had gotten what he came for. "I think we can still make it if we hurry!" is all he said, as he started the car and drove off.

The problem was our detour had cost us quite a bit of gasoline. We were still a good twenty minutes from the airport when the needle on the gas gauge hit empty. By some miracle we made it without running completely out of gas and boarded our flight with just a few minutes to spare. (Of course, when we got back to the car after the trip, it refused to start, and a friend had to bring Forgacs a can of gasoline just to get out of the airport.)

The whole ordeal left me very edgy and more than a little annoyed. We had followed all of the government's rules to the letter, and yet we still barely made it onto the plane. Why did everything have to be such a battle? I hoped things would be easier once we got to England.

I wasn't disappointed. The whole place just felt alive. There were women in gorgeous colorful dresses and men in well-tailored suits. Pop music blared from car radios, and the stores were stocked with more kinds of products than I knew existed. People just didn't have this kind of choice and variety back in Hungary, and they certainly didn't express themselves through what they wore. It was against the official ideology to stand out too much, to portray yourself as an individual. And, at least in my case, we didn't have much money for things like clothing. Whatever products we had access to were usually quite simple and functional. Compared to that, England felt like something out of a fashion magazine. Even the playing facilities were nicer. I can distinctly remember the sprawling green lawns at the boarding school where we were playing. In between games, the other girls and I would gather, and I'd practice my English, which I was only just starting to learn.

I spotted Teresa Needham not long after I arrived. She was the local favorite and received a lot of extra attention from tournament organizers and local press. I mostly kept my distance from her. Even though I had nothing against her personally, I knew she was one of my chief rivals, and I really wanted to beat her. When I finally got my chance, I didn't hold back.

Playing with the black pieces, I countered Teresa's king's pawn opening with a sharp Sicilian Defense that culminated in a swarming middlegame attack in which my queen, rook, and both bishops overwhelmed white's king. The game ended with a nice bishop sacrifice that made mate impossible for Teresa to avoid. It's not out of the question that I could have won the tournament even if I didn't beat her. But that victory—beating the top British player on her own turf—made it so much sweeter.

I finished the tournament in first place and without losing a single game. It was only during the closing ceremony, when the organizers gave me a large engraved glass bowl as my trophy, that the weight of what I had just done really sank in. A girl from Hungary had fought her way to the West, taken on the best players around, and left a world champion.

As a reward for my victory, my parents agreed to take me to London for a few days. I couldn't believe they had the money for such a trip. The Hungarian government had only allowed us to exchange a total of thirty pounds' worth of currency for all three of us, which had to last us the entire trip. But by some miracle, my parents worked it out. An Esperantist family they had contacted earlier in the trip had agreed to put us up in their home just outside London. As long as we didn't spend too much on food, we could last a few days in London before we ran out of cash. Forgacs, sadly, would not be joining us.

At that point I was only twelve years old, but I had seen quite a few large cities in my part of the world. London was something else—not just its size and energy, but also the little things. An entire store selling nothing but cheese! An exotic new chocolate treat called a Kit Kat (still one of my favorites)! Department stores were so massive they seemed to go on forever. At night, the town was lit up in bright neon lights—which would have never happened back home, where electricity was rationed and the city went mostly dark every evening.

Had it not been for our hosts, we could have never put together the money to stay even a single night in London. They served us a hearty breakfast each morning. And for the rest of our meals, my parents and I would get by on a loaf of bread, a few bananas, and a bottle of milk.

The British chess community used the opportunity to organize a four-game blitz exhibition with a fifteen-year-old local hero, who also happened to be the Boys' Under-16 World Champion—a match I won in an upset in the final game.

The reaction I got really shocked me. Back home, my wins against boys were rarely celebrated. But here in the UK, they were happy to see me succeed. There was actually applause as the match ended. In fact, the Western media in general often praised my achievements during this period. A British chess writer, the grandmaster Murray Chandler, wrote around that time that "the Hungarians may have found their Kasparov [the most promising Soviet player and future World Champion], only she is female!" If this was life outside the Iron Curtain, I thought, I sure could get used to it.

SIX

Back in Budapest, the reaction to my success was far more complicated. We hadn't unpacked our bags yet from our trip to England when my mother got a phone call saying that she had gotten in trouble at work.

My mother had taken a few days off from work at the school where she taught in order to travel with me that summer. The school year hadn't even started, so it didn't seem like a big deal. All she had missed were a few staff meetings. But it was grounds enough for her school's principal to put her on probation. It didn't matter that her daughter had just brought pride to our country on the global stage. My mother had broken the rules, and that would be that.

I was still giddy from my triumph in England, and I was looking forward to celebrating a little and living for a moment in those fleeting few days of ecstasy that can accompany a big win. With one phone call, they had managed to bring this celebration to a screeching halt. I was only twelve, and I was already getting tired of the authorities acting as if my family was doing something wrong.

My mom was so angered by the decision that she quit her job not long after that. Looking back years later, it might have been a blessing, because she had more time to devote to me and my sisters' careers. In fact, that was the year that my mother taught Judit chess. My youngest sister had been eager to learn the game for a while. And my mother had picked up the basic rules by then. So she spent many afternoons giving Judit the same introductory lessons my father had given me.

It's impossible to say whether the reprimand from my mother's school was a targeted attack by the authorities on me and my family (communist governments are good at hiding what they don't want you to know). What's undeniable is that the people in charge had grown increasingly hostile to us, in no small part thanks to the work of another female chess player who happened to share my first name, Zsuzsa Veroci.

Zsuzsa was twenty years older than me and had been a big celebrity in Hungarian women's chess long before I came on the scene. At the time, she wrote a chess column for one of the country's leading newspapers, *Nepszava*. She was also the daughter of Bela Veroci, who, in addition to being a board member at the Hungarian Chess Federation, happened to write a chess column of his own for the sports paper *Nepsport*.

I didn't know either of them well. But it was clear even in those days that they both resented the attention I was getting. I had overtaken Zsuzsa in the national rankings earlier that year and would soon surpass her in the international rankings, too. They didn't like that I represented a changing of the guard in female chess. And they used their influence to advance a media narrative that portrayed Zsuzsa Veroci as the unrivaled queen of Hungarian chess, and Zsuzsa Polgar as not only overrated but an outsider and a troublemaker as well—a narrative that soon became the party line in the mainstream press.

The two of them also happened to be close with the head of the chess federation, Sandor Szerenyi. And they used their influence to turn him into an "anti-Polgar" partisan in the extreme. Szerenyi wasn't the kind of person one wanted as an enemy in those years, as he was quite friendly with Hungary's top government official, Janos Kadar. In fact, he would often drop Kadar's name during meetings, perhaps as an intimidation tactic. It was only once the Verocis put us on Szerenyi's radar that the chess federation started picking fights with my family again.

The chief bone of contention was Szerenyi's insistence that I play primarily in female-only tournaments. This was the standard career path for talented female players not just in Hungary, but throughout the Soviet empire. And my win at the World Girls' Under-16 Championship in England—as well as another tournament victory at a women's event in Bulgaria not long after that—had marked me as one of the top young female players on the planet. The thinking within the Hungarian Chess Federation was that if I stuck to girls' events, many more high-profile victories would follow, which would be good propaganda for both the Hungarian Chess Federation and the country.

There was also a prevailing assumption—even among my friends and supporters—that no women, even me, were good enough to compete at the same level as men and boys. "Why put yourself through all that?" was the general attitude I'd hear at tournaments and even at my own chess club. "You're setting yourself up for failure."

Sure, I might be able to beat some of the weaker male players. But I would never be able to compete against the best in my country, much less the world. These naysayers often pointed out that no woman had ever earned the grandmaster (GM) title, chess's highest designation. The category of woman grandmaster (WGM), meanwhile, had been created a few years earlier. But the requirements for that title were much less stringent than for the traditional GM or even the international master (IM) title—which, in part, reflected the view that women shouldn't be expected to measure up to men in this game.

This plan didn't appeal to me in the least. As far as I was concerned, I had already proven myself at female-only tournaments. Now I was ready to move on to more challenging events which included higher-rated (usually male) opponents. This was, in part, a matter of principle for me. I didn't want anybody telling me who I could and couldn't play, especially if those dictates were based on the assumption that women couldn't measure up to men. But I also had my career to think about. I was racing to become an international master—the second-highest title in chess after grandmaster—as soon as possible. This required me to play in tournaments with a certain number of IMs. And since there were only a few female IMs in those years, it would be impossible for me to get the title if I stuck to women's events. The federation's demands, in other words, would have stalled my career just as it was starting to take off.

So when I was invited to compete in the Hungarian Women's Championship that year, I politely declined. Of course, the federation didn't like that very much. Like so much of Hungarian society in those years, the chess federation, as a part of the sports ministry, was just another arm of the government. And nobody could stand up to the government and not pay the price.

Not only had I stepped out of line, but I had also done so in a way that went against the federation's long-standing belief that women should not compete against men.

It wasn't the existence of female-only tournaments that bothered me. I understood that these events served an important purpose back then, as they still do now—not least because they create a safe and friendly environment for women and girls in what has historically been a male-dominated culture. But I always saw these tournaments as a temporary measure—one that would eventually be unnecessary once more great women players broke into the game and the male-centric norms of the chess community began to shift.

I was already coming to see myself as a person who could change those norms. But for that to happen, I would need to show the world that I could hold my own against the toughest competition on the planet, male or female. That meant continuing to work hard on my game and playing in open tournaments in which most of my competitors would be men. The Hungarian authorities didn't want to see any of this happen. But I really didn't care what they wanted, especially after how they had treated my mother.

I wasn't fighting this battle on my own. Both of my parents, and especially my father, were firmly against the federation's plans for my career. In his mind, my freedom to play in the best tournaments, regardless of gender, was essential to my development as a player.

"There are two ways to climb a mountain," he would say, sometimes drawing a crude upside-down *V* on the back of an envelope to help illustrate the point. "One way is to take a winding path, zigzagging from side to side across the mountain's face, gradually making your way up, setting small goals and hoping that you get to the top one day. The other is the direct route, scaling the mountain at the steepest angle, making big jumps on your way straight to the summit." The main reason women hadn't excelled at chess as much as men, he believed, was because they had been forced to take the winding path. But to become the best, I had to set my sights high, not limit myself to whatever the government allowed.

My father even made this argument to the chess federation president in person. But Szerenyi was having none of it. He screamed at my father, calling him a "crook" and an "anarchist," and sent him away.

At first, the federation's hostility manifested itself in subtle ways. For example, I had already satisfied the requirements for the woman grandmaster title by then, which would have made me the youngest person in history to do so. In fact, I would ultimately earn eleven separate WGM norms. But, in what I can only interpret as an act of spite, the Hungarian Chess Federation "forgot" to submit my paperwork to FIDE. I didn't make a fuss about it. I needed to pick my battles. Becoming a grandmaster was my real goal, anyway.

There was another conflict between my parents and the chess federation that blew up around that time. The organization's higher-ups insisted that one of their own officials—and not my parents—accompany me on my trips to tournaments, and especially to tournaments in the West.

It was an entirely self-serving demand on the federation's part. They just wanted an excuse to travel to the West, which was a rare privilege in those years, even government officials. It was also a money-making opportunity for those who were so inclined. Many Hungarians who were granted permission to visit England or France or Holland would use their trip to acquire hard-to-find products and bring them back to Hungary, where they could sell for a significant profit. And with me, the federation's leadership saw a chance to enrich themselves personally. They would accompany me as a "chaperone" whenever I competed in the West. Along the way, these functionaries could enjoy some free drinks, stay at nice hotels, purchase a few Sony Walkman cassette players, or VCRs, or whatever else they could get their hands on, and make a tidy sum at the end of it all.

I remember getting this tense sickening feeling in my stomach when my father told me all of this. The memory of my attack in Yugoslavia was still fresh in my mind. And just the suggestion that I might have to leave the country without my parents was physically terrifying.

It wasn't just the emotional aftermath of the attack that was affecting me. At that moment, the world outside of my family just felt threatening in a very visceral way. Every person and institution seemed out to get me, and for reasons that just didn't make sense. I wasn't going anywhere without my parents, and I definitely wasn't traveling with some stranger from the chess federation. I didn't explain any of this to my parents—I never had to.

The whole "chaperone" idea was a nonstarter for them, and they refused to go along with it.

Of course, the more we refused to accept the chess federation's demands, the more beating we took in the media. As the respected Hungarian journalist Tamas Karpati would later write about that period: "The press was characterized by massive resistance to the Polgars. This manifested itself in different ways in misinformation, information withholding, open and covert accusations, falsifying the facts. It would be unfair if I didn't mention that in the anti-Polgar chorus, there were also a couple 'false' voices, supporting the girls and their father. There was also a period when there was deep silence around them, which according to my well-informed colleagues was due to orders from the highest levels." With the phrase *"false" voices*, Karpati was ironically referring to the few writers who broke with the official line to publicly support me.

It was around this time that my father officially resigned his membership in the Communist Party—the boldest act of protest he could think of, and one that was sure to invite yet more of the government's ire. This was an era of one-party government. And it was expected that most citizens would be members in good standing. This was especially true for teachers, given their influence over young students. So, cutting ties with the party could have easily cost my dad his job. My mother and I didn't know he was going to do this. And we were both a little surprised when he broke the news to us after returning from work one afternoon. But we never once doubted that he was right.

My father continued to support communism as a political philosophy. But he'd had enough of the corrupt leaders who were abusing the Communist Party's power to hurt our family.

"If they want to punish us for standing up for principle," he said to me, "there's nothing we can do to stop them. But I am not going to be part of an organization which treats us like this."

It was the purest act of courage I had ever witnessed. He was well aware of the dangers of turning his back on the party. And he had no guarantee that things would turn out well for us. But he did it anyway. Right then, I wanted to be brave like him.

My father wasn't trying to escalate the situation on purpose. He just wasn't willing to live in such a debasing and demoralizing arrangement—and he didn't care who knew it. In fact, a few days after leaving the party, my father paid another visit to Szerenyi, the head of the Hungarian Chess Federation, to share the news. "I'm no longer a member of the party," he told him. "And you're the reason why."

The press had managed to turn public opinion so strongly against us that we started to fear for our safety. Returning home from work one day, my father found a strange letter in the mail. It had no return address. Inside was a photo of him with his eyes cut out. There was also a one-page handwritten letter, which he refused to let me read. He only said that it was dripping with antisemitic remarks and violent threats.

In that instant, none of what we were doing seemed worth it. There wasn't a principle in the world worth losing my dad over. His reaction showed me that there was another way to get through this situation.

He didn't get scared. He got angry, storming off to the police to report the incident. What was happening to him was unjust. And the only proper response to injustice is opposition and action—even if that action is in vain. Overt acts of antisemitism were technically against the law and were often persecuted. The police agreed to investigate the threat, but they never found anything.

That was the first time I really understood the stakes of the battle we were fighting—that it was me and my family against the world. I knew what side I was on. And I was ready to go to war.

A lot of my chess friends didn't understand what we were doing. The general attitude I would encounter at my club or around tournaments was that I shouldn't be putting up such a fight. What difference did it make if I played in female tournaments or male tournaments? It's not a hill that is worth dying on.

That other people couldn't understand this didn't really faze me. I knew my father was right to push back against the federation, to put my interests ahead of any ideology or political party. And his strength became my strength. His act of protest became my act of protest. That thought alone gave me confidence that we'd come out on top in all of this. We had done it a few years earlier, when the authorities tried to stop me from homeschooling, and I really didn't expect this time to be different.

SEVEN

The following year, in 1982, my father made arrangements for me to work with a new coach for a couple of weeks in Moscow. The Soviet capital was far and away the center of chess culture in Eastern Europe in those days, if not the world. And it was widely believed that Soviet coaches were among the best on the planet. My father didn't want me left out of that tradition, and neither did I. So my family headed to Moscow's Central Chess Club for a special coaching session with a grandmaster named Alexey Suetin.

In a part of the world where chess is treated like a religion, the Central Chess Club is Mecca. The building itself is a vast nineteenth-century mansion in the center of Moscow on Gogolevsky Boulevard. And throughout the Soviet era it had served as a site of countless historic tournaments. It was a place where giants of the game like Tigran Petrosian, Mikhail Tal, and Vasily Smyslov walked the halls. A fifteen-year-old Bobby Fischer even traveled there in 1958 to get his own peek at the Soviet chess machine in action.

Moving through the rooms at the Central Chess Club, it was hard not to feel humbled. Every inch of the place—from the rugs to the draperies and even the molded ceilings—gave off a sense of nobility and weightiness. The walls were covered in old photographs of the great Soviet masters, and everywhere you looked there was some evocative artifact from the game's past. At one point, I walked through a nondescript door in the mansion to find the offices of the Soviet chess newspaper 64, which I would read back in Hungary every chance I got. I even got a quick peek at the layout for the following week's cover, which felt like a glimpse into the future!

I had never seen chess venerated in this way. At that moment, in that building, chess seemed like the most important thing in the world. But it was hard to ignore the fact that almost all of the names and images adorning the club's walls were of men. I knew that for many girls, this would have been taken as a sign that women didn't belong, which was a genuinely sad thought. But I didn't take it that way. If anything, the noticeable absence of women lit a fire in me. There was still a lot of history to be written for this game, and I was going to do my best to write it.

Suetin came out to greet us not long after we arrived. He wasn't what we expected, and he gave off the distinct impression of being hungover. After a few pleasantries, he alerted my parents that the price they had agreed on for my chess instruction was too low, and that he would need ten times that amount in order to take me on as a student. The discussion got a bit tense after that. Suetin apologized for the surprise. He explained that he was afraid to mention his actual price in his correspondence with my parents, since the government was likely reading his mail. Had the Communist Party discovered that he was charging such a high rate, it could mean trouble for him.

He did have another proposition for us, though. Since we had traveled so far to meet him, Suetin offered to have a less experienced coach, a candidate master, teach me instead. I, for one, was open to the idea. Soviet candidate masters were rumored to be as strong as international masters elsewhere in the world—which is just one rung below grandmaster. So it was at least worth considering. I agreed to play several blitz games against the young instructor so that we could size each other up.

Part of me was just itching to play even a few games in this cathedral of chess—it was impossible not to. My opponent and I found an out-of-the-way spot, put five minutes on each of our clocks, and over the next hour or so, showed each other what we were made of.

Even I was surprised at how lopsided the results were. I didn't just beat him—I demolished him, winning at least eight of the ten games (nine, as my father remembers it). My dad was a little irritated that Suetin would even consider passing his daughter off on such a weak player, but I didn't take it personally. I was used to people underestimating me, and I actually enjoyed the chance to set the record straight. This young player, we all agreed, should not be my teacher. Even Suetin couldn't argue with that. We ended the meeting and went our separate ways.

I wasn't in a hurry to leave, though. In fact, we went back nearly every day after that for a few games of blitz with whoever happened to be at the club. At one point, I spotted the father of the Soviet Chess School himself, former world champion Mikhail Botvinnik, which left me just a little starstruck—as did my brief encounter with grandmaster Yuri Averbakh, whose series of books on endgames had been a staple of my chess education.

For my father, though, the most impressive thing about the Moscow chess club was its enormous library card catalogs, which held more than a million important games sorted by opening and player. It wouldn't be long before he invested in some card catalogs of his own for our apartment and got to work on his own library of games.

We spent the next week or two enjoying the city. We visited Red Square, played chess in the park, and sampled some of the local cuisine. I especially liked the black bread sold in the bakeries throughout Moscow, as well as the kefir, a fermented milk drink that is one of my favorite Russian delicacies to this day. I also used the chance to practice my Russian, which had gotten a little rusty by then.

One of our last stops before leaving was at an international tournament somewhere near the Olympic Village the city had built for the recent summer games. Mikhail Tal happened to be competing, and I wanted to see him with my own eyes. Tal was one of the chess world's biggest celebrities, and with good reason. He was only twenty-three when he won the World Championship in 1960, making him the youngest person to have ever held the title up to that point. His games were so dazzling and inventive that players took to calling him "the Magician from Riga" (the Latvian capital where he was born). But I tend to think of him as the Mike Tyson of chess, because of his aggressive attacking style. Until somewhat recently, he still held the record for the longest unbeaten streak in competitive chess, having gone ninety-five games without a single loss in the 1970s. I wasn't going to leave Moscow without at least seeing him.

When I finally caught sight of him, I was a bit taken aback. The Tal I had seen in photographs was handsome and dashing, with a head of dark hair and a youthful mischievous smile. That was not the Tal I saw in Moscow. Although only forty-four years old, a life of heavy smoking and drinking had added years to his face. He had lost all of the hair on top of his head, yet he wore the sides excessively long, which lent him an air of mad-scientist eccentricity that seemed fitting for a magician. Behind this odd appearance, though, was one of the most generous souls I would ever encounter in competitive chess.

I was still quite shy as a thirteen-year-old, and the thought of approaching him was too much for me to bear. Sensing this, my mother intervened. She walked over to Tal while he was pacing in the hallway chain-smoking, as he so often did. She introduced herself as my mother, and explained that it was a dream of mine to play him in a blitz game, if he could find the time. His eyes lit up. He obviously knew who I was. It would be his pleasure, he said.

I got very excited. I could hardly imagine what was about to take place. He disappeared from our sight to resume his tournament game. A short time later he came out, and said, "I am ready for some blitz." He had offered his tournament opponent a draw just so he could play me.

It didn't seem real. Tal—one of the greatest players to ever touch a chess piece—had actually heard of me. Even better, he would rather play with me than continue with a far more consequential game in an official event. This just couldn't be happening. I can only imagine his reasons for sitting down with me. Maybe he was curious about how good I actually was. Or maybe he was just being kind. Probably it was a bit of both.

I can still picture the confident way he moved the pieces, evidence of a lifetime spent at the board; the big-eyed facial expressions he'd make when evaluating a position; and his oddly shaped right hand, which was deformed from birth by a congenital disorder. Based on his playing style, I had imagined his personality might be a bit no-nonsense, or even a little hostile. I was pleased to be proven wrong. The whole time he showed me nothing but warmth and kindness, peppering our games with jokes and funny observations.

As we blitzed out moves in a series of games, a crowd of people swarmed the table, which made me a bit nervous. But anxiety was a small price to pay for spending time with one of my heroes. I couldn't wait to get back to my chess club in Budapest and tell all of my friends that I had tested my mettle against the great magician himself. Would they even believe me?

I surprised myself in that first game, sacrificing two pieces in Tal-like fashion, and forcing a draw by perpetual check, which prompted an approving smile from the former champion. After that, Tal took over, winning the remaining few games. But I didn't mind. I was having the time of my life.

The graciousness Tal showed me that day was a revelation to me. He didn't know me, and he didn't need to be nice to me. And yet he saw a chance to encourage an up-and-coming player and give a young girl a story she'd never forget—and he didn't hesitate. That was the kind of champion I wanted to be.

We left Moscow not long after that and headed back to Varna for another tournament. The train ride took more than twenty hours in a sleeper car. With two small children to look after, my parents were at their wits' end by the time we reached Bulgaria, but not me. I was still buzzing with excitement from my encounter with Tal.

EIGHT

For the next few years, I became a prisoner of sorts, locked behind the Iron Curtain, not sure if I would ever be allowed to leave again. At first, it seemed inconceivable to me that my own government would go to such lengths to keep a young girl who was barely a teenager from playing a game. I couldn't help but wonder if I had made a wrong move somewhere along the way, if I maybe should have given the authorities just a little of what they were asking for, if for no other reason than to spare my parents the strain and stigma of yet another controversy.

For most of my life, every spare penny they had went toward my coaches, chess books, and tournament travel. And here, I had made these two people who had sacrificed so much for me into enemies of the state. I would have backed down and did as the government asked if my parents had asked me. I owed them at least that. But they never did. In fact, the message I got from them was always the same: If you want to fight this battle, we'll be here, fighting right along with you.

It's a profoundly lonely feeling, being singled out by such a powerful regime, denied the right to pursue your dream. What I hated most was the sense of helplessness I felt. The government had made its decision, and there was nothing either I or my parents could do about it. We simply had to bide our time and hope for an eventual change.

I was thirteen years old and just hitting my stride as a chess player, moving up the rankings faster than ever before. The next few years were supposed to be the culmination of all that I had worked for—a period in which I traveled the world, making a name for myself on the global stage, and testing myself against the very best. This was the stage of my career I had been looking forward to most. And now, it had all been canceled, without ceremony or justification, with a single decry from the sports ministry.

But one thing chess had taught me was that simmering in these sorts of emotions usually makes bad situations even worse. If I was going to weather this, I had to keep a level head, and I would need to be strategic. I kept returning to something my father had taught me. It's useless to fixate on things you can't control, he used to say. And, of course, he was right.

The authorities might be able to keep me away from top tournaments for a little while, I thought, but they couldn't keep me from getting better. That part, at least, was in my control. And so, I did what I always did when faced with a bad position: I went to work finding ways to improve it, however incrementally.

For starters, that meant continuing to play as much chess as I could against the strongest players I could find. Since I couldn't travel very far, my parents had the inspired idea to open our house to masters and grandmasters from places like Denmark or Holland or the Soviet Union to stay with us for a few days—all of them men. If there was an especially strong tournament happening anywhere near Budapest, I would often get in touch with a few of the top players and let them know they had a place to stay after the competition. We didn't have much space in those days—five people in a tiny six-hundred-square-foot apartment. Still, there were times when we had four or five guests staying with us at once.

I recall distinctly the few days we spent with the Dutch players Leon Pliester, Herman Grooten, and Johan van Mil, who had
driven together to Hungary for a tournament. I had never met
anyone from Holland before. And I was immediately charmed by
how funny they were. The kind of humor I was used to in Eastern
Europe was generally quite wry and ironic, a symptom of living
under an authoritarian government. But not these guys. They were
playful and lighthearted, always laughing. I was the only person
in the family who spoke English—the main language our Dutch
guests and I shared—so I had to act as their interpreter. And yet,
it never felt awkward. We all loved having them around. They
brought a little bit of optimism from a part of the world, which at
that time felt so far away.

Our guests would usually spend part of their days sightseeing
in Budapest. At night, my mother would cook dinner for the group
and make palacsinta (Hungarian crepes) or some other delicacy for
dessert. After dinner, my father might tell a couple of the jokes he
had collected over the years. I loved the one about the man who
had gone to pray at the Wailing Wall in Jerusalem every day for
sixty years. When asked by a journalist what it felt like to pray so
intensely for so long, he replied, "Like I'm talking to a wall."

At night, my sisters and I would stay up late playing game after
game of blitz chess with whoever was staying over. For someone
who was banned from traveling, these little gatherings felt like the
next-best thing, and it made these bleak years at least tolerable, and
at times even fun. Not only was I developing as a chess player, but
I was also meeting new people, learning about different cultures,
and getting to practice my foreign languages.

At times our home felt like an overcrowded boardinghouse
for offbeat chess geniuses. We would have so many pull-out beds
in our closet-size guest room that there was sometimes no space
to walk! I can only imagine what my neighbors thought, with all
of these grown men constantly coming and going from our tiny

apartment. But for my sisters and me, nothing could be more normal.

Both Sofia and Judit had shown a serious interest in chess by then. And I would often find myself serving as part babysitter, part chess coach, spending hours a week in our apartment's back room teaching them endgame technique or analyzing classic games by Capablanca or Alexander Alekhine or Fischer.

These lessons were gratifying for me on so many levels. Here I was, welcoming my sisters into a world that mattered so much to me and inspiring in them the same passion for the game that my own coaches had given to me. I was also playing the role of teacher for the very first time, and I was delighted to find that it fit me very well. I remember having dreams at night about the chess school I would open one day—a sprawling campus with wood-paneled classrooms and playing areas and a grand lecture hall with stadium seating and a giant two-dimensional demonstration board at the front.

After our lessons is when the fun began. My sisters and I would often challenge each other to ten-game blitz matches, the winner of which would earn a half bar of chocolate or some other small prize from my father. Early on, I'd start the game without one of my rooks to level the playing field—or give them "rook odds," as it's known. I'd also give them "time odds," playing with just one minute on my own clock while allowing each of them five minutes. As Sofia and Judit got stronger, we'd adjust the rules to keep things competitive. I'd give them knight or bishop odds. Within a few years, we were playing with only time odds until eventually neither of them needed an advantage.

These matches were always fiercely contested events full of laughter and trash talk. Both Sofia and Judit were determined to beat their big sister, and I was just as determined not to let them. Since I often had just one minute for the entire game to deliver checkmate (or else lose on time), our games frequently devolved into adrenaline-fueled scrambles in which I was forced to make my moves almost as quickly as I could think. The board would become a tempest of rushing hands, wobbling pieces, and increasingly violent clock punches. Captured pieces would fly off the table as my movements grew more frantic. Sofia and Judit were already growing into their particular playing styles, which, in both their cases, was far more attacking and aggressive than my own solid, positional approach to the game.

Once the match ended, I'd replay the games with them, pointing out where they'd miscalculated or missed a tactic or overlooked a stronger move. When we needed a break from chess, we'd tell jokes or turn on the radio and listen to whatever music was trending at the time. Any pop music considered subversive in any way was banned by the government. So the music that made it through the censors—ABBA or Boney M or Modern Talking—became our portal to a forbidden world.

While I was staying put in Budapest, though, Szerenyi was doing whatever he could to ruin my reputation. He even made his case to the world chess federation, known as FIDE, at that body's annual meeting in Manila in 1983. There, before an audience of FIDE delegates, he insisted that my name be scrubbed from the official women's world rankings, since I had continued to play mostly against men. As the English journalist and grandmaster Raymond Keene wrote in *The Spectator* a few years later, Szerenyi "complained in comically broken English that Mr. Polgar only wants his girls to play with the boys." Fortunately, his arguments against me weren't well received by the delegates at FIDE, who refused to remove me from the world rankings. It was becoming clear to me that Szerenyi didn't merely disagree with us. This was personal for him.

If anything, all of this hostile treatment was the best motivator I could have hoped for, because my chess improved by leaps and bounds during that period. By January 1983, I had become among the top ten female players in the world. And even with the travel ban in place, I was able to meet the first of the three performance requirements—or "norms" as they are called in chess—for my international master title that same year at just fourteen years of age, a title I would officially earn in 1984. To put it in perspective, the world champion at the time, Anatoly Karpov, didn't become an IM until he was around eighteen. Kasparov was about sixteen. So the fact that I was advancing even more quickly than these great players was a very encouraging sign.

But the accomplishments that stand out to me from that period had little to do with formal titles. In 1984, I became the highest-rated fifteen-year-old chess player on the planet, male or female. This flurry of achievements only raised my hopes for the future. The government had tried to derail my career, and in response I just kept getting better. I could just feel that it was only a matter of time before this terrible episode would finally be over. As it turned out, my enemies weren't finished with me just yet.

NINE

When the phone rang early on the morning of July 1, 1984, I was hoping it would be good news. The official world rankings were scheduled to be published that day, and I had a strong suspicion I would be at the top of the female list. I couldn't be sure, of course. There was no internet in those days, which made it difficult to keep close tabs on other players. Back then, the rankings were released only twice a year—first in January and then in July—and there was at least a chance that one of my rivals might have pulled ahead of me.

I can't say for sure which friend was the first to call that morning—the phone hardly stopped ringing all day. But when they told me I now shared the number one spot with Pia Cramling, I screamed. I had experienced the rush of a big victory plenty of times before that. But this was another thing entirely: pure euphoria and vindication and contentment, like the entire world had just given me a great compliment. I remember my sisters rushing out of their bedroom to hug me and the look of pride and satisfaction on my parents' faces. "Did you hear that, Klara?" my father said to my mother. "Our daughter is the number one female chess player on the planet." My mother just smiled, tears of joy welling up in her eyes.

It was the best news I had heard in years, and nothing could spoil my good mood. I imagined that this is how people must feel when they win the lottery. Only this was better. This I had earned.

My family immediately walked down to the newsstand to buy several copies of the major newspapers where the rankings were published. It wasn't until I saw the list, right there in black and white, that it all felt real. I was the number one female player in the world—and just barely fifteen years old. All of that hard work, sacrifice, practice, and study had led me to this moment. I pictured the Verocis and the top officials at the federation reading the news. They had made it their mission to cast doubt on my abilities and defame me in the press. Now not even they could deny what I had just achieved—or at least that's what I thought.

It took just a day or two for my critics to prove me wrong. By July 3, in fact, Zsuzsa Veroci's paper, *Nepszava*, was at it again, insisting that I still hadn't proven myself as the top female player in the world. In a column subtly titled "When the First Is Not the Best," one journalist wrote that I had somehow gamed the system by "regularly playing in men's competitions (weak men's competitions), cunningly collecting rating points."

Since the men's tournaments I played in generally featured higher-rated players, she argued, I was able to increase my rating more quickly than if I had played in female-only tournaments. I could never understand this argument. I had played—and beaten!— much better opponents than most of the other female players in the world. In other words, I had proven myself at the chess board. How on earth could this be construed as cheating? I nearly threw the newspaper across the room when I read that column, I was so livid. How could they write and print this garbage!?

As usual, though, my father was there to put things in perspective. "Stop reading whatever nonsense they're writing in the papers," he told me. "This is chess. All that matters is who makes the better moves. And the world now knows that of all the women in the world, nobody plays better than you do."

I knew this already, of course. My parents had said some version of this to me countless times over the years. But being reminded of it at that moment gave me an idea. I was scheduled to do an interview on a popular Sunday radio show that week. And it seemed like the perfect time to settle this dispute in a way that nobody could ever question. So, when the interviewer asked me what I thought of the negative coverage in places like *Nepszava*, I had my answer ready. If Veroci really thinks she's the better player, I said, then she should have no trouble playing this fifteen-year-old in a twelve-game match.

With that one interview, I managed to put my biggest critic in a tough spot. For the next week the Hungarian papers were full of speculation about a possible match between Hungary's two most well-known female chess players. And, just as I had suspected, Veroci found a way to refuse to play me.

When a reporter at her own paper asked about all the buzz surrounding our possible match, she brushed it off. "I don't pay attention to it. On such a basis anyone in the country could ask me to play a 12-game match. Zsuzsa Polgar has not achieved any kind of results, neither in the Hungarian championship, nor in female competitions. When I feel that she will be a worthy challenger, I will accept it. But until then..."

It was such an obviously ridiculous response that I almost felt sorry for her. She was really trying to argue that the world's number one female player wasn't worthy of a match with her. The reality, of course, was that Zsuzsa Veroci was afraid to play me and be embarrassed by the results. Anybody paying attention could see for themselves. It felt good to finally defend my reputation so publicly. But I also took a special pleasure in outplaying Veroci at her own game, at using her favorite weapon—media perception—against her. The fight wasn't over, but it felt like this round had gone to me.

None of my success stopped the head of the Hungarian Chess Federation, Szerenyi, from continuing his anti-Polgar campaign. That same year that I rose to number one in the world, he had deliberately insulted me by offering me the third board at the Hungarian women's Olympiad team.

The Olympiad is chess's equivalent of the Olympic games. And every two years, each country's chess federation chooses two teams—one men's and one women's—to represent their home nation in competition. Based on my rating alone, I should have been the obvious choice for playing first board—that is, for facing off against the best players for each other country. By asking me to play third board—and restricting my parents' involvement in the run-up to the event—he had made it impossible for me to accept. And so, I would not be part of that year's team.

This would be like the United States putting together the 1992 basketball "Dream Team" without Michael Jordan. The federation told the press that I had refused to represent my country, which, of course, made me mad. But what was different about this dispute was that the rest of the world was starting to take notice of the unfair treatment I was getting from my federation.

Now that I was at the top of the female rankings, invitations to elite tournaments in the West began flooding in. The chess community couldn't wait to see Hungary's girl prodigy in action, and I was just as impatient to let them. As usual, the only thing standing in my way was my own government, which was still refusing to grant me the passport I needed to leave the Eastern Bloc. We had settled into a routine, the authorities and I. After each tournament invitation, my family would submit an official request to the sports ministry (through the Hungarian Chess Federation) for permission to travel to the Netherlands or England or America or wherever the big event was being held. My mother would bring our paperwork down to the government office, and a week or so later we'd get a call or a letter stating that our request had been denied.

But the punishment didn't end there. That same year, the federation issued a disciplinary notice that revoked my license to play under the Hungarian flag—not just in the West, but anywhere. A year earlier, this would have devastated me. But not this time. What the federation had failed to realize is that they were no longer dealing with a promising young player. They were dealing with the world women's number one. And that gave me some influence of my own—particularly in the Western media.

After the federation completely banned me from playing, journalists and chess players all over the world started to ask a very inconvenient question regarding my situation: Why? Especially to Western observers, it made no sense that my government would bar such a high-profile player from competing around the world. If the authorities—and, specifically, the Hungarian Chess Federation— wanted to keep me sequestered, they would need to give a reason.

The actual reason was that I hadn't done as I was told. The state was used to dictating the career paths of talented people, whether musicians or artists or athletes. The future they had mapped out for me was one in which I played primarily in female-only tournaments, won the Hungarian Women's Championship each year, represented Hungary in female competitions around the world, and played the part of a compliant, reverential subject of the communist government. My chief crime, if you wish to call it that, was to take control over my own career and insist on playing in strong tournaments against men.

The powers that be couldn't admit any of this to the press, of course. So, when journalists started to take note of my success and question the Hungarian Chess Federation about why I was banned from traveling, things got a bit uncomfortable for my "jailers." I'm sure it came as a shock to many in the government that their campaign against me would inspire such a strong response. State-sponsored sexism and oppression had been standard practice in that part of the world for generations. Now it seemed that the feminist movement that had transformed so many Western institutions years before was beginning to exert some influence in Hungary. I didn't see myself as a revolutionary for women's liberation. I was just fighting for the right to excel at the thing I loved the most—it was really that simple. Yet, in retrospect, a revolution was exactly what we were waging. And, at least in this particular battle, my side won.

Sometime early in 1985, the sports ministry and the chess federation probably got tired of defending their policies against me and decided it was easier to leave me alone. I had just been invited to play in an exhibition match against the grandmaster John Nunn in Hamburg, Germany. And, purely as a matter of principle at this point, my family dutifully submitted an official request that I be allowed to travel there. We were expecting the usual rejection. But not this time. One afternoon, my mother received a phone call from the sports ministry regarding our trip. She mostly just listened, as some official on the other end spoke. From the stunned look on her face as he hung up the phone, I was sure something awful had happened.

"What is it? What now?!" I asked her.

"You're not going to believe this, but they've approved our trip to Hamburg. We can pick up our documents next week."

This was outrageously good news. And there was plenty of shouting and celebrating and phone calls spreading the news that day. But it felt less like a victory than a reprieve.

Since flights within the Eastern Bloc were cheaper for us in those days, my mother and I flew to East Berlin first. From there, we would take a train under the wall to West Berlin. But first, we needed to get past the checkpoint at the Friedrichstrasse railway station. It was no easy feat.

Friedrichstrasse was one of the major border crossings in those days, the site of so many heartrending goodbyes and dashed hopes that it was known as the "Palace of Tears." I had heard stories of all the families separated by the wall, unable to see each other ever again—and here I was, about to make my way across. I felt a pervasive sense of seriousness and danger as we waited in line to have our documents stamped, which was almost certainly by design. Reinforced fences surrounded the place on all sides, and every few feet stood an armed police officer, sometimes accompanied by an unnervingly well-behaved dog. Just outside the station sat row upon row of little booths, in which border agents would inspect each traveler's papers before deciding that person's fate. My mother and I waited silently, doing our best not to attract attention. Even though we had our papers in order and we had every right to be traveling across, I was still consumed with the sickening fear we had done something wrong.

As a fluent German speaker who had taught the language for years, my mother did the talking during our meeting with the border agent, answering each question succinctly and confidently, like a student sitting for an oral exam. We were waved through without incident. But things didn't get any less tense once we were inside the station. I remember waiting on the platform, watching as a policeman guided a leashed dog underneath each train car in search of stowaways. It was such a disturbing sight, watching a person being hunted like an animal right before my eyes, surrounded by businessmen and mothers and children in strollers. I got a shiver when it occurred to me that some of these guards were old enough to have been Nazis. I thought about my grandparents. The worst part of what I was seeing was just how routine the procedure seemed, as if this agent of the government were just delivering the mail. I tried my best not to imagine what I might see should some poor soul be discovered under one of the cars. If anyone was hiding, I thought, I hope they make it.

Just minutes after our train pulled away from Friedrichstrasse, we arrived in West Berlin. I remember asking myself, *Was that really it?* The past few years of uncertainty and anguish and hopelessness about ever being able to leave my small part of the world, all of it had culminated in a one-stop train ride. It would have seemed funny to me were it not so tragic.

It was a fitting way for me to reenter the West after all of those years. The Berlin Wall, I now saw, was little more than an arbitrary line meant to keep people in their place, a tool of enforcement and confinement—concepts that had come to shape my life in so many ways. As we walked out into West Berlin, it felt like I was escaping someplace desolate and forbidding for a new world of excitement and possibility.

That such a staggering transformation could occur by moving just a few feet—it was difficult to make sense of. These two places may have shared a language and a history and even a name, but the artificial barrier between them had given rise to two palpably different ways of life. And it was fast becoming obvious which of the two I preferred.

One of the people I was most excited to see on that trip was Frederic Friedel, who was one of several chess journalists who had come to my defense earlier that year in my disputes with the federation. He had also organized the exhibition event with Nunn. I had met him two years before in Budapest at the World Microcomputer Chess Championship, an event in which different chess computers—or "chess engines"—competed against each other. He would have been about forty by our trip to Hamburg, and he had already made a name for himself as a pioneer in applying computer technology to chess.

Frederic invited me and my mother over to his house in Hamburg to give us a sneak peek at his latest project, a digital database of chess games he would soon market as ChessBase. Although it might seem elementary in today's age, the idea of using computer software to organize a searchable collection of chess games was revolutionary back in 1985. Ready access to important games and opening lines is essential to how top-level players train and prepare for tournaments. Before ChessBase came on the scene, assembling that information was a tedious undertaking. Games had to be copied by hand or clipped from magazines and organized in vast file systems. My father had spent countless hours compiling a collection of hundreds of thousands of games, which he recorded on index cards stored in the long narrow drawers of a giant library card catalog we had in our apartment. Each month, we'd buy two copies of the leading chess publications, like the Russian *Shakhmatny Bulletin* or the Hungarian *Magyar Sakkelet* or the Yugoslav *Chess Informant*, cut out each of the games, paste them to cards, and file them away. Although it took years to build, the system itself was quite fragile. If you return a card to the wrong drawer, you may never find it again. Do that enough, and the system would fall into disarray. Taking care of our files over the years instilled in me an attention to detail that would serve me well on the chess board. Those card catalogs weren't very portable, of course. So, when I traveled to tournaments, I always carried several notebooks full of openings and games I had transcribed by hand—as well as any number of chess books—which I'd use to stay fresh in between games, and which we would lug from city to city in big suitcases in the days before suitcases commonly had wheels.

ChessBase promised to replace these old analog systems by creating a single, comprehensive game database that, in theory, would be available to anyone with a computer. By today's standards, the program he showed me that day was dreadfully slow and clunky, as most software was in that era. But the seismic potential of what Frederic had helped build was impossible to deny. Frederic later admitted to me that my father's system, which he had seen for himself while visiting Budapest, was one of the inspirations for ChessBase.

Frederic was always on the cutting edge of chess computer technology. In fact, it was during a visit to his home sometime later that I first met Matthias Wullenweber, who was already at work on the chess engine Fritz, one of the most sophisticated chess programs of its day. Testing out Fritz at Frederic's house that day, it was clear that with just a few more breakthroughs, this technology could change the game of chess forever. And I got my first glimpse of this future during my visits to Frederic's house.

Frederic and Matthias were helping to build a future for chess that just a few years earlier would have been unimaginable. Seeing what they had created filled me with a kind of hope and optimism that I had never felt before.

TEN

Really, though, the Hamburg trip was just a prelude to my first visit to the United States later that spring. The Hungarian government had approved our request for me, my mother, and Sofia to travel to the New York Open, which was being held at the Penta in Manhattan (formerly the Hotel Pennsylvania). I would play in the tournament's top section, while Sofia would compete in the amateur group.

The only catch was that my father and Judit would have to remain back in Hungary. The government was afraid that if we were all allowed to leave the Soviet-controlled world, we might never return. And forcing the two of them to stay put for the duration of our trip was their insurance policy against our defection.

It was the strongest event I had ever entered. So it seemed like the perfect venue for my US debut. The progress I was making in those years was undeniable, yet I had still to beat a single grandmaster in an official classical time-control game. I saw this tournament as my best chance to cross that item off of my list. It didn't hurt that the tournament organizer, Jose Cuchi, generously agreed to cover our travel and accommodation costs.

Had you told me, weeks earlier, that I would soon be packing my suitcase for an all-expenses-paid trip to New York City, I wouldn't have believed it. Yet I remember feeling this odd mixture of elation and anxiousness in the run-up to the trip. New York was the farthest away from home I had ever traveled, and I had no idea what I might find there. I'd been told that it was unlike any city in the world, but what exactly did that mean? For all I knew, I was heading into a hostile environment that I was ill-equipped to navigate.

Complicating matters even further was that my sister and mother spoke very little English, which meant that I would have to serve as both spokesperson and interpreter for the group in almost every situation. I had picked up some basic English a few years before, in a five-week intensive course taught by a gregarious old Hungarian man who had lived for a time in Australia. Since then, I had practiced speaking the language every chance I got, but still had no real sense of how my English would hold up when truly put to the test in a place like New York. Lucky for me, all of these worries turned out to be unfounded.

Flying over the Atlantic Ocean for the first time was a bizarre experience. It was the longest flight I had ever taken. And I found it deeply unnerving that for all of those hours, there was nothing below us but a massive body of water.

When we first caught sight of Manhattan on the horizon from the window of our airport taxi, the three of us were instantly transfixed. The sheer scale of the place was difficult to believe. And those buildings—so impossibly sleek and tall that they looked like they'd been painted onto the sky by some skilled artist. On the street in front of our hotel near Madison Square Garden, another city revealed itself, one entirely distinct from the architectural wonder we had viewed from afar. Great crowds of humanity rushed from every direction, dashing across streets, emerging from subway stations, and shuttling into and out of buildings with a speed and determination that felt completely foreign to me. I can only imagine what we must have looked like, the three of us, staring up in disbelief at this colossus of a city for the first time, our suitcases sitting beside us on the sidewalk like classic tourists.

Manhattan was somehow both larger than life and, at the same time, intimately human. I had never seen so many different kinds of people walking the same streets, or such a variety of stores and restaurants with signs written in so many languages. Hungary was a fairly homogenous place where people spoke the same language and ate the same foods. New York was something wholly different, a chaotic mix of people with radically different origins, lifestyles, traditions, and values all coexisting on a single, densely packed strip of land. Yet somehow, it all made sense. I was just a fifteen-year-old Hungarian girl with only passable English, and yet I felt comfortable immediately.

The thing that stood out most about America was just how earnestly upbeat everyone seemed. I had grown up in a place where irony and pessimism defined the default temperament of most people I knew. It was a way of staying sane in a world where so much of our lives was outside of our control. The Americans I met on that first trip seemed to have none of this negativity. They spoke about the future with such hope and confidence that, at least at first, I wasn't sure if they were serious.

Even more shocking was the media reception I got in New York. Days before I sat down at a chess board for the first game of the tournament, I was giving interviews with news outlets from around the country that were eager to tell my story. Without exception, every American journalist who interviewed me was pleasant and enthusiastic, which was refreshing, considering how the press had treated me back home. On the first day of the tournament, *The New York Times* even ran a picture of me and Sofia on its front page, along with an article that was more flattering than anything that had been written about us back home. "She has a mind of her own," *Times* journalist Harold C. Schonberg wrote of me, "she fights the bureaucracy and she has announced that, since she is strong enough to meet men on their own terms, she will play only in tournaments that challenge her." I had grown so tired of seeing my given name, Zsuzsa, misspelled in tournament cross-tables and news articles that on this trip, I went by "Susan" in all of my interviews—a name I would use more and more in the years ahead, especially in English-speaking countries.

I enjoyed all of this media attention, there's no denying it. But I tried not to let it get to me. I hadn't played a single game in the United States, after all. And yet I had found my way onto the cover of one of the nation's leading newspapers. Despite being the top female player on the planet—which is certainly newsworthy—I couldn't shake the feeling that I was being rewarded for something I hadn't done yet. And in that sense, the chocolate bars I won in my informal blitz matches with my sisters back home felt more satisfying than the press coverage I was getting in New York. I didn't want to be the subject of a puff piece that would be forgotten a few days later. I wanted to make history. For that, I would need to use this event to show the world I was more than just a public interest story.

I got my chance in the tournament's seventh round. I had come to the tournament determined to defeat my first grandmaster. But I had still yet to sit down across from one. My opponent in round 7 was a person whose name I had grown up hearing, thirty-three-year-old Filipino Eugene Torre. This wasn't just any grandmaster. At one time, Torre was ranked twentieth in the world. And he had competed as a candidate for the World Chess Championship just a few years before our game. He was also a boundary breaker in his own right, having been the first Asian in history to earn the grandmaster title, which I deeply respected. Distinguished and well dressed, with long dark hair, Torre was an absolute gentleman in the few interactions I had with him before our game. Once we sat down at the board, however, he was all business.

I was playing with the black pieces, so the odds were tilted against me before a single move was made. Despite this, my strategy going into the game was to play for two results. Instead of trying to win at all costs, in other words, I would keep open the option for a draw as well as a win for as long as the game allowed. Torre opened with 1. d4, a move directly from my own playbook. And for the first few moves I played my usual solid, positional game, gradually maneuvering my pieces to optimal squares. By the end of the opening phase, the position felt pretty equal, although looking back on it today with the aid of a computer, Torre technically had a slight advantage. That changed after the seventeenth move, when I laid an elaborate trap. At first glance, it appeared that Torre could just capture my pawn on c6 with his knight, attacking both my queen and rook. In fact, I had calculated a ten-move continuation that left me much better off. If all went to plan, we'd each have roughly equal material at the end of this sequence of moves. But my pieces would be beautifully coordinated to mount an attack. It wasn't the easiest continuation to see over the board, but then again, this was Eugene Torre we're talking about, so I couldn't be sure.

Sure enough, though, on his eighteenth move he snatched up my pawn with his knight, just as I had hoped he would. I felt a jolt of adrenaline coursing through my body. I wanted nothing more than to blitz out the next series of moves, but I stopped myself. Had he really missed it? Or had he just analyzed the position more deeply and found a continuation I hadn't considered? *Stop*, I told myself. *Think this through.* I spent the next few minutes checking my calculations, but couldn't see a way out for him.

I had him.

After my eighteenth move, his whole posture changed. The momentum of the game was about to shift in my direction, and even he knew it. Normally quite stone-faced during games, I could see the occasional hint of a grimace appear on his face as he played out the next few moves in his mind. After a quiet opening, the game was now full of action, as pieces disappeared off the board in one exchange after another. By the thirty-third move, everything had gone as I had anticipated. My queen, bishop, and knight were working in perfect harmony, ready to mount a lethal assault. His king and queen were on the verge of being trapped. I was no longer playing for two results.

We played on for another thirteen moves after that, during which I did my best to make sure Torre never got back in the game. On the forty-sixth move he resigned. My very first victory against a grandmaster was officially on the books.

You can tell a lot about a player by how they handle themselves in defeat. Emotional losers are everywhere to be seen. But Torre was a class act. With a friendly face, he shook my hand in resignation. We sat analyzing the game for a little while together. "You have a great future ahead of you," he said to me, as we got up to leave. The rest of the tournament, he would check in with me to see how I was doing.

The euphoria from that game stayed with me for the rest of the tournament, which wasn't without its share of disappointments. I lost my final game against the grandmaster Dmitry Gurevich, which put me out of contention for a cash prize. Had I won, I would have left New York with at least some of the event's $50,000 purse, which would have been a huge windfall for my family. Still, beating Torre was sweet consolation, as was my draw against William Lombardy, who, in addition to being one of the best American players of his generation, had helped Bobby Fischer train for his 1972 match against Boris Spassky. The day after the tournament finished, the *Times* ran a picture taken during my game against Torre on its front page, along with yet another story. "Girl Wins

Respect, Not Cash, in Chess," the headline read. This was the kind of attention I could feel good about.

With that tournament out of the way, my mother, sister, and I could finally spend some time taking in the sights. We walked through Times Square and went to the top of the Empire State Building. The chess community there was happy to take us in. It seemed as if everyone we met wanted us to visit their chess club or do a simultaneous exhibition in the area.

Frederic was also in town as well. And he invited us to spend some time with the renowned computer scientist Ken Thompson, who happened to be a huge fan of chess. Ken was so excited to meet us that he took us on a private tour of Bell Labs, where he worked. He had made groundbreaking progress on endgame tablebases— computer programs that can perfectly analyze endgames where only a few pieces are left on the board. And it was on our visit to Bell Labs that I saw the software in action for the very first time on one of the facility's high-powered computers.

By the end of the trip, my confidence in speaking English had reached a new high—so much so that when it came time for my oral language exams back in Hungary, I entered the room believing my English might even rival my own teacher's knowledge of the language. I was technically enrolled in a local high school, which happened to be named after Anne Frank. But the school was very accommodating of my chess career and let me continue homeschooling most of the time on the condition that I come in at the end of each school year to take my exams.

In response to one of my teacher's questions I went on at length about my recent trip to New York, the things I had seen and the people I had met, determined to wow her with my well-practiced English. When I explained how we had stayed in a hotel directly across the street from Madison Square "Jarden," the teacher quickly corrected me. "Do you mean Madison Square Garden?" she asked in a patronizing tone. My face went red as I thought about all of the times I had said this ordinary word incorrectly, and of all the people who didn't bother to correct me. What else had I gotten wrong? I left the exam room with a badly bruised ego and only a B in English for the year. It was a potent reminder that all of that media hype about the chess prodigy from Budapest had gone to my head a little.

ELEVEN

Now that I had my first GM victory under my belt, I was hungry to earn the title for myself. This elite designation is reserved for the world's most special players, a group, in 1985, that still numbered in the few hundreds. There is a reason why the club of grandmasters was so small. To attain the title, players have to meet a strict set of requirements, arguably the most difficult of which is the achievement of three GM norms. To earn just one norm, you must perform at a high level in a tournament in which at least three of your opponents are GMs. These events must also include players from different countries and meet a number of other criteria as well.

There weren't that many grandmasters back in those days, which meant that finding qualified events was a challenge in its own right. Performing well enough in one of these events to earn a norm was a gargantuan feat. And I would need to do so three times to get the title. At that time, no woman had ever done this. I knew I could be the first—there was no doubt in my mind. But to do so, I'd need to play in the strongest tournaments I could.

My father had already quit his job in order to devote himself full-time to managing my career. With my travel privileges now reinstated, he was able to line up a steady barrage of international tournaments all over the West that year. Looking back on it now, it's difficult to believe how much ground we covered.

Over the course of just a few months we found ourselves in Amsterdam, Baden-Baden, and Dortmund before heading back to New York that fall. And even with all of this traveling, I still remained an active player for my chess club in Budapest in the Hungarian team championships.

Few things give me more pleasure than chasing a difficult goal. Here that goal was the grandmaster title. And the road to my destination happened to run through European capitals and stunning countrysides and new restaurants—not to mention the booming metropolis of New York, a city I was quickly coming to love. My family's material circumstances had also improved, since many of the events I was playing in provided appearance fees in addition to any prize money I might win.

Even the playing conditions at tournaments were far nicer than anything I'd known. Everything had gotten better for me all at once. The year finished on a high note with our trip to Brussels for the OHRA Tournament, which was held in the last two weeks of December. This time, both parents were allowed to come along, as well as Sofia—who, at eleven years old, was becoming a bit of a chess celebrity herself—and nine-year-old Judit. Both would compete in the tournament's lower section.

Even for a Jewish family like ours, Brussels at Christmastime was simply magical, particularly the Grand-Place at the city's center, which was blanketed with lights of every color, a Christmas tree, and a massive nativity scene at the center of the square. It was a perfect backdrop for an event that I still remember with a certain childlike enchantment. I can still picture the little Belgian chocolates in the shape of a seashell that my parents bought us, and the feeling of pure ecstasy I felt as I savored every bite.

Competing against me in that event were some of the most famous players in the world. Most notable among them were political dissident Viktor Korchnoi and the former world champion Boris Spassky. Both of these men were practically mythological figures for me at sixteen. Spassky, of course, was best known for having lost his world championship title to Bobby Fischer in 1972, which was easily the most-watched chess battle in history. He had, by then, relocated to Paris after marrying a Frenchwoman, a decision that, at the time, had landed him in some political trouble with the Kremlin.

If Spassky was the most globally famous Soviet grandmaster of his generation, Korchnoi was the most controversial. He was, without question, among the greatest players of the twentieth century and, at fifty-six years old, was still considered among the top players on the planet. His World Championship matches against then champion Anatoly Karpov were the stuff of legend—as was his defection from the Soviet Union in 1976. He now lived as a Swiss citizen, as well as an official enemy of the Soviet regime, all of which only intensified his ongoing rivalry with Karpov. Their consecutive World Championship matches in 1978 and 1981 were such politically charged spectacles that they inspired *Chess*, a Broadway musical featuring songs by Benny Andersson and Björn Ulvaeus from the band ABBA.

Being invited to join these two giants in Brussels that winter was a rare privilege. Sharing meals with them throughout the tournament was a kind of fantasy come to life. It was one thing for Tal to have agreed to a few blitz games with me back in Moscow. That was a kind gesture from a gallant soul. Here, I was being treated as a member of a very special club, one that few players are ever invited to join. I might not have been their equal as a player—in fact, I lost my games against both Korchnoi and Spassky—but I was at least in their league.

I also felt a deep connection toward these two, and not just because we shared a vocation. All three of us had suffered the wrath of an unfriendly communist regime, in one way or another, although none more dearly than Korchnoi. After enduring years of persecution in the Soviet Union—including being banned from traveling to international tournaments—he had risked his life to seek asylum in the West. His son and former wife remained trapped in the USSR for years, which I'm sure tormented Korchnoi. He lived every day with the knowledge that his enemies in the Soviet Union might one day get their revenge.

At dinner each night, many of the players would sit around a large restaurant table and listen as Korchnoi and Spassky traded long stories about famous players they had known or celebrities they had met or their run-ins with the government. Spassky had this wry, knowing humor and a knack for playful comments and cunning wordplay. Referring to his previous two marriages at one point—he was then married to his third wife, Marina—he remarked that he had "exchanged queens." But he could also be quite serious. I asked him about the 1972 match with Fischer. As he put it, he was treated as a "black sheep" and even a traitor by his own government after losing to Fischer, and life got much more difficult for him. A few years earlier, I would have found Spassky's stories baffling. What sense does it make to punish someone for losing a chess match? Did the Soviets think he had lost on purpose? Now that I had witnessed just how irrationally cruel governments could be in our part of the world, his experience seemed all too predictable.

Korchnoi was a much more dynamic figure, full of forceful complaints and bold declarations, and rarely without a cigarette in his hand. One night at dinner, I finally got the chance to ask him how he found the strength to stand up for his government for so many years.

"I didn't do anything wrong!" he screamed, his voice animated with righteous rage. "Why would I let them win?!"

Then he looked me in the eye and said calmly, "They're going to try to destroy you the same way they did with me. Don't let them."

"I won't," I told him.

"Good."

At the chess board, Korchnoi was a completely different person—focused, reserved, completely unflappable. I had a pretty good position at one point in our game together, and I even managed to put Korchnoi in time trouble. But he never once seemed the least bit bothered, even as his time ticked down. Defending a tough position under time pressure is one of the hardest things to do in chess. But Korchnoi made it look easy. He just kept going about his business, improving his position little by little with each move until eventually he had the upper hand. He actually ended up winning that game, as he deserved to. It was a kind of self-possession I didn't know was possible. If the Soviets thought they could beat him, I thought, they had seriously misjudged their opponent.

But it was Korchnoi's wife, Petra, who made the biggest impression on me. I was just beginning to take an interest in clothes and fashion. And Petra was the most stylish woman I had ever met. She dressed almost exclusively in bold solid colors. And every item of clothing she wore—from her scarf to her blouse, skirt, coat, and shoes—was always perfectly coordinated. I still consider her one of my fashion idols to this day. And yet, her glamour and beauty never came at the expense of her strength. It didn't matter how intense or blustery Korchnoi would get; Petra could always disarm him with a subtle comment or a knowing look.

With us at many of these meals was Bachar Kouatly, who would become a lifelong friend. In fact, it's striking to me just how many people I met that year would remain a part of my life to this day. It was just by coincidence that I briefly crossed paths with a college student named Paul Truong at the New York Open the previous spring, a man who I'd eventually marry.

Sometime in the middle of the Brussels tournament, my entire family sat down for an interview with one of the leading chess magazines, *New in Chess*. My father recited anecdotes about our home life, which we'd all heard hundreds of times before. And he'd point out that only Bobby Fischer had reached my level of play at such a young age, one of his go-to talking points in those years. I talked about my newfound love for the music of Lionel Richie, especially the love ballads like "Hello" and "Truly," which I had only recently discovered while traveling in the West. Had you told me back then that more than thirty years later I would become friends with Lionel and his family, I wouldn't have believed it.

I remember that Walter Tevis's 1983 novel *The Queen's Gambit*—the basis for the 2020 Netflix series—came up, as it often did in those kinds of interviews. The novel, which had been published just two years earlier, tells the story of a young female chess prodigy. And the overlap between her story and mine was difficult to miss. At one point near the end of the interview, the reporter turned to me and asked bluntly, "Are you happy?" I suppose he was worried that my parents were forcing us all into this career, or that I'd much rather have the life of a typical teenager. I answered with a firm "Yes," but what I really wanted to say was "That's a ridiculous question."

Here I was in Brussels, sitting comfortably with the likes of Korchnoi and Spassky, forging new friendships, and earning the respect of people I admired—all after a year spent jet-setting around the world as a minor celebrity. Whatever I had given up getting here was more than worth it. Sure, I had missed out on some of the simpler pleasures of young adult life—dressing up for high school dances or sharing gossip with friends my own age. But that was a small price to pay. "Happy" didn't begin to describe it. I didn't know life could be this good.

Several weeks later, my mother and I boarded yet another plane across the Atlantic, this time for a tournament in San Francisco.

I remember that the games took place in the back of a restaurant, which was quite unusual. After each round, my mother and I would walk to the front of the house for a big meal. After each good game, I would reward myself with an exotic American delicacy I had just discovered known as a banana split.

From there, the two of us made a short hop to Las Vegas for the National Open. We had been invited by the event's organizer, Fred Gruenberg, who went out of his way the entire tournament to make us feel welcome and taken care of. What I mostly just remember is how outlandish Las Vegas seemed, this city-sized amusement park. Nothing about it made sense. So much excess in the middle of the desert; so many blazing lights even in the middle of the night. The only gambling I knew was the blitz chess games I'd played in the park for pennies. Yet in Vegas, I walked through a crowded casino each day just to get to my hotel room. The night after the tournament we treated ourselves to the *Jubilee!* show at Bally's. And at night, we'd walk the strip, marveling at the lights and stopping at the buffets. Oh, the buffets! Every kind of food one could imagine, laid out before us in preposterously large quantities—and for so little money! As someone raised in a world of compulsory rationing and thrift, such flagrant overabundance made me giddy.

We'd eventually end up back on the East Coast for the New York Open in April 1986, where we'd meet up with my father and sisters. With Sofia and Judit both playing, the tournament marked a kind of East Coast debut for all three Polgar sisters. It wasn't my best tournament, although I did have several good games. I was pretty disappointed that I narrowly missed out on my first grandmaster norm.

That was the year I beat the thirty-seven-year-old grandmaster and six-time US champion Walter Browne. Normally a very pleasant guy, Walter was so enraged after our game that he violently swept all of the pieces off the board before storming out of the playing hall. It was one of the strangest things I had ever seen at a tournament, which are usually very quiet affairs. Every eye in the room turned to me to see my reaction. I was startled, of course. But not scared. I had seen more than a few players—usually young men—throw tantrums after losing to me, although none this dramatic. Regardless, Walter was clearly more angry with himself than he was with me. I just figured he had never lost to a girl before, which I later learned was the truth. That thought put a small smile on my face. *These guys will get used to it,* I told myself. *Just wait.*

There must have been something in the air at that tournament, because another high-profile player, the Danish grandmaster Bent Larsen, did the exact same thing to a young Vietnamese American named Paul Truong, who I had met briefly at this same event the previous year. Paul and I ended up bonding over this shared experience and spending some time together at that tournament. He was funny and easy to be around and as passionate about chess as I was. I liked him right away.

My sisters, however, were the ones who really shined in that event. Sofia ended up sharing first place in her section. The star of the show was nine-year-old Judit, who took the top prize in the unrated section after winning her first seven games—and despite being the second-youngest player in a field of around a thousand. I remember Judit used to carry a little wooden lion figurine with her, which she'd place on the table next to her as she played. She thought the lion might scare her opponent, but most just found it to be cute, which, of course, it was.

The New York Times took notice of Judit's performance. "The three chess-playing Polgar sisters from Hungary are doing well in the New York Open at the Hotel Penta," wrote Harold C. Schonberg, the same writer who had covered me the year before. "But it is 9-year-old Judith who is tearing her section apart."

I took a lot of pleasure in how well my sisters were doing. One of the biggest reasons I was fighting so hard for the right to compete against men, after all, was so that my sisters—and all the girls who would come after them—wouldn't have to face the same obstacles I had. I saw myself as their mentor, their role model, their protector. And when they performed well and got the praise they deserved, I was unabashedly proud. The fact that I was also their big sister—that I had grown up babysitting for them and helping to change their diapers—made their triumphs all the more rewarding for me. We were a team.

I was also enjoying watching the two of them develop into unique personalities. Sofia had already discovered her love of art and literature at that time. Even at a young age, she could express herself in these beautifully eloquent sentences. It always impressed me how that creative sensibility would show itself in her chess, whether in some elegant tactic or beautifully coordinated mating attack. A lot of her drawings featured chess pieces and other related imagery. (Years later, she'd combine all of these passions in a chess book featuring a selection of her paintings and drawings.)

Although she was the youngest, it was clear from an early age that Judit was also the most serious and ambitious of the three of us. Her single-minded obsession with chess was even more intense than mine at her age. In any other household that might have seemed odd, but in ours it was encouraged. Judit was also the most fearless and self-confident over the board, a style that seemed to be an extension of her no-nonsense personality.

Somewhere near the end of the New York tournament, a man named Shiloh approached my family about an event he was organizing in Ottawa, Canada, for Nancy Reagan's "Just Say No" anti-drug campaign. His idea was to have me play in an exhibition against my good friend Yasser Seirawan, then the top active American player. Under normal circumstances, my parents probably would have declined. But Shiloh's wife happened to be Hungarian, and she helped put my parents at ease.

They flew all five of us first class from New York to Ottawa and put us up in a suite in one of the city's finest hotels, right across the street from the American embassy. I remember just how floored we all were by the size of the accommodations, and how my sisters would run from room to room playing hide-and-seek. The event with Yasser had this strange format, in which we played ten games against each other simultaneously. Exhibitions in which one player faces multiple opponents at the same time are pretty standard. But simultaneous games between the same two players are quite novel. It proved to be a great time, with Yasser and I running around like maniacs from one board to the next, snapping out moves as quickly as we could. Yasser is one of the most warm and fun-loving people I know in chess, so I couldn't have chosen a better partner for the little show we put on.

After the event, Shiloh and his wife approached my parents with another idea. They were on their way to Vancouver for the Expo 86 world's fair, they explained. And wouldn't it be great if Sofia—then only twelve—could travel with them for another week and do a few chess events? It would be a chance for her to learn some more English. She'd even get to meet Prince Charles and Princess Diana, who were scheduled to appear at the fair. And it would all be for a great cause.

Even I was a little surprised when my parents agreed. That said, I never thought for a moment that Sofia would be in any danger. Even in these years, I was still very cautious about going anywhere without my parents, but Shiloh just seemed trustworthy. He was effortlessly positive and enthusiastic, and he seemed to have a real interest in seeing me and my sisters succeed. He had one of those easygoing ways about him that made you feel like you had known him for years. It didn't even occur to me how strange it was that he was putting together an event for Nancy Reagan in Canada, of all places. I also liked that Sofia would be traveling with someone who spoke Hungarian. We said our goodbyes and the rest of the family headed home to Hungary without Sofia, confident that we'd see her in a week.

When Shiloh phoned our home in Budapest a few days later asking to extend Sofia's trip another week, I didn't think much of it. The events were even more popular than Shiloh had anticipated, he said, and he'd already added a few more to the schedule. Sofia seemed to be having a great time, at least from what little I spoke with her on the phone. When Shiloh called to talk about extending the trip yet another week, my parents once again said yes— although somewhat reluctantly. It wasn't until his next call, asking that Sofia stay with them for a fourth week, that we started to get a little frightened.

Talking to Sofia on the phone, I could tell she was not enjoying herself, even though she said otherwise. In fact, I got the distinct impression that someone was in the room with her—perhaps Shiloh's Hungarian wife—making sure she didn't say anything that would raise suspicion. I knew my sister, though, and something felt fishy.

We tried calling her again that day, and again the next morning, but Shiloh stopped picking up the phone and never once returned any of our messages. My parents did their best to remain calm, but I knew from the look on their faces and the edgy tone in their voices that they were actually terrified. Both had tried so hard to keep their daughters safe, at times to the point of being overprotective. They had let their guard down just once, and their little girl had been taken from them.

"Should I go there?" I remember my mother asking.

"Where? To Canada? You don't even know where to look," my father said.

"I'll figure it out when I get there. I just need to do something."

"Even if you left right now, it would be at least a day before you got there, and then what?"

While they sorted out the details, I kept calling the number Shiloh had given us. Eventually, Sofia picked up. I handed the phone to my mother.

"Is there anyone else there with you?" she asked Sofia, trying desperately to sound like she had the situation in hand.

"Yes."

"Okay. I know you want to come home, and we are going to get you back here right away, I promise. Just tell me: Is there anyone there that you trust?"

"I trust Max."

"Go find Max and put him on the phone."

We had all met Max in Canada. He worked with Shiloh. And he did, in fact, seem like a decent person—although we had all thought the same about Shiloh. I spoke the best English in the family, so when Max got on the line, my mother handed the phone to me.

I explained to Max that Sofia needed to come home right away, and that we didn't think Shiloh was going to let her leave. He hadn't realized what was going on, he said. And he promised to do what he could to get her away without Shiloh noticing.

Somehow, Max managed to get Sofia away and over the next few days drove her back to New York, where my mother had flown to meet him. Sofia arrived home a different person. Once a sweet, innocent girl with an artistic sensibility, she was now a little more sober, a little less trusting, and fluent in English, a language she hardly knew just a month before. As we would soon learn, Shiloh was a complete fraud who had lied about almost everything, including his connection with the "Just Say No" campaign. Sofia never even got to play in many exhibitions. She mostly just tagged along with Shiloh's crew, watching as the situation got more and more hostile. I think we all became a little less trusting after that.

TWELVE

In a year in which I would cross the Atlantic multiple times and play in about a dozen countries, it was an event in my own backyard that I was looking forward to the most: the 1986 Hungarian National Championship, which was being held in Budapest that April. I was the first woman to qualify for the tournament since its founding in 1906. And I wanted to show my nation's chess community that their campaign against me had been in vain. The stakes got even higher when the Hungarian Chess Federation officially announced that the top three finishers in that year's championship would earn a place at the upcoming Zonal Tournament—the first of a series of events that would determine the next Men's World Championship challenger.

Walking into the playing hall for my first game, I felt like I had made it, in some way. It was one of the most magnificent venues I had ever played in up until that point. The room itself was enormous, with beautiful high ceilings. We played on a large stage before an audience of at least a hundred spectators. And the boards and pieces were of a noticeably better quality than I was used to seeing in competition in that part of the world. The hall was outfitted with giant two-dimensional demonstration boards, which were set up behind each game. Every time a player would make a move, one of the "board boys" would put it up on the big board, so that the spectators could follow along from the audience.

I remember that a close family friend, Hungarian-born Laci Katz, had traveled to the event from his home in France just to cheer me on, and he even brought me some delicious Swiss and Belgian chocolates, which were almost impossible to get in Hungary.

As chance would have it, one of my opponents in the event was a former coach of mine and fellow club member, Levente Lengyel. I knew his style quite well, and I used that knowledge to prepare an opening with the black pieces designed specifically to throw him off his game. I remembered that against the King's Indian Defense, he would almost always respond with the fianchetto variation. With the help of another competitor in the tournament, Peter Szekely, I worked out a sixteen-move variation that would at the very least force Lengyel to burn time thinking during the game. The strategy worked better than I could have hoped, giving me a decisive win at a crucial moment in the competition.

By the end of the nearly three-week tournament, and after hours of exhausting play, I had tied for second place. Proving myself in such an important event really made me feel like I had entered a new stage of my career. I was playing chess at a level that most other players on the planet could not match—which was my goal all along. But the symbolic importance of what was happening wasn't lost on me either. It would have been a coup for any seventeen-year-old to qualify for the Zonal Tournament. The fact that I am female made my achievement genuinely historic. Best of all, I had reached this place while fighting off a coordinated effort to derail my career orchestrated by my own country's officials.

I half expected my old nemesis Szerenyi to somehow downplay my achievement, as he had with so many of my past successes. But not even he could deny the importance of what I had done. During the closing ceremony, he even said a word of congratulations, which was later published in the official journal of the Hungarian Chess Federation, *Sakkelet*:

> [O]n behalf of the presidency of our Federation, I must point out that Zsuzsa Polgar achieved the greatest success at the chess championship. Zsuzsa Polgar, who is currently in 26th place in the Hungarian rankings, deservedly finished tied for second/third place. This is an achievement that should be eminently recognized. This result also means— and it serves us with pleasure—that we can present to FIDE our nomination of Dr. Laszlo Hazai and Zsuzsa Polgar to the world championship zonal competition.

I couldn't believe what I was hearing. Was he really changing his tune after all of this time? He hadn't said a kind word about me publicly in years. I could only hope that this wasn't some kind of maneuver, that maybe my relationship with the federation was thawing. But I was still skeptical.

Regardless of his motivations, I at least felt confident I would advance to the next round of the World Championship cycle, the Zonal Tournament. Szerenyi himself had just said so. If I held my own there, it would be on to the Interzonal Tournament and eventually the Candidates Tournament—the winner of which would play Kasparov for the World Championship title. If I'm honest, I knew that my chances of making it that far weren't great. But I still dreamed it was possible—if not this time around, then one day soon.

Exhausted though I was from weeks of nonstop travel and competition, this was no time to slow down. I committed myself to an even more intensive training regimen and continued to play in tournaments around Europe. I got a huge vote of confidence that June at the International Open in Albena, Bulgaria. In a field rich in grandmasters, I won the tournament without a single loss. It was my biggest tournament victory to date, and helped make me the second-highest rated seventeen-year-old on the planet, just 5 rating points behind Vasyl Ivanchuk, and above future world champion Viswanathan "Vishy" Anand. A year before, I was content to notch my first win over a grandmaster. Now I was dominating events full of higher-rated players. I could see the path to my own GM title opening up in front of me.

I got yet another boost of momentum later that year, at the Politiken Cup in Copenhagen, where I would face Vasily Smyslov, a former world champion whose books on endgames I had devoured as a young girl. Unlike some of the top players I had met, Smyslov was incredibly reserved and polite, always showing tremendous respect for me both on and off the board. He was a truly sweet man, who I would get to know a lot better in the years ahead.

This would be the second time in less than a year that I played against a former world champion. Sometime in the early middlegame, Smyslov offered a draw, which, after some thought, I accepted.

Even as my playing schedule got busier, I would still find time to coach my sisters. In fact, this was the year that I began traveling with them to international tournaments purely to serve as their advisor or "second," as it's known in chess. The first of these events was the inaugural World Under-14 Championship, which took place in Puerto Rico. We stayed in this little motel right on the beach just outside of San Juan for a few days before the tournament, to help us recover from jet lag. Every morning, we'd each order a virgin piña colada from the hotel restaurant, made from coconuts picked fresh from the tree. Then we'd head to the beach with a chess board and enjoy our sweet drinks as we prepared for the approaching competition.

At first it felt strange to be the coach at one of these tournaments, not the one playing. Having to watch my sisters' games from afar for hours at a time, unable to intervene, was difficult for me.

At times, it took every ounce of my willpower to keep from shouting out some game-winning move that I could see one of my sisters had overlooked. As a player, I was used to being the author of my own games, choosing moves and executing strategies in real time. Being a good coach meant giving up that control, which required a special sort of discipline that I was only beginning to develop.

Later in the year, the entire family crossed the Atlantic yet again so that my sisters could play in the World Under-16 Championship in Patagonia, Argentina. Here, too, I assumed the role of coach, helping my sisters prepare each morning and analyzing their games after each round. On one of the rest days, we all went for a hike near the Chilean border. We didn't realize that Argentina's seasons were the opposite of what we were used to in the northern hemisphere, a mistake we soon came to regret. Those few hours were the coldest I had ever felt in my entire life, yet the scenery made it worth it. Climbing over a hill at one point, we came upon a massive crowd of penguins in the middle of mating season. Spread out before us were hundreds of waddling birds, many walking hand-in-hand, others burrowing into little holes. For just a moment, we forgot about how freezing cold we felt, and we all stood watching in silence.

———————

The first sign of trouble for me came in late 1986. My family and I were preparing for a trip to Adelaide for the Australian Open when the news came in from the Chess Olympiad in Dubai, which was underway at the time. The event was mired in political drama, with many countries boycotting in protest of the United Arab Emirates' refusal to recognize Israel. The International Chess Federation, known as FIDE, used the opportunity to make one of the most controversial decisions in the organization's history. It was there that FIDE announced a plan to award up to 100 additional rating points to every female player on the planet. Every female player except one, that is: me.

It's hard to overstate the brazen unfairness of this decision. In competitive chess, there is no statistic more important than a player's FIDE rating. The number is used to determine who qualifies for the grandmaster title, to set requirements for playing in various tournaments, and, of course, to rank the best players in the world (the number one player in the world is the player with the highest FIDE rating).

What's more, ratings are supposed to reflect players' actual performance in rated games of chess. Usually, the only way to gain points is to win or, when playing against a higher-rated player, at least draw. But FIDE's decision in Dubai dispensed with these rules by handing out free points—and in a way that discriminated against just one player. This would be like letting all but one of the runners in a 100-meter dash start the race at the 90-meter mark.

FIDE bent over backward to justify this move, claiming that my participation in men's events gave me an unfair ratings-point advantage—the same argument the Hungarian press had used against me for years. But the ruling's actual purpose was plainly political. The Soviets held a lot of sway in international chess in those years. And the USSR Chess Federation didn't appreciate that a teenage girl from Hungary—and not the reigning women's world champion, the Soviet Union's Maia Chiburdanidze—was the world's highest-rated female player. Simply inflating the rating of every other woman in the sport brought Chiburdanidze back to number one.

I must have read that article a dozen times, hoping I had misunderstood it. There was just no way that the world chess federation would single me out like this. I knew that Hungary's federation had it out for me. But FIDE had usually taken my side. They had refused to comply with Szerenyi's demand that I be stricken from the world rankings a few years before. Why would they come after me now?

I felt this sense of physical panic come over me, the same feeling I would sometimes get after making a horrible blunder at the chess board. My face turned red and my stomach turned inside out. I remember handing the newspaper to my father, hoping desperately he'd tell me I was mistaken.

When it dawned on him what he was reading, I saw his whole face change. His eyes got big, and his mouth dropped open. At first, my parents and I were outraged and determined to set things right. But as we discussed our options, we came to grips with the fact that there was nothing we could do. The decision had been made at the highest levels of professional chess. There would be no appeal, no reconsideration, no public debate. This was happening.

Once the news got out, our phone started ringing. First an old coach called. Then a friend from the chess club. Everyone wanted to express their sympathy, as if a family member had just died in a public accident. But nobody had any ideas for how to fix this.

I can't say I was surprised when the Hungarian Chess Federation strongly encouraged the decision. Szerenyi might have praised me a few months earlier, but I never really believed he had come over to my side completely.

That FIDE would sometimes tip the scales in favor of the Soviets was widely known by then. Just a year earlier, the organization had sparked another controversy when it paused the World Championship match between Soviet favorite Anatoly Karpov and the outspoken critic of the Soviet Union Garry Kasparov. The move was seen by many as a flagrant attempt to stunt Kasparov's momentum so that Karpov could retain the title. It didn't work. In the end, Kasparov triumphed, becoming the youngest world champion in history.

Equating the two scandals, the British journalist Raymond Keene wrote: "Whatever the machinations of reactionary or chauvinistic sports officials, apparently allergic to aggressive young talent, Kasparov could not be held back, and neither will the Polgars."

The support we received from the Western media gave me some comfort. But I knew it wouldn't help anything. The official rankings were released in January, I had fallen to number three. The whole situation just made me furious—a feeling that my mom and dad not only supported, but shared. My parents were so incensed, in fact, that they felt the need to do something radical once the whole family arrived in Australia.

"Maybe we don't go back," my dad said to me one day in our hotel room.

I, of course, knew what he was suggesting right away, and it caught me completely off guard. He was talking about defection to the West. He was talking about becoming fugitives from our own country. The idea had been floated to us by friends and acquaintances during one of our recent trips to the United States, but we never really considered it as a serious option until that night in Adelaide.

"We shouldn't decide anything right now," I told him. "But we can at least talk to some people while we're here."

My mom chimed in with a word of caution.

"If this gets out, things will get even worse for us back home."

My stomach felt sick.

Over the next few days, we quietly arranged some meetings with several friends we thought could help us secure support and Australian residency. This included Gary and Evelyn Koshnitsky, who were two of the biggest figures in Australian chess in those years and fast becoming close friends of the family. Both Gary and Evelyn were furious that FIDE would come after me in this way, and they wanted to do everything in their power to help us fight back.

It quickly became obvious that we never had to return to Hungary again if we didn't want to. This was no longer hypothetical. One night at our hotel, my parents sat me and my sisters down for a long discussion. We weighed the pros and cons of relocating, as if we were considering a chess move. The more we talked, the more we started to see that, for all its challenges, none of us wanted to leave Hungary.

I, for one, still wanted to bring pride to my country, and especially to the friends in the Hungarian chess community who had supported me for so long. I really believed that the battles I was fighting with the authorities were winnable, and I would rather keep fighting those battles than abandon my home and play under another flag. I could only imagine what the press might write about me and my family if we left, and the anger it would inspire. We'd be playing into the old antisemitic narrative that we weren't "real" Hungarians and potentially inviting a backlash against our fellow Jews throughout the country.

And what about the rest of the family? My mother and father just couldn't imagine leaving their own parents behind. What if the Hungarian government took revenge? If that happened, we'd never forgive ourselves.

There were also practical concerns to think about. For instance, there was no guarantee that either my parents or I could make a living in Australia. My father didn't even speak English.

I also wasn't thrilled by the prospect of moving so far away. I love Australia, and the people there were some of the kindest I had ever met. But even the top Australian chess player, Ian Rogers, spent only half the year there. The rest of the time he lived in Europe, where most of the biggest events took place.

So it was settled. We had to stay in Hungary.

I was still reeling from the rating scandal when the Hungarian Chess Federation delivered its next attack on me in February 1987. In a move that, in retrospect, I should have seen coming, the organization refused to include me in the upcoming Zonal Tournament. Women, they argued, shouldn't be allowed to compete in the Men's

World Chess Championship cycle. There was no official rule to this effect. The federation just didn't want me playing.

It was a devastating blow. I was not yet eighteen years old. And for the first time in my life, I was face-to-face with the possibility that my own discipline and perseverance were no match for the political forces conspiring against me. My father's philosophy—to disregard those things that you can't control—offered little comfort. There was no disregarding what had just happened to me.

I had fallen in love with this game in no small part for the consistency of its rules—rules that applied equally to all players all of the time. Yet within a matter of weeks, I had watched the highest authorities in organized chess rewrite the rules in a way that harmed nobody on the planet but me. My heart was broken.

For months after that, I lived in a world drained of joy or hope or excitement. There were entire weeks when I struggled to sleep and had little appetite. Never one to cry much before then, now I would erupt into uncontrollable sobbing from time to time. It was a level of emotional pain so intense and all-consuming that there was no running from it. I continued my normal training routine, but more out of habit than anything else. *What's the point?* I kept thinking. Even if I became the greatest player in the world, FIDE or Szerenyi or some other powerful person would probably find some way to sabotage my career. Why fight a battle you simply can't win?

But there was still a part of me that saw all of this negative thinking as a mistake, as something to be resisted. In the end, it was a remark from my grandmother that gave me the strength to move forward and fully recommit myself to the game—a saying she'd used many times before. As a survivor of the Auschwitz concentration camp, she had endured some of the most monstrous acts of cruelty, hatred, and discrimination in human history. Yet she wasn't defeated by those experiences. She emerged from that horrific period eager to start a family and live a gratifying, loving life.

"You think this is tough?" she said to me. "You don't know what tough is."

It was time to get back to work.

I could tell right away that if I was going to rebound from this defeat, I would need a new way of motivating myself. I had spent the last few years chasing rating points. But I now knew that those points could be redistributed without explanation if the right bureaucrats decided they didn't like me. My commitment to the game needed to come from someplace purer, someplace that the organized chess world couldn't touch. I needed to treat this beautiful game as an end in itself, not as a means to some number or title bestowed upon me by a corrupt committee someplace.

Once I started seeing the game this way, everything changed. I returned to my daily training regimen more fired-up than I'd been in years. The tournament invitations kept coming in, and I'd spend 1987 playing in Biel, New York, and Brussels, among other places.

At the second round of the New York Open that year, I played Julio Granda Zuniga, a gifted and good-looking twenty-year-old Peruvian player. These were the years when I started noticing boys more and more. But at seventeen, I was still under the near-constant supervision of at least one of my parents, both of whom were pretty protective of me. It didn't help that the chess tournaments where I was competing were mostly male environments where lewd comments flowed freely and unwanted advances from obnoxious men were to be expected. Once, while selling some chess books at a tournament in Vienna when I was thirteen, a man approached me with a proposition. He didn't want to buy any books, he said, but he'd be willing to pay for a certain kind of favor.

I knew enough by then to ignore these comments. Had I made a scene every time some idiot made a blue joke at my expense or bragged about their "bishops" in front of me (a double entendre I heard more than a few times over the years), there would have been little time left for anything else. So I mostly just put up with it. Unfortunately, this locker-room atmosphere made my parents much more protective of me. They rarely let me out of their sights whenever we traveled. This could be frustrating.

On the one hand, I was a full-fledged professional chess player on equal terms with most of the adults around me. On the other hand, I was a conflicted teenager, desperately wanting more independence but also plagued by insecurity and a keen awareness that I was still not completely ready for adult life. The residue from that attack in Yugoslavia hadn't completely worn off, so I still harbored some apprehension about being alone in strange cities. But I was also developing an interest in the opposite sex for the first time.

I suppose my teenage awkwardness got the best of me in my game against Granda. It started off well enough, and my position was technically winning by the middlegame. Then I got into time trouble and started playing poorly. My big mistake was trying to win in style instead of playing simple, methodical chess. At one point, I sacrificed my queen—a flashy tactic I thought was irrefutable. When Julio refused to take it, my position started to crumble. Soon, my position was merely equal, and eventually he had the decisive advantage, which he gradually converted into a win. It was such a frustrating loss, and I had only myself to blame.

Afterward, we talked. He spoke very little English at that time, and I had limited Spanish. But we still managed to fumble our way through. At one point I remember speaking to him in Esperanto, hoping that it was similar enough to Spanish that he might understand me. Even with the language barrier, we'd still manage to chat here and there throughout the tournament, and we met up after the tournament at the Manhattan Chess Club, which my parents weren't too pleased about. I was completely charmed.

ABOVE LEFT: With my mom in 1969, when my whole story began.

ABOVE RIGHT: Learning math with an abacus around 1971.

RIGHT: With my first coach other than my dad, Eva Karakas. *Photo originally published in* Daily News *(Hungary), 1974.*

BELOW: Early chess lessons with my dad in 1974 while my mom watched. *All photos from the Polgar family album unless otherwise noted.*

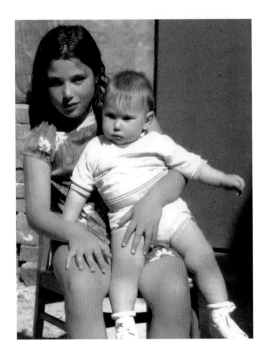

ABOVE: Holding the red-haired baby Judit in 1977.

ABOVE RIGHT: With the two "little ones" in 1979.

RIGHT: Showing my mom my first World Championship trophy in 1981.

BELOW: In full focus in a final round game in 1982.

ABOVE: At home with my sisters around 1982.

RIGHT: A cherished memory: playing the Magician from Riga, Mikhail Tal, for the first time in Moscow in 1982. *Photo originally published in* Shakhmaty v SSSR, *1982.*

BELOW: At home with our library of chess books in 1982. *Photo by Gyorgy Lajos.*

ABOVE: Around 1986, when we finally could travel as a family.

BELOW: The "Golden Team" after winning the 1988 Women's Chess Olympiad.

ABOVE: With my sisters in 1988. Where in the world next? *Photo by Csilla Cseke.*

BELOW: With my sisters and Laszlo Hazai before our match against Cuba at the 1990 Chess Olympiad.

LEFT. With my sisters, my maternal grandma Manci, paternal grandpa Armin, and my mom in the middle, around 1991.

ABOVE: Sitting in the middle (in red jacket), holding Melody Amber with the participants of the 1992 World Blitz Championship.

LEFT: Analyzing with Viktor Korchnoi after our game in Monte Carlo in 1993, with his wife Petra and Gata Kamsky (on his left) observing.

ABOVE: First meeting with Bobby Fischer in 1993 in his hotel room in Kanizsa. He is explaining his new invention, the digital Fischer clock.

RIGHT: With Bobby Fischer and the kitten at our summer home in Nagymaros in 1993.

BELOW: With the father of the Soviet chess school, Mikhail Botvinnik, in Tilburg in 1994.

ABOVE: World Championship match in 1996, at the beginning of the game.

LEFT: The "crowning" moment, receiving the laurels and the silver "olive tree" from FIDE president Kirsan Ilyumzhinov in 1996.

BELOW: At the closing ceremony of world championship in Jaen, Spain, in 1996, with FIDE president Kirsan Ilyumzhinov and Xie Jun.

One of my fondest memories from that year was a tournament in Cannes—not just because of the beautiful surroundings, but because of the time I got to spend with Boris Spassky. Some mornings, he'd come by the hotel room where I was staying with my mother. She'd make us savory and sweet crepes, like she had for the players that visited our home in Budapest, and he'd make us laugh with one of those long stories he was so good at telling.

That June I was in Bilbao, Spain, facing some of my stiffest competition to date, including the former world champion Anatoly Karpov. There were doubts among some people that I even belonged at a tournament that strong, doubts that at least one player, the Serbian Ljubomir Ljubojevic—number six in the world at the time—didn't mind airing publicly. Before the competition even got underway, he asked rhetorically in the press why a woman would bother playing in such a tournament. It was a personal affront to me as well as Maia Chiburdanidze, the only other female player in Bilbao. But I took it as a challenge. *If he wants to know whether I belong here,* I thought to myself, *I guess I'll just have to show him.*

And I did, beating him pretty handily with the white pieces in the tournament's second round. It was my most important victory up until that point. Ljubojevic had underestimated me, and I made him pay for it in front of some of the best chess players in the world.

It was such an upset that the national news took notice. Writing in *El País*, one of Spain's largest newspapers, the journalist Leontxo García wrote: "Polgar's victory was highly applauded by the spectators and was a great surprise for the specialists, who barely remember similar events." When Maia beat Ljubojevic later in the tournament, Leontxo penned another article, this one featuring the headline "Chiburdanidze and Polgar Question the Theoretical Inferiority of Women in Chess." Over the years, Leontxo would become a great champion of mine as well as a dear friend. But it was that win in Bilbao which first piqued his interest.

My game against Karpov didn't go nearly as well. I held my own against him for a little while, launching what I thought was a devastating kingside attack. But eventually Karpov worked his magic. Using his perfectly coordinated pieces, he somehow found a way to defend on his kingside while simultaneously attacking my queenside. It was a classic display of the same Karpovian style that had inspired much of my own approach to the game. As cold and unforgiving as he was over the board, Karpov was a generous and surprisingly friendly person when he wasn't playing. At dinner one night, he taught me how to eat oysters and clams. I still think of him often whenever I eat seafood.

In the final round I faced off against Ulf Andersson of Sweden—a former number four in the world—in one of the most tense games of my career. Andersson needed to win that game in order to win the tournament ahead of Karpov, and everybody was watching to see if I'd let him. I had made it clear that I was no pushover days before. But I still don't think anybody expected me to give Anderssen such a hard time. He was known as an endgame virtuoso. And, true to form, he simplified things quickly, trading queens within the first few moves, and applying gradual pressure, waiting for me to slip up, a strategy he'd employed successfully countless times before. But I hung in there.

I could sense his frustration build as we entered the seventh hour of play and then the eighth hour and then the ninth hour. By the time the sun went down, we were the only two people left playing on the floor of the gymnasium where the tournament was taking place. Most of the others, including Karpov, stayed around to see how things panned out, sitting patiently in the bleachers and watching the game's progression in real time on large digital screens that had been installed for the spectators. They might have reconsidered had they known how long they'd be there.

We played late into the night, sitting in near complete darkness, with only a single spotlight illuminating the board. I was long past the point of exhaustion by our one-hundredth move. Now I was playing on adrenaline and instinct and my own stubborn refusal to give anything away. Maybe all of my battles back home had made me tougher, or maybe it was just my years of experience showing through. But I seemed to have this unlimited reservoir of grit that night. It was sometime around 4 a.m. when the game finally ended in a draw. Andersson had thrown everything he had at me, and he still couldn't find a way to victory. The result made Karpov the tournament's winner and secured me $20,000 in prize money— the most I had ever won. Anyone who had questioned my abilities going into that tournament now had their answer.

THIRTEEN

B y my eighteenth year, I had seen enough of life to consider myself a relatively savvy person. Nothing, I felt, could surprise me anymore. Then I visited Iceland twice in one year.

The first trip was to the Reykjavik Open in February 1988. During nearly two weeks of competition, the sun barely ever appeared in the sky. I had been warned about Iceland's long winter nights, some of which can last for nearly twenty hours. But there's really no preparing for something this strange. That day inevitably follows night is one of those beliefs that are so fundamental that you can't actually doubt them. You might as well try to convince yourself that for a few months a year, two plus two will no longer equal four, or gravity won't work. So when you actually experience weeks of time consisting almost entirely of night, you start to wonder what else you might have been wrong about all of your life.

Disoriented as I was for those first few days, I managed to have a decent event and an enjoyable time seeing the city. In the years since hosting the 1972 "Match of the Century" between Fischer and Spassky, Reykjavik had embraced its identity as a cultural landmark in the chess world. And the excitement from that match sparked a local chess boom that had helped make Iceland home to more grandmasters per capita than any nation by the time I visited.

It also meant that a few of the other top players and I were greeted as honored guests. Upon arriving there, the Icelandic prime minister treated us to a reception at Hofdi House, the site of the 1986 Reykjavik summit between US president Ronald Reagan and Soviet leader Mikhail Gorbachev. For me and the other players, though, the highlight came during a stop at the Icelandic Chess Federation, which still housed the chess table, pieces, and even the chairs used in the 1972 Fischer-Spassky match—items we had all seen countless times in old photos and TV footage. At one point, somebody pointed out that we had visited the site of two of the most historic Cold War meetings—one between Reagan and Gorbachev, the other between Fischer and Spassky—in a single day. (Or was it night?)

It was just a few weeks later that my mother and I arrived in Wellington, New Zealand, for the Plaza International Chess Tournament. I had already grown quite fond of the region during our trip to Adelaide a little over a year before, so we were happy to return. Also, the tournament gave me and my mother a chance to spend some more time with Spassky, who was by then a great friend of ours.

During one of my long chats with Spassky—always in Russian—I mentioned my recent trip to Iceland, and how I had seen the famous chess table from his World Championship match. I wasn't sure how he'd react, given all of the grief that match had caused him. To my surprise, the whole episode no longer bothered him. He admitted that he was the weaker player in that match, having passed his peak sometime before then. But he also saw the big picture. It was clear to him that Fischer was an important historical figure, one who raised the game's profile and gave it a new cultural status. Because of Fischer's lobbying, playing conditions and tournament prizes were now larger, which benefited all high-level players. "Fischer needed to win," he kept saying. It really impressed me to see this great champion could admit that his most famous defeat was, in the end, a good thing. Spassky loved winning. But he also had a deep love of professional chess as an institution. And he truly appreciated what Fischer had done for the game. He showed me, during those chats, that a killer instinct at the board didn't have to come at the expense of sportsmanship and maturity.

We spent a few days following the tournament touring the countryside, and even attended a performance of the Maori, New Zealand's indigenous Polynesian people, which we both found quite moving. It reminded me just how vast and diverse this world is, and how much of it I had still yet to see.

My entire family returned to Iceland that June for an invitational grandmaster tournament in Egilsstadir—during which the sun never once seemed to set. It was also surprisingly warm, even though it still looked like winter. There's a great photo of my two sisters sunbathing in bikinis in the middle of a snow-covered field. It just didn't make any sense, this place.

If made to choose, I would have much preferred these "white nights" to the oppressive nighttime darkness we had seen just months before. But it was still quite a shock to my system. Luckily, it didn't affect my play much, nor either of my sisters'. Sofia ended up winning the tournament's open section. For my part, I played well enough to finish in a tie for first place with my youngest sister, Judit.

The real novelty during that second trip to Iceland—even stranger than the endless daytimes or my shared first place finish with Judit—was my father's decision to compete. It was the first and probably the only time he would play in a serious tournament. I'm amazed he waited so long. So many hours spent studying with us, overseeing our training, clipping and collating every published game he could get his hands on—and yet, until that summer, he had not tested his skills in actual competition since high school.

I'm still not sure what compelled him. My guess is that now that all three of his daughters had clearly surpassed him, he finally felt free to enjoy the game on his own terms. A few times during that tournament my sisters and I went over his games with him, offering advice and doing what we could to summon the same attentiveness and patience he had shown to us our entire lives. Thinking about it all these years later, it's almost poetic. In a part of the world where day was night, his most cherished pupils were now his teachers.

My run-in with FIDE a few years earlier had definitely made me less reverential toward official titles and ratings points. Nevertheless, my number one goal was still to become a grandmaster. I knew it would take a lot of work, a lot of focus, and a lot of travel. What I didn't anticipate was how much luck I would need.

It was just by bad luck that the tournament in Egilsstadir that year was short by just a single GM to qualify me for my first norm. Fortune finally smiled on me in Royan, France, that summer. We had started visiting the country fairly often for chess events while also spending time with our family friend Laci Katz and his wife. I remember being in Paris for that year's Bastille Day celebrations, wandering through streets overflowing with exuberant French people, all of them raising glasses to their nation's birth—something one would never see in the Hungary of my youth.

In Royan, I would stage my own unlikely revolution, beginning with a game in the tournament's second half. I was playing with the black pieces against Jacob Murey, a talented Soviet-born Israeli GM with a penchant for creative and surprising openings. I knew going into the game that a win would give me a good chance to clinch my first GM norm and maybe even win me the tournament. With that in mind, I broke from my normal strategy and instead chose a sharp line of the Dutch Defense to maximize my chances for a win. The game quickly took on a double-edged character, a situation in which even minor inaccuracies can lead to catastrophe.

After twenty moves or so I had built up an aggressive attack on the kingside, while he was assaulting my queenside and hoping to checkmate me before I could do the same to him. We were both trading punches well into the middlegame until, on move 35, I made a fatal mistake. I had just minutes on my clock, and the time pressure had gotten to me. Under tournament rules, players would get 150 minutes to play their first forty moves, after which another hour would get added to each side's clock. So my error couldn't have come at a worse time.

I soldiered on for the next few moves, doing everything I could to keep his attack at bay, but it all looked pretty hopeless for me. As a last-ditch attempt to turn things around, I set a trap for Murey on move 40—a bishop sacrifice I expected him to see through, especially now that he had a fresh hour of time to play with.

No longer under time pressure myself, I took a bathroom break, exiting the stage on which we were playing and skulking down the aisle past a crowded audience, just a little ashamed of my performance. When I returned, I couldn't believe what had just happened. I saw it from the back of the theater, right there on the giant presentation board at the rear stage. Murey had taken my bishop on g4 and fallen right into my trap. I could also see Murey sauntering around the stage, looking at the other games and stretching his legs. I thought to myself, *He doesn't even know he's lost!*

I headed directly for the stage, picking up speed as I approached. After one last check of my calculations, I delivered a decisive blow, giving a check with my pawn on the f3 square, opening up a discovered attack and winning his queen. When he came back to the board, Murey couldn't believe what had just happened. He had plenty of time to find the right move, and yet he had thrown away a winning game with a single careless decision. He resigned immediately. That win gave me a huge boost of confidence, allowing me to finish the tournament strongly and secure my first GM norm. *One down*, I thought. *Only two to go.*

I can't say I was looking forward to another twenty-plus hour plane trip that August for the World Junior Championship in Adelaide. But there was no way I was going to miss this particular tournament. Our friends Gary and Evelyn Koshnitzky had helped organize the event. The Koshnitzkys became great advocates of mine after witnessing how FIDE and the Hungarian Chess Federation had conspired to keep me out of the World Championship cycle the year before.

In his capacity as a FIDE delegate from Australia, Gary had fought to change the rules surrounding the Men's World Championship, as it was then known. In no small part because of Gary and Evelyn's efforts, the event eventually would simply be known as the World Championship. It was a long-needed change, one I take some pride in helping bring about. It was the most public evidence to date that my efforts to break down chess's gender barrier were having an effect. From that day on, no young girl would grow up thinking that the top honor in professional chess was reserved solely for men.

On top of that, after years of insisting that I play in the girls' section of that event—despite being the top player in my age group of either gender—the Hungarian Chess Federation finally backed down and agreed to let me play against the boys this time. There was just no way I was going to let the opportunity go to waste.

I was the only woman playing that year, and just nineteen years old. Still, I came very close to winning that event. I ended up finishing just one point behind first place in a field that included some of the best players of my generation—among them the Belarusian Boris Gelfand, who would become a very close friend after that tournament. Boris and I had a lot in common, as well as very similar senses of humor, having both been raised in Jewish families in Eastern Europe. We often found each other between rounds and took long walks around the beautiful boarding school campus where the event was being held.

I visited Judit for a few days at the Boys Under-12 Championship that year, which was held in Timisoara, Romania. It remains
one of the most bizarre trips of my life. The country was still under
the firm control of Nicolae Ceausescu, the brutal dictator who by
then had completely crippled the Romanian economy. I remember cans of Coca-Cola being offered to us as if it were a rare delicacy. But the oddest part of the visit was our hotel. At first, we were
impressed that our room was outfitted with both a television and a
telephone, which we didn't expect at all. It was only when we tried
to use these devices that we realized they were purely for show.
The television was nothing but a big hollow box, and the phone
had been gutted as well. The symbolism hit me right away. Those
fake appliances seemed to encapsulate the tragic absurdity of life
in a totalitarian state. Despite all of the nice people we met—some
of whom would become friends—under this regime, even seemingly nice things, on closer inspection, were merely hollowed-out
versions of themselves.

FOURTEEN

The 1988 Chess Olympiad took place in Thessaloniki, Greece, that November. With the exception of the World Championship, the Olympiad is far and away the most important chess competition on the calendar. It is literally the Olympics of chess. And although the men's competition dates back to the 1920s, it took until 1957 for FIDE to establish a Women's Chess Olympiad, which today takes place alongside the men's event, as it did in 1988.

Until that year, the Hungarian Chess Federation had always found some excuse or other to keep me out of the games. But a lot had changed by 1988. To begin with, my sisters and I were the top female players in Hungary: me in the first spot, followed by Judit, and then Sofia, who was tied for third. So keeping all of us off the Olympiad team would be difficult to justify, even by the tortured logic of the Hungarian chess bureaucracy.

We knew that the federation had read the writing on the wall and knew that they couldn't deny my sisters and me a spot on this year's squad without facing some serious international backlash. My father had the idea to use this leverage to put our battle with Szerenyi behind us for good. In return for my playing in the Olympiad, we asked the federation to sign an official memorandum in which we all "let bygones be bygones" and agreed to work together. The federation went even further, officially admitting that in the past it had taken steps to hinder my career—and agreeing to get out of my way from now on. I really wanted to believe the Szerenyi was finally warming up to me and my family, but I had been fooled in the past. And it would take some time for me to really believe they were on my side. Until then, I decided, I would remain cautiously optimistic.

Of course, I still had Zsuzsa Veroci to deal with. My performance over the previous few years had made it impossible for her to insist that she was somehow the better player. But she continued to argue in the press that my sisters hadn't proven themselves yet and that they had no business representing Hungary at the Olympiad. As a veteran of several Olympiads herself, Veroci believed that she was the natural choice to send to Greece that fall. The final decision would come down to a man named Janos Tompa.

As the captain of the women's team that year, Janos had free rein to recruit whoever he wanted. Most other countries simply choose the highest-rated players—which would have been me and my sisters. But he understood that politics was involved, and he wanted to make the process as fair and open as possible. It was a foregone conclusion that I would lead the team that year. It perhaps helped that I had played Janos in competition a year earlier and beat him convincingly. So he had seen what I could do with his own eyes.

That left three other spots to fill. In order to appease the pro-Veroci faction of the federation, Janos proposed a twelve-round qualifier event in which my two sisters—as well as Veroci and another top player, nineteen-year-old Ildiko Madl—would compete for the chance to represent their country in Greece. I saw no harm in this. In fact, I was looking forward to my sisters putting Veroci in her place, which I was confident they could do if given the chance. Judit was in the middle of the best year of her playing career so far, and Sofia continued to make steady progress up the rankings.

But when Janos invited Veroci to play, she scoffed at the suggestion. It was an insult, she said, to have to play in such an event given her distinguished history at the Olympiad. And she wouldn't dignify the request with an answer. I half-figured this would happen. It was the same tactic she had used years earlier when I had challenged her to a match of my own. And it only confirmed for me that she was more interested in bad-mouthing my family than proving herself over the chess board. The federation gave all of the players until August 2 to either accept or decline the qualifier event. Even then, Veroci refused to give her answer. Janos waited a few more days out of courtesy. When she still didn't reply, it was settled. My sisters, Ildiko, and I would be going to Greece that fall.

I suspect this is the outcome Janos secretly hoped for all along. Having Veroci in the group would have been horrible for the team's chemistry. And based purely on our ratings, it was undeniable that the four of us gave Hungary its best chance to date to take home Olympiad gold in the women's section. But gold was still far from guaranteed. The Soviet women's team had the highest average rating of any team that year, making them the favorite, as they had been every year before. In fact, the Soviets had taken gold at every single Women's Olympiad they had entered, stretching all the way back to 1957. The only Olympiad they hadn't won was the 1976 tournament in Haifa, Israel, which the Soviets had boycotted for political reasons. Had the Soviet women's team competed that year, they would have very likely won. In other words, my sisters, Ildiko, and I were attempting what no other Olympiad team had ever managed.

As the highest rated and most experienced player among the four, I would play board 1. Judit would take board 2, with Sofia and Ildiko taking turns on the third and final board, depending on the day. Judit would also sit out a few games, if needed. But those decisions would be left to Janos.

I had mostly stayed away from female-only tournaments in those years. So, I barely knew my fourth teammate, Ildiko, before Janos introduced us at the airport in Budapest. We all got along right away. It couldn't have been easy being the one non-Polgar on the team, but Ildiko handled it with grace. She had this very ironic, self-deprecating sense of humor that set her apart from my sisters and me but that we really enjoyed. Like a lot of people back in Hungary, she was skeptical that we'd actually beat the Soviets. She even joked in our first meeting at the airport that "if they agree to give us the silver medal today, maybe we can all go home and save ourselves a trip."

My sisters and I were more confident in our chances. We invented a ritual for getting into a fighting spirit during the event—a kind of pump-up exercise. Before we left our hotel room for that day's round, we'd sing one of our favorite songs, "Rasputin" by Boney M. After belting out each verse with all the energy we could muster, we'd linger on the song's last line: "Oh, those Russians." We had nothing against Russians personally, of course. They just happened to be our biggest rivals.

The setting for the Olympiad that November couldn't have been more picturesque than the ancient Greek city of Thessaloniki, which sits right on the Aegean coast. From time to time, we could make out Mount Olympus shooting up out of the horizon off in the distance.

Inside the playing hall, mingling and laughing and saying their hellos, was a seemingly endless crowd of the world's best chess players. A quick glance around the room revealed more living legends than I had ever seen in one place before. People like Kasparov, Karpov, Seirawan, Nunn, Ivanchuk.

The room itself was an enormous, utilitarian space, lit from above with long strips of fluorescent light and filled to capacity with row upon row of tables at which participants from more than a hundred countries would do battle over the next two and a half weeks. Each table held three basic wooden chess boards and a set of regulation-sized plastic pieces, each one accompanied by a manual-wind Garde chess clock from East Germany, the standard for that era. Punctuating the rows every few boards were white rectangular plaques hung high off the ground from L-shaped metal stands, which displayed the flags of the two countries facing off on the boards below along with the names of the players. I remember scanning the hall that first day, looking for my country's flag and the jolt of excitement I felt when I finally spotted it. There in the distance was Hungary's red, white, and green tricolor. Beneath it, in bold, clear letters were three names: POLGAR, POLGAR, POLGAR.

My first order of business before the round began was to find the bathroom, a common habit among chess players settling in for a long tournament. And I was stunned to find that the women's room lacked a standard toilet and instead housed just a porcelain drain in the floor, something I had encountered only a few times before. It would make the next couple of weeks of competition... well, interesting.

I played my entire first game against the Australian Anne Slavotinek in a kind of heightened state, viscerally affected by the significance of the moment. Here I was, representing my nation on a global stage and sharing the privilege with my two young sisters, both of whose talent I had nurtured for years. It was hard to believe how much attention we received from the other players. From time to time, even the reigning world champion Garry Kasparov would walk over to watch our games.

The swirl of emotions I felt—gratitude and pride, determination and anxiety—was intoxicating. And the elation that came after we swept all three boards that round was more intense still. We repeated that feat in the second round against France, this time with Ildiko playing on the third board, proving that our team could work together. Everything just felt *right*.

But it didn't last.

We got the bad news at the end of our second day. While traveling to meet us in Thessaloniki, Ildiko's fiancé, Bela Perenyi, had died in a car accident. I had known Bela for years and liked him quite a lot, as everyone did. Hearing what had happened, though, I immediately thought of Ildiko and how happy she had seemed talking about Bela just hours before. This young woman, who was my age exactly, had found someone she wished to share her life with, just as her career was reaching new heights. The life she had always wished for—the life we all wanted for ourselves in our own way—was finally laid out before her. And then, at the worst possible moment, it was all over. We all assumed that Ildiko would want to head back to Hungary right away to be with her family. But she insisted on staying. She had a job to do, she said. And she wasn't going to let down her team. It was one of the greatest shows of strength I had ever witnessed.

All of a sudden, winning the Olympiad felt much less important. But Janos managed to put things in a new perspective for us. He told us that if Ildiko was willing to fight through her pain, then we owed it to her—and to Bela—to salvage something good from this nightmarish episode. It was exactly the motivation we needed to refocus and get back to work. And it completely changed the nature of the competition for us.

Ildiko would sit out the next two rounds, and in the evenings we'd all eat dinner together and try to distract her a little. We were giving her whatever time she needed to get back into a state of mind where she could play. And we were ready to let Sofia take the rest of the third-board games if we needed to. But Janos had a different idea.

During round 5—our one face-off against the Soviets—Janos chose Ildiko for board 3. It was a bold move, and one that could have easily backfired on our captain. There was no telling how Ildiko would respond to the situation. And a loss against the Soviets would have put us in a tough spot, with regard to both the tournament standings and our own team morale. It's a testament to Janos's judgment and leadership that this extraordinary gambit paid off.

In a stunning display of fortitude and concentration, Ildiko managed to win with the black pieces that round, playing against the higher-rated Soviet player Marta Litinskaya. It was a stellar performance on Ildiko's part, and it came exactly when we needed it. We had gone to Thessaloniki to defeat the Soviet team, and since Judit and I drew our games, Ildiko's upset win was what ultimately gave us the victory.

The Women's Olympiad became the center of another drama a week later, after Elena Akhmilovskaya—the Soviet team's second-strongest player—failed to show up for her eleventh-round game. This meant that the Soviets would need to use their reserve player in order to avoid a forfeit.

The playing hall was buzzing with speculation about where Elena might be. After Bela's sudden death just days before, I had this sickening feeling that something horrible had happened to her. News got around pretty quickly that Elena had eloped with the captain of the American team, John Donaldson, escaping to the United States just a day earlier. They would divorce about a year later, but Elena would remarry and remain in the United States until her untimely death in 2012.

We entered the final round of the Olympiad tied for first place with the Soviets. But whereas the Soviets were paired against a relatively weak Dutch team, we would face a Swedish team led by Pia Cramling, a world-class player with whom I once shared the top spot on the female rankings. I knew my game against Pia would be a difficult fight. I had no idea how difficult.

I began with a queen's pawn opening, to which Pia replied with a version of the Benoni defense. I was able to secure a positional advantage after fifteen or twenty moves and would continue to build on it gradually over the course of the middlegame. But somewhere around the thirty-fifth move or so, I lost the thread.

My advantage had evaporated. By the time we adjourned for lunch, Pia was back in the game.

Thankfully, Judit notched a quick win on board 2. But after Ildiko's subsequent draw in her game, things got even tougher for me. Our path to the gold medal was getting narrower. In a surprise result, the Soviets crumbled under the pressure and drew all three of their last-round games. This meant that all I needed was a draw in my game for Hungary to take home gold.

Analyzing the position during the break, it became more and more obvious that Pia had multiple ways to win. It was a heartbreaking realization. But I was experienced enough to know that lost games can turn around fast if your opponent gets careless. I had seen it happen that year in France, in my game against Murey. So I set my emotions aside and returned to the game determined to improve my position as best I could. I just needed to stay focused and fight on.

If I lost, we would end the tournament tied with the Soviets, and the gold medal would go to whoever came out ahead in a tiebreaker. This is a system in which the total points scored by each of the teams Hungary faced is compared to the points of the Soviets' opponents. So my father and Janos spent the rest of my game frantically calculating points and watching the other remaining games in the hopes that things would break our way.

Something changed over the next dozen or so moves. Pia kept thinking for long bouts—longer than seemed reasonable. Pretty soon, she was in time trouble. The luxury of a winning position can be burdensome. And, in this game at least, it proved Pia's downfall. She had several promising paths to victory. But she made a decisive error. The position was still winnable for her, but it wouldn't be easy, and she knew it. Still flustered from the mistake, she played yet another inaccurate move, which made a draw all but inevitable. Once again, fortune had smiled on me. A few moves later, we agreed to a draw. Gold now belonged to Hungary.

I shook Pia's hand and immediately ran to my sisters and Ildiko, squeezing them close in celebration. For weeks, I had tried not to imagine what it would be like to win in Greece. The moment it was over, though, a tsunami of emotion came rushing into me—a sensation that went beyond happiness or contentment or pride. This was pure joy. I don't remember another victory meaning so much or feeling so good. It would have been gratifying enough simply to unseat the Soviets and do my country proud. The fact that I played every round of the tournament on the top board without losing a single game was a particular point of pride. But sharing this achievement with my own sisters—and being there as Ildiko rose to the occasion during one of the most horrific moments of her life—there was just nothing to compare it to. I recall watching Judit's astounding performance on board 2—in which she won twelve of her thirteen games, with one draw—and the mix of big-sisterly pride and professional respect and competitive glee it still gives me. Judit was an absolute rock for our team in that tournament, and it gave us all a glimmer of what she would do in the years ahead.

The hours that followed are still mostly a blur in my memory. I can remember posing for pictures with my teammates and Janos, struggling to stand still from all of the adrenaline. I especially remember standing onstage during the medal ceremony as the Hungarian flag was raised just a little bit higher than the Soviet flag, our national anthem playing triumphantly. I remember Garry Kasparov's toothy smile as he congratulated me and encouraged me to "keep it up," and the look of relief in Janos's face, and the tears of joy welled up in my parents' eyes.

Most moving of all, however, was what awaited us back home in Hungary. As we stepped out of the Budapest airport, a crowd of hundreds greeted us, applauding and holding up homemade signs and chanting our names. We had left Hungary as black sheep and returned as golden girls. It had been just months since Hungary's historic eleven-gold-medal performance at the Olympic games in Seoul, Korea. Now, my sisters, Ildiko, and I have brought that total to twelve.

The government, once hostile to me and my family, awarded me and my two sisters top national honors. The Hungarian Chess Federation also changed their tune, as they rushed to take credit for the decision to send us to Greece. A flattering book-length account of our long journey to Olympiad gold was published not long thereafter. And many of Hungary's most prominent businesses—from insurance firms to computer companies—lavished endorsements on me and my sisters. It took me a while to really believe it, but the feud between my family and Hungary's power elite had ended overnight. And nothing in our lives would ever be the same again.

FIFTEEN

This was the heyday of "Polgaria." That was the name the press gave to me and my sisters after our gold-medal coup at the 1988 Olympiad, as if we were a nation unto ourselves or a cultural institution like the Beatles or the Rat Pack. For the next few years, it felt like nearly everybody in the chess world wanted to test themselves against our little three-person country. We'd get invited to Denmark or Slovenia or France or Greece for an exhibition against some of the top male players in each country. We'd sit for photo shoots and press interviews and attend receptions, like Hollywood stars promoting a new movie.

We had several endorsement deals, including one with an early chess technology company called Mephisto. They made these computerized chess boards with touch-sensitive squares. You'd make a move on the physical board, and the computer would spit out a response on a little digital screen, enabling you to play games against it. The company called their latest model the Polgar to capitalize on the buzz we were creating. We'd travel to toy fairs all over Europe promoting the product, giving simultaneous exhibitions, and playing chess blindfolded (without looking at the board) against anyone who came to the booth for a game. We saw it mainly as a helpful source of income. But it was also a little bit of low-pressure fun, a break from the serious work of competition and training that filled up most of our days in those years.

A very special bond developed between me and my sisters during this period, one that went beyond the normal ties of sibling-hood. Celebrity can be a lonely condition, but we were going through it together, and at an age when we could all really enjoy it. The two little girls I had helped raise were now on the verge of becoming young women. At the time of our Olympiad win, Sofia was fourteen, Judit was twelve, and I was nineteen. We had a lot more in common socially, even though they were fast developing into unique and interesting people right before my eyes.

These differences were most obvious when we were on the road together. Especially in those years, I had this bottomless appetite for meeting new people—it was my favorite part of traveling. I had no trouble striking up conversations with absolute strangers on planes or in airports, just to hear about what they did for a living or where their family was from. As the most artistic of the three of us, Sofia had her own interests. Before each trip, she'd study the history and culture of wherever we happened to be traveling and spend whatever time she could touring the local landmarks and visiting museums. Judit was completely different. Chess was almost her only focus in those years. Nearly every aspect of the game gave her pleasure. She could study openings and solve puzzles for hours on end without her enthusiasm ever waning. But she was also a relentless competitor with a fierce determination to get better as quickly as she could.

We did everything together in those years. When we were back in Budapest, our days would always begin with several hours of table tennis training, our favorite form of physical exercise. We took it very seriously and even worked with a coach for several years. We'd follow that up with several hours of chess study—always working right alongside each other.

While traveling, we'd often start each day with a private fashion show and take turns voting on what each of us should wear. After the day's events were over in whatever city we were visiting and we had finished working on chess, we'd relax together in the hotel room and talk about the things we'd seen or some cute boy one of us may have noticed and sometimes do each other's hair. We'd listen to music and watch movies—*Coming to America* with Eddie Murphy or some goofy comedy like *Foul Play* with Chevy Chase and Goldie Hawn. On tournament rest days, we'd go on shopping trips around town, wandering in and out of boutiques and department stores, hunting for sales and trying on different outfits. And if there was time to kill at an airport, or after dinner at a restaurant, we'd sometimes play a version of the game Battleship we had invented, which used a chess board we would draw on a piece of graph paper. It was like a globe-trotting sleepover with your two best friends, one that didn't ever seem to end.

There with us through all of it, as usual, were my father and mother, both of whom had long before adopted specific roles in our traveling entourage. My mother, our unwavering source of affection and comfort, would see to it that we ate well and slept enough and had clean clothes. Her gift with languages also came in quite handy throughout our travels. My father, who was also our manager in those years, did a lot of things. But he was particularly good at keeping things in perspective for us professionally, making sure that all of the Polgaria publicity didn't get in the way of our serious chess work. The recognition we were getting was all well and good. But I was still chasing the grandmaster title. And it was clear that, pretty soon, Judit would be as well. My father was there to keep us on track. No matter how busy our schedule got, he always made sure to block off six to eight hours for chess study each day.

One of the earliest stops on the Polgaria world tour was Mexico City. The international master Roberto Martin del Campo had arranged for us to visit. He had competed with us in Greece as part of Mexico's men's team. When he saw the attention we were getting there, he quickly got to work organizing the trip, lining up sponsors, and scheduling promotional events in record time. As a member of a chess family himself—his sister Astrid and brother Jorge were both serious players—he and his siblings felt a connection to me and my sisters, which was mutual.

The Martin del Campos were outstanding hosts, especially considering we had only just met them. I can still remember driving around Mexico City, Roberto pointing out historic landmarks from behind the wheel, and the inside joke my sisters and I had about the Bosque de Chapultepec, one of the city's largest parks, which, to a Hungarian ear, sounded so funny that we'd giggle each time someone said it. We took a brief detour to see the pyramids outside the city. Also, Mexican food was a revelation. The quesadillas and tacos and tortillas and guacamole and pico de gallo—it wasn't like anything we'd ever eaten before.

Mexico City was just the first of two stops during that trip. The main reason we had come to the country was to compete in Mazatlan at the very first World Rapid Chess Championship, which was then known as the World Active Chess Championship (an unfortunate name which didn't last for long). *Rapid chess* refers to games in which each player gets anywhere from ten to sixty minutes to make all of their moves (in the case of the Mazatlán tournament, each player got thirty minutes). This intermediate time control makes rapid chess a kind of hybrid of longer classical chess and much shorter blitz chess.

Serious rapid tournaments really didn't exist yet. So FIDE's decision to create such a competition—as well as the new titles of world active champion and active grandmaster—marked a major break with tradition. Some people saw it as a threat to chess, world champion Garry Kasparov being chief among them. If there was going to be a world active chess champion, he joked, "did that mean I played passive chess?" Even with all of the controversy, the tournament was still able to assemble a distinguished group of players, including Karpov, Seirawan, Bent Larsen—and, of course, my sisters and me.

I was rooting for rapid chess to succeed as a legitimate format in high-level competition. At its best, classical chess can be a transcendent experience. But when you're not playing well—when you're forced to spend hour after hour defending a difficult position, fighting for your life with little hope of prevailing—games can feel like absolute torture. That kind of suffering can take a toll on even the best players. Say what you will about rapid chess, but at least the games are over quickly. I also liked that, in rapid chess, there's always the possibility that your opponent might make a last-minute mistake that turns your losing position into a win, which meant that no position was ever truly hopeless.

Also, rapid events take up a lot less time overall. At classical tournaments, I'd often prepare for three or four hours before a game even started. That game could stretch on for another seven hours, after which I'd have just enough time to eat, go to sleep, and start the process all over again the next day. Over the course of a dozen rounds or so, this routine can be exhausting. So the chance to play the top players in a quicker format just seemed too good to pass up.

It didn't hurt that the event took place at a beach resort in Mazatlan, which even in December felt like a tropical paradise. The place was packed with vacationing families in bathing suits, lounging by the pool or listening to one of the live mariachi bands. It was not the typical setting for a world chess championship. There was even a celebrity tournament going at the same time as the rapid event. I remember the American television actor Erik Estrada played, which was exciting. I liked that the chess world was experimenting with different venues and formats and trying new ways to make chess accessible to and fun for a wider audience.

At one point, Sofia and my mother went parasailing, strapping themselves to a parachute and flying thirty feet in the air as a boat pulled them across the water. You couldn't have paid me or Judit or my father to try something like that. We were too scared. Not Sofia, though. She was always looking for new experiences. Nothing gave her more pleasure.

Judit had such an impressive string of tournament performances in 1988, and accumulated so many rating points that by January 1989 she overtook me as the world's number one female player—and at just twelve years of age. It was a unique experience, watching my little sister make such incredible progress, building her own career right beside my own. I had seen it coming for quite some time. It was just a few years earlier that I was still giving both her and Sofia knight odds or time odds in the little ten-game blitz matches we'd play at home. By 1987, we had changed the rules, playing on equal terms—although I still had to win seven out of ten games to "take the match." I knew it was only a matter of time before at least one of my sisters started to give me a run for my money. The intensity with which Judit studied and worked and fought over the board—even as a young girl—made it clear she'd be the first to do it.

Part of me wasn't happy to fall from the top of rankings. Nobody would be. At the same time, if I had to lose my number one position to anybody, I'd prefer it be to either Judit or Sofia. Just as long as it stayed in the family. Being the best female player was never that important to me, anyway. What I really wanted to be was a grandmaster and a top player.

There was something deeply validating about watching both of my sisters excel. That they were ascending up the chess rankings and competing against men without any of the opposition I had faced from the authorities meant that the battles I had fought for so long actually counted for something. I might not have changed the culture as much as I wanted to. Professional chess was still a boys club, and in many ways it remains so today. But at least I had cleared a path for my sisters and made it just a little bit easier for other girls to follow our lead.

⸺•◦•⸺

Few people had a greater effect on my career than a Dutch gentleman named Joop van Oosterom. Even today, I still refer to him almost exclusively as "Mr. van Oosterom" when he comes up in conversation, out of an innate sense of respect and gratitude for what he gave to me and my family. He was a promising junior player in his youth. But, as he used to tell the story, a game against Spassky during the third World Junior Championship in Antwerp made him doubt he could ever go very far. He could see that Spassky had a kind of greatness that he himself would never have. He turned his attention to computer programming and ultimately earned a significant fortune in the software business.

From then on, he became a great benefactor of chess, financing two separate Dutch-league chess teams. A good friend of my family's, the international master Leon Pliester, happened to be playing for one of those teams. And in 1989, he arranged an introduction between my family and Mr. van Oosterom. We all hit it off right away, and before long, my sisters and I were playing for one of his Dutch teams as well. Mr. van Oosterom also agreed to finance nearly every aspect of our careers and pay for whatever coaches we chose to hire or books we needed. He'd use his connections to secure us invitations to top Dutch tournaments, and even gifted us a laptop computer—which were hugely expensive in those days—for organizing our chess files, so that we no longer needed to travel with suitcases full of books and notebooks. It was one of those life-changing strokes of fortune that sometimes appear from nowhere.

It was clear from very early on that Mr. van Oosterom genuinely wanted us to succeed and was willing to do whatever he could to make that happen. He wanted to see just how far we could advance in the male-dominated world of chess. At one point he even pitched my father on a plan to repeat the "Polgar experiment" with a group of randomly selected four-year-olds, to see if my father could make them into grandmasters. Mr. van Oosterom would finance the project completely, he insisted. My father was actually interested, but only if he could adopt the children and work with them full-time while also raising them. I'm convinced my father would have moved forward with it all had my mother not intervened. She had raised her children, she said. And she wasn't interested in starting over again.

Mr. van Oosterom also had plans for a documentary about our family. This time, it was my father who wasn't interested. He knew that having a camera crew follow the family around for months on end would have distracted from our careers too much. People sometimes portray my father as a publicity hound or someone who was out to make money off of his children, but he's never been that way. Outside of his children's safety and well-being, chess was always what mattered most to him. And anything that might interfere with that work—no matter how lucrative or flattering to our egos—was always out of the question. A beautifully produced feature film about our daily lives would have very likely brought us more money and celebrity. And if we were all grandmasters already, he might have even agreed to it. But we still had history to make.

If asked to name the most outstanding individual achievements in the history of chess, a few stand out. There's Bobby Fischer's twenty-game winning streak in the run-up to the 1972 World Championship, in which he convincingly outplayed some of the strongest players on the planet in a series of matches against the likes of Tigran Petrosian, Bent Larsen, and Mark Taimanov. After being swept by Fischer 6–0 during a match at the Candidates Tournament, Taimanov famously quipped, "Well, I still have my music."

For me, though, Sofia's 1989 performance at the Magistrale di Roma tournament is high up on my list—and not just because she's my sister. Fischer's run might have been unlikely, but what Sofia did that winter in Rome is simply inexplicable. She just turned fourteen. In a field that included five grandmasters, Sofia absolutely dominated, winning the first eight of her nine games, and drawing in the final round.

She was strong for her age but, at least on paper, nowhere near the strength of the grandmasters she was competing against. So the idea that she could finish near the front of the pack was a little fantastical.

When she won her first two games against unrated players, I wasn't all that surprised. When she won her third game, against the Soviet GM Sam Palatnik, I was fairly impressed. But when the victories kept piling up, neither I nor my parents nor Judit could believe what we were seeing. She beat the young Italian phenom Carlo D'Amore in the fourth round, and followed it up with a route in round 5 against the GM Alexander Chernin—who was rated nearly 300 points higher than she was. Then she went to work on Romania's best player, the GM Mihai Suba. Another win! And another after that! She drew her final round against another top Soviet GM, Sergey Dolmatov, for a final score of 8½ out of 9—a full 2 points ahead of the second-place finisher.

Up until that point, Sofia had been the lowest-rated player of the three of us. But watching from the sidelines, Judit and I got the distinct impression that if Sofia kept playing like this, she might eclipse us both in the very near future.

I wish I had some sort of theory about what went on at that tournament, or some closely held secret to her success to reveal. The truth is, I was just as floored as anyone. I was sure Sofia was a gifted player, and I'd seen moments of brilliance in her games for years. Not even I knew she was capable of a performance like this, though. I can only speculate that it had something to do with the food. Sofia was fairly petite at that age and never had a very big appetite. But throughout the entire tournament in Rome she couldn't get enough to eat. At lunch before her games she'd start with a generous portion of pasta. Then she'd order her own meat or fish course and, after cleaning her plate, move on to dessert. I remember making eye contact with my mother during meals as Sofia devoured her plate of pasta and sharing a look of puzzlement. *Who is this girl?*

Whatever she was doing, it worked. Because for those two weeks in Rome, my middle sister couldn't lose. She left Italy with a beautiful first place trophy, a massive metal chalice nearly one-third her size. Over the next few months, almost every chess publication on the planet put her photo on the cover. It became known as "Sofia's Sack of Rome."

SIXTEEN

For most of my life, the idea that the Communist Party would ever relinquish power in Hungary seemed unthinkable. By the spring of 1989, it seemed inevitable. In order to avoid social unrest, my government had already begun to embrace liberal reforms, gradually adopting some capitalist policies. It also removed most travel restrictions for Hungarian citizens. And there was even talk that multiparty elections might be on the horizon.

The biggest sign that things were changing came in May of that year, when Hungary removed the barbed-wire fence along our border with Austria. It was the very first puncture in the Iron Curtain, the first sign that the Cold War I had grown up in might soon be over. And I was overjoyed.

I knew firsthand just how transformative it could be to experience a different kind of life in the West. And I wanted more of my fellow Hungarians to see what I had seen and be changed by it. What I found most heartening was that this process happened peacefully, with leaders from both nations agreeing to open up to one another.

In my wildest dreams, I wouldn't have imagined that the destruction of Hungary's border fence with Austria would inspire a wave of similar actions across Eastern Europe. But that's exactly what happened. By that fall, the Berlin Wall—the greatest symbol of Cold War oppression and division and control—was no more. I didn't know what would happen next, but I was hopeful that it would be better.

After a year of dashed hopes and near misses on my way to the grandmaster title, the stars finally aligned for me in Leon, Spain, that June.

It was good timing, as I was beginning to get impatient. For whatever reason, things just seemed to gel for me in Leon. I always loved the deliberate rhythm of life in Spain, and Spanish had already become one of my favorite languages by then. There was also the pinball. Some nights after dinner at a restaurant near the playing hall, Sofia, my mother, and I would hold these little pinball and foosball competitions with our fellow Hungarian, the grandmaster Jozsef Pinter, who was also playing in the event.

Whatever the reason, I was at the top of my game, finishing tied for first. I would enter the new decade with some wind at my back, a second GM norm under my belt, and hungrier than ever to get the title I had dreamed about for so long.

A few weeks later we found ourselves back in Holland for the OHRA Tournament in Amsterdam. With the exception of the weather, I loved nearly everything about Amsterdam—the gorgeous canals, that playful spirit that the Dutch bring to every interaction. But I really loved the Indonesian food. I had never had it before coming to Amsterdam, but right away it became one of my favorite cuisines. Each time I visited the city, I'd make a stop at one of the same few restaurants and order a sampling of little "rice table" dishes, or "rijsttafel" as the Dutch call them—delicious little portions of food.

It was also a pleasure to play in a country that held chess in such high regard. There was a certain respect that the Dutch showed for chess players, and it came through in lots of little ways. The playing conditions were a little bit better, and you'd sometimes get recognized on the street by total strangers. Judit made a real stir at this particular event, securing her very first grandmaster norm not long after turning thirteen. The Dutch press went so crazy over the story that one chess publication described the atmosphere as "Polgarmania."

Predictably, she and I were peppered with questions about whether a rivalry was brewing between us, now that she was hot on my heels in the race for the GM title. And in every interview, Judit would deny any kind of competitiveness between us. "No, [Susan] is happy when I make good results," she told one reporter—which of course I was. I wasn't just her sister. She was my student, or at least she used to be, and I still saw her in that light.

It was during that trip that we visited the Anne Frank House. I had known Anne Frank's story for as long as I could remember. My high school was even named after her. So I didn't expect to be as stirred by the experience as I was. Seeing the tiny rooms where she had hidden for those years, scribbling in her diary, and knowing what would become of her was just so sad. I felt connected to her in many ways, this bright young Jewish girl, victimized by forces wholly outside of her control. But I also felt humbled.

———◆•◆———

It's impossible to grow up in a Jewish family without thinking of Israel as an almost mythical place. Even though we weren't religious ourselves, the culture and tradition of Judaism was still an important part of our lives. My father's father, Armin, was still a practicing Jew, and at that time ran the synagogue in the town my father had grown up in. So it was only natural that we had all

manner of preconceived notions about what we'd find in Israel—
few of which proved very accurate.

When we first landed at Ben Gurion airport, we couldn't escape
the sense that this place was special. Some of our fellow passengers kissed the ground of the Holy Land as we exited the plane.
What struck us most after arriving in Tel Aviv was just how many
people walked the streets carrying guns. Not pistols, either, but
long, intimidating-looking rifles and automatic weapons, always
at the ready, as if an enemy assault could break out at any moment.
When we entered a hotel or a restaurant or a department store, it
was standard practice that our bags be searched. I knew all about
Israel's conflict with the Palestinians, its constant fight for existence, and its system of compulsory military service. I just didn't
expect to find evidence of it right there on the street—and not
just in the disputed areas. Even as a tourist, it's impossible not to
feel part of the struggle. The only guns I'd seen were holstered
in the belts of police officers or attached to East German border
guards. For me, wars and terrorist attacks and deadly shootings
were things that happened someplace else. In my naïveté, I had
failed to comprehend what it was like to actually be in one of those
places, to walk the streets knowing that violence might erupt at
any moment.

Just as shocking was the extraordinary variety of people who
called Israel their home. When I thought of Israel before that trip, I
always pictured a country populated mostly by Ashkenazi Jews like
us, although perhaps a bit more observant. Judaism meant something very specific where I grew up, and I had just assumed it was
the same everywhere, and certainly in Israel. I was plenty familiar with Orthodox and Hasidic Judaism. But I knew little about
Sephardic Jews. And I definitely didn't expect there to be so many
Muslims, Christians, and even atheists. On any given day, you'd hear
people speaking Russian or English or French or what I later learned
was Amharic, a Semitic tongue from Ethiopia. Most of the Jewish

population wasn't even all that religious. Many were risking their lives simply to be in Israel, and they saw this as observance enough.

As our family rode camels in the desert one day, I felt a profound connection with a distant past. I thought about my grandparents and all of the relatives we'd lost in the death camps, and how none of them ever lived to see the promised land our people had dreamed about for thousands of years. I felt sad and grateful, but also a little insignificant. The historical forces that had made this place possible were so much bigger than me. I felt lucky to be there.

Genuine physical danger is rare in the game of chess, I'm happy to admit. But that's exactly what I felt in the summer of 1989, at the World Junior Championship in Tunja, Colombia. It was my predictable reaction to the armed guards we saw everywhere we went—muscular, serious-looking men forever scanning our surroundings and peeking around corners, military-grade firearms in hand. There were guards at the airport when we arrived and on every street we passed in town. Even during our games, the guards were there, manning the exits, protecting the chess players from some ever-present mortal threat, the nature of which was left distressingly vague for the duration of the tournament.

We visited Bogota after the tournament. And by comparison to Tunja, the city felt positively welcoming. As it turned out, I could have used some armed security there as well. Crossing a street to meet my coach outside of his hotel at noon one day, a young man bolted past me, ripping my necklace from my neck with a precision and speed that suggested it wasn't his first time. The gold chain was mercifully thin and left only a faint scratch as it snapped against the back of my neck. I took it as a good omen that the thief didn't get away with the necklace's pendant, which had slipped off of the chain and fallen to my feet. It was a Star of David that I had worn proudly for years.

It was just by coincidence that weeks after nearly losing my favorite symbol of Judaism to a street criminal, my family and I found ourselves back in Israel for the European Team Championship in Haifa. I was already proud to represent Hungary in the men's championship for the first time. That it took place in Israel, which had already become so meaningful to me, made it so much more significant.

—•—

The first thing I noticed about Viswanathan Anand—or Vishy, as he liked to be called—was his speed. Nobody played as quickly as Vishy. I had been hearing about the blistering pace of his games for quite a while. But it was only in January 1990 in the Dutch village of Wijk aan Zee that I got to see it myself for the first time.

The annual tournament in Wijk aan Zee (pronounced something close to "vike on zay") is a very special event for chess players—the "Wimbledon of Chess," it's sometimes called. (Today it's technically known as Tata Steel, the name of the event's chief sponsor.) The tournament has been held, in one form or another, in the same coastal village for nearly nine decades—and, unfortunately for players, almost always in January. The North Sea of Holland in the middle of winter has some of the most brutally cold winds of any place I've ever been. Wijk aan Zee winds seem to come from every direction, chasing after you down narrow alleys and attacking you as you turn a street corner, knocking off hats and filling your ears with frigid static. The town itself is incredibly pleasant to look at, with its historic churches and charming little Dutch beach houses. And the locals are always incredibly welcoming to the hundreds of chess players that swarm the village each year. Those winds, though, could really wear you down.

Braving the harsh weather over the two and a half weeks of the tournament is like a rite of passage for chess players. It's tradition for the organizers to serve hot pea soup from an enormous bowl in the analysis rooms outside the playing hall to help keep the players warm. I was playing in the tournament's B section in 1990, just below the top group players. As in previous years, the A section boasted an impressive roster, which included John Nunn, Lajos Portisch, Korchnoi, and, of course, Vishy. Everyone plays in the same giant room at Wijk aan Zee, and I would always find myself wandering over to Vishy's table to catch a glimpse of his lightning speed. He was even faster than I expected.

In games where each player had as much as three and a half hours to make their first fifty-six moves, Vishy would sometimes use just thirty minutes for the entire game—and still end up winning. He spent most of his time casually wandering around the playing hall, waiting for his turn to move. To outside observers, his speed looked like a parlor trick, or like he was late for an appointment across town. There was almost a comedy to some of his games. His opponent would calculate for thirty or forty minutes, head in hands, marshaling all of the concentration they could before finally making a decision and punching their clock. Then, before they had even written their move on their score sheet, Vishy would snap out a reply, with an attitude that said, "I knew you were going to do that an hour ago. What took you so long?!"

There was an element of psychological warfare to his speed, for sure. But mind games can only get you so far in chess if you can't find the right moves when it counts. And more often than not, Vishy could find them. He and I might have been neck-and-neck in the rankings for our age group (we were born the same year), but Vishy had a superpower, and we all knew it.

Away from the board, he was another creature entirely. Kind, soft-spoken, always relaxed and joking around like he had all the time in the world. He loved to laugh and would make silly jokes in nearly every conversation. For years, we had followed each other's chess. By the time we finally got to talking in Holland, it was like we were already old friends. I invited him to come to Budapest after the tournament and stay with my family for a week. In classic Vishy fashion, he replied yes immediately.

We all loved having Vishy around. We were a chess household, after all. And he could talk about chess for hours. He had other interests, of course. A huge fan of pop music, he was rarely without his Walkman cassette player when not playing chess. But chess was the subject he never got tired of. I offered to show him around Budapest one day. Just thirty minutes into our walking tour, he had had his fill. He'd rather turn around and get back to chess. That it happened to be a very cold day certainly didn't help.

We spent all day replaying our games from the tournament, going down various rabbit holes to see where certain continuations led. My sisters and I would take turns playing him in blitz games, and he'd browse through our ever-growing card catalog (although, by this point, the advent of ChessBase made our collection a little less impressive). He'd pick out games he had never seen and talk about how it reminded him of this line he'd once considered, or that blitz game he once played.

We were from different cultures, different continents, different religions. But we spoke a common language: chess. And in that sense, we were compatriots. My mother would cook our meals, always conscious of Vishy's vegetarianism (as recently converted pescatarians ourselves, it was no stretch for her). We didn't know we were in the presence of a future world champion, but we knew Vishy was special. And each of us was happy to make him feel like a part of the family.

That fall, I enrolled at the Academy of Physical Sports and Education in Minsk Belarus, at the urging of Boris Gelfand, who I had met years earlier at the World Juniors in Australia. He was also a student there. I had always wanted to go to college. I just assumed that earning a degree while maintaining a full tournament schedule would be impossible. Boris set me straight. The university in Minsk was very hospitable to professional chess players, he explained. They even had an entire department devoted to chess and checkers. All I would need to do was show up a few times a year for exams, which sounded great to me. I'd usually meet up with Boris on those trips, and we'd train a little while I was in town. And my classmates in the chess program were always more than happy to supply me with class notes and other course materials. I was used to studying at home or in hotel rooms, so the arrangement felt pretty natural. It wasn't a typical college experience by any means, and I can't say I have many special memories of being a student. But I did graduate after four years with a teacher's degree in physical education—and a minor in chess and checkers, of course. I didn't know exactly what I'd use this for, but I felt that having a college education could be useful one day.

SEVENTEEN

The process of choosing the next World Championship challenger was gearing up again in 1990. And I was finally in the running, having qualified for the Zonal Tournament, which would take place in the Bulgarian city of Stara Zagora that February. As in previous cycles, the top finishers would advance to one of a couple Interzonal Tournaments, which would then determine a final list of candidates, and eventually a single challenger to reigning champion Garry Kasparov. I had met all of the requirements for this stage of the competition all the way back in 1986, but had been deliberately excluded on the grounds that I was female. To find myself back in contention after all of that controversy felt like a victory in its own right. I was ready to make my mark—not in some symbolic sense, but by playing some great chess.

Since there were an odd number of players, I was able to sit out the first round, which gave me time to settle my nerves and observe the other players a little more closely. Then, in round 2, I went to work, playing with the white pieces against the Czech Zbynek Hracek. It's still one of my favorite games. He answered my queen's pawn opening with a Queen's Indian Defense. His mistake was not to castle quickly enough—an error I didn't hesitate to punish. The position was so one-sided after seventeen moves that he had little choice but to resign. I was off to the races.

Over the next few days, I made a string of seven draws in hard-fought games, playing solidly in order to gradually put points on the scoreboard. After my tenth-round win against the German grandmaster Rainer Knaak, I felt like I might actually have a shot to win the whole thing and make it to the Interzonal. If nothing else, I could finish undefeated, which would have been some consolation. But the final round didn't go my way. I ended up losing to another German grandmaster, Uwe Boensch. Had I found my way to draw, I would have tied for first place and moved on to a playoff, the winner of which would have secured a spot in the Interzonal.

It stung. It still stings. But I wasn't about to hang my head. I had finally played for the first time in the World Championship cycle, and I remained a strong contender until my very last game.

—•◦•—

One of the things I loved the most about life as a professional chess player is the unique social dynamics that emerge at tournaments. For the duration of a game, the person sitting across from you is your opponent, your rival, maybe even your enemy. You spend hours facing this person in silence, trying to get inside their head, outsmart them, read their thoughts. But once a game is over, everything changes. Until recently, it was pretty standard for players to engage in lengthy postmortem analyses after every game, right there at the board, each player sharing the strategies and calculations that, seconds before, had been their most closely held secrets. In that instant, you stop being enemies and become fellow forensic investigators, dissecting the game you had just shared in search of the truth, pointing at squares emphatically, and hastily recreating positions while reciting strings of chess notation that only each of you fully understand. Sometimes, these conversations would last an hour or more. This kind of postgame analysis has since gone out of fashion, now that chess engines have gotten so strong. Although players still go over the game briefly, most of them are more eager to get to a computer to find out the engine's assessment of the "truth." Back then, though, the conversations would usually go something like this:

"Why didn't you capture on e5 with your knight?"

"I was afraid that after you pinned me with rook to e1 I would lose the piece."

"But then after the exchange on e5, you had that brilliant move rook d8 to d1, deflecting my rook, and you come out ahead."

"Yeah, I missed that."

It's like you both just watched the same movie, and now it's time to share your own personal interpretations. But there's something more going on. You learn a lot about a fellow player during these exchanges. I've always believed that a person's playing style is an extension of their personality. Some are more materialistic; others are more cautious; others still are natural risk takers. When professional players open up about their thinking—especially right after a game—they're sharing something very special about who they are, how they operate, and what they value, simply by revealing how they think about chess.

There's actually some scientific basis to this idea. Several years ago, I was asked by a Columbia University neuroscientist to undergo an fMRI brain scan for a National Geographic documentary, *My Brilliant Brain*. They wanted to see what happens in my brain when I look at a chess game. The researchers showed me a variety of chess positions. In some cases, the pieces were just randomly arranged on the board. In others, the positions came from actual games, some of which I recognized instantly. The surprising result was that the familiar positions activated the same part of my brain that's used to recognize faces. In a sense, I saw chess positions as old friends, with their own histories and personalities. It's really no surprise, then, that so many of my closest friendships got their start during and after chess games.

Another very special relationship got its start in Dortmund, Germany, that same year, after my game with the Georgian grandmaster Zurab Azmaiparashvili. Zurab was one of dozens of elite players who had been sequestered within the USSR for much of their careers. Like the Hungarian Chess Federation, the Soviet chess establishment kept tight control over which players were allowed to compete on the international circuit, which wasn't many. As a result, Zurab—like so many other talented players at that time— had spent some of his peak years unable to prove himself at top events. Within the Soviet Union he was well regarded for his deep knowledge of openings, so much so that none other than Garry Kasparov had recruited him as a second. Now that the communist empire was crumbling, Zurab was finally free to come out from behind the scenes and ply his trade. Even though I won the game, I could tell I was up against a true artist and a graceful competitor. But it was during the postmortem that I really came to like him. A tall, well-built gentleman, he emitted a level of enthusiasm and friendliness that defied the unfairness he had endured for so long. This combination of personal kindness and mastery over the board made it clear to me that he was the kind of person who could help take my chess to the next level—as well as the kind of person I would enjoy working with. We didn't know it at the time, but we were laying the groundwork for a professional relationship that would span years.

The Dortmund tournament took place a few weeks after my loss to Boensch at the Zonal in Stara Zagora. Painful defeats like that one can have lasting psychological effects if you let them. The person you lost to in that one critical game can get inside your head and make it difficult for you to play your best game the next time you face them. It happens all the time. That's why it's always a good idea to replace the bad memory with a good one as soon as possible—that is, to beat the person who just beat you the first chance you get. And, as luck would have it, Boensch and I were paired against each other in Dortmund. This time I would play with the white pieces. It was perfect timing. Not only would I get to even the score against him, but I would get to do it in his own country.

I got control of the game right out of the opening—the exchange variation of the Queen's Gambit Declined. By the middlegame, I had achieved near-perfect coordination of my pieces, which led to an all-out attack that Boensch couldn't manage to fight off. I would have much rather beaten him weeks before at the Zonal. But at least now we were even.

Sadly, my performance in Dortmund wasn't good enough for a third GM norm. However, it did gain me a few more ratings points, which was a positive sign that I was moving in the right direction, that I hadn't yet plateaued as a player. I had become pretty good at not letting these disappointments get to me. It wasn't always easy, but I knew that there was no forcing the third and final norm. All I could do was stick to my process, keep working, keep improving, and wait for things to fall into place.

In November 1990 my sisters and I joined up with our old teammate Ildiko Madl for the Olympiad in Novi Sad, a city in what was then Yugoslavia. I still remember how the city was covered in advertisements for the film *Pretty Woman*, which my sisters and I couldn't wait to see.

Whereas we had been the underdogs just two years before, this time we were the team to beat. It wasn't just that we had the highest average rating of any team. We were playing near the Hungarian border, which gave us a kind of home-field advantage. For instance, we appreciated that one of the chefs at our hotel was Hungarian and could cook some of our favorite foods, which was no small matter during a tournament that lasted for nearly three weeks— especially given that we were strict pescatarians. A large number of Hungarians even made the trip to cheer us on. In many ways, though, having so many things working in our favor became its own sort of burden. We had gone to Greece to prove something—it was us against the world. Now we were expected to defend our title. But even though we were up against a field of lower-rated players, we were expecting a tough fight, especially from the Soviets, who were the more experienced team.

I would describe our play as uneven in that event. We ended up losing to the Soviets 2–1, although I did manage to beat the reigning women's world champion, Maya Chiburdanidze, in that round, my first ever victory against her. Judit walked into an opening line that the Soviets had prepared especially for her and never found her way to safety.

Throughout the competition Judit and I both drew more games than we would have liked. And by the second-to-last round, the Soviets had opened up a 1½-point lead. This meant that things would have to break our way exactly if we had any hope of catching them, much less winning gold.

It's a tough position to be in, staring down the barrel of defeat, watching your fiercest rivals steal back the title you had won just two years before, and with a crowd of compatriots watching. We didn't dwell on that, though. Our attitude was to focus on the things we could control and forget about everything else.

In the end, we got lucky. The Soviets drew all three games in their penultimate round against Czechoslovakia, while Judit, Ildiko, and I swept the Argentinian team. We were now tied for first with the Soviets and remained in a dead heat after both our teams scored 3–0 in the final round. In situations like this, tournaments are decided by tiebreakers. This meant that our fate rested on the outcome of games that were still being played by other teams. It would be hours before all of the results were in. But by some small miracle, we ended up on top.

It was such a relief. We had succeeded in our chief objective, although just barely. And that made it all the more sweet. Once again I played every game on the top board without once losing— just as I had in Greece. And my sisters and I each won individual gold medals, in addition to the gold we won as a team. What really felt good was that we had shown that the last time wasn't a fluke— that Polgaria wasn't a fad, but a dynasty, and a force that was only getting stronger.

We barely had time after Novi Sad to head home and pack our bags for our next long adventure. This time we were off to New Delhi for an invitational tournament. My first reaction to the place can only be described as culture shock. Every aspect of it was governed by its own strange logic and aesthetic principles, from the food to the architecture to the music to the ways that drivers behaved in the city's cramped streets. What really took me aback was the stark contrast between wealth and poverty. The event's organizers had put us up in a five-star hotel that was as luxurious as any we had ever stayed in. Right outside our window, though, we saw people who were visibly malnourished, young children begging for money, makeshift homes, and families sleeping on the streets.

Within minutes of our arrival in the city I found myself struggling to breathe due to the poor air quality. When I confined myself to the hotel room, I'd begin to feel claustrophobic. I'd return to India several times after that, and never had the same reaction. But on that visit, I never quite found my bearings.

I'd play Vishy for the first time in an official tournament at that event—a game that he won. And I finished in a tie for third place with Judit. At the closing dinner, India's prime minister Rajiv

Gandhi made an appearance. It was so rare that a leader of his stat-
ure would make the time to visit a chess tournament. And yet he sat
with me and the other players, ate with us, and showed his respect
for the game and the people who make it their living. It would be
less than six months later that Gandhi was assassinated, just as
his mother, Indira Gandhi, had been years before. It's unsettling,
having a chance encounter with a public figure like that and then
seeing him perish not long after. When I heard the news, I found
myself mourning for someone I'd spoken to only once.

The few times we had met a world leader, the interactions were
brief—usually consisting of some pleasantries. A year earlier, I was
introduced to President George H. W. Bush and First Lady Barbara
Bush during their trip to Budapest. Both of them seemed perfectly
nice, but we didn't get to know them very well. It's easy to think
of these individuals not as regular flesh-and-blood people, but
as symbols or representations, like the wax figures I had seen at
Madame Tussaud's years before. But it was different with Gandhi.
I felt like I had actually met him, and not just posed for a photo
op with him.

We ended the year back in Spain, for a tournament in
Pamplona, the city best known for its famous running of the bulls.
Locally, it's just as famous for its New Year's Eve carnival, which
was about to get started when my mother and I arrived. Every
year, people flood the city dressed in all kinds of crazy costumes,
moving between bars and dancing in the streets. You wouldn't
expect a citywide street party would be a good backdrop for a
chess tournament. In my case, the setting couldn't have been more
perfect. I had come to see Spain as a lucky place for me after I
secured my second GM norm in Leon the year before. And there
was something about the energy from the festival that seemed to
propel me in Pamplona.

This was my best chance to date to finally earn the GM title.
And I couldn't help but feel the pressure. Everything I had worked

toward was right there in front of me. I just needed to take it. If anything, though, the stakes of that tournament helped me to play some of my best chess. I went undefeated in that event and even played Korchnoi to a draw. But what put me over the top for the final norm was a win against Leonid Yudasin. At the time, Yudasin was among the top ten players in the world, and Soviet co-champion. He had also won Olympiad gold that year and was a candidate for the World Championship.

I played a solid line of the Sicilian Defense. And by move 15, I had launched my attack, aiming all of my pieces directly at his king. I could feel the game shifting in my favor. I had a chance to finish him off in the middlegame, but I made an inaccuracy under time pressure, and Yudasin was able to defend. This wasn't going to be decided in the middlegame. Luckily, after we transposed to an endgame, I still had a clear advantage. I quickly marshaled my resources and regained the momentum. Little by little, I was able to pin his pieces, depriving him of any opportunity to fight me off. By move 41, it was hopeless for him. I had done it. Beating such an elite player—and doing so with the black pieces—was about as perfect a finish to my grandmaster quest as I could have asked for.

It's difficult to describe the torrent of emotions that came pouring out of me the moment I became a grandmaster. This was something I had wanted more than anything; it's what got me up in the morning and kept me at the chess board for hours a day. I had built my entire life around this goal for years, and now I had it. My immediate response was more physical than emotional. My legs went numb, and I felt a buzzing in my ears, as if my entire body was recalibrating itself to this new reality. Once that subsided, I was left with this warm glow of contentment that seemed to emanate from every part of me. A need that had become a deep part of my psyche was now, at long last, fulfilled.

It just happened to be the Feast of the Three Kings, and the city was once again in a state of celebration. I made my way around the streets of Pamplona with my mother, eating and laughing and running around. It was as if the entire city was acting out what I was feeling inside. The chess gods had smiled on me, delivering me my three norms—and on the very same day that the three wise men delivered their gifts. *What could be more perfect than this?*

EIGHTEEN

I had put off adult life for too long. I was almost twenty-two in early 1991, and had spent most of my days in the near-constant presence of my parents and sisters. They were not only a source of affection and meaning; they were my team, the only people in the world who treated my interests as their own and who were as devoted to my career as I was. But now that those two glorious letters *GM* were permanently affixed to my name, my more personal needs and aspirations began to assert themselves with new urgency. I had made a name for myself as a chess player, yet outside of that world, I had only a faint understanding of who I was. I desperately wanted to find out.

I moved into my own apartment around this time, a small unit I purchased in the same building where my parents and sisters lived. I saw it as a baby step toward independence. To really feel like my own person, I knew I'd need to learn how to drive.

Nobody in my family had a driver's license at that point, nor did most people I knew in Budapest. Even now that the communist regime had fallen, owning a car remained prohibitively expensive for many families. I had seen how young people in America—many far younger than me even—treated driving as a gateway to freedom. I wanted that for myself.

I don't think I had even unpacked my bags after returning
from Pamplona before signing up for driving lessons. As I soon
learned, Budapest in the dead of winter isn't the best setting for
an inexperienced driver. About a couple of weeks into my driving lessons, I found myself on an iced-over hill on the Buda side
of town. For someone who had not yet grasped the nuances of
a manual transmission, it was a daunting situation. I remember
reciting the complicated handbrake-clutch-accelerator procedure
to myself in preparation, as if it was a series of chess moves, and
executing them as formulaically as I could as I moved up a slip-
pery hill, my instructor looking on nervously from the seat next
to me. I had never spent much time in cars even as a passenger,
so the sensation of actually operating such a machine felt unnat-
ural and more than a little frightening. When cars aren't part of
your everyday life, the mortal dangers involved with driving are
much harder to ignore. The thought that a single misstep, sluggish
response, or ill-positioned mirror could result in multiple deaths—
my own among them—made me painfully tense during those early
weeks of driving instruction. I ended up taking a few extra lessons
just to get my confidence up. But by the end of February, I was my
family's first and only licensed driver. I celebrated the milestone
by purchasing a brand-new tan VW Passat.

I fell in love with driving that year. I'd look for every excuse to
take the car out. Sometimes I'd knock on the door of my neighbor
Emese, just to see if she wanted to take a spin or needed a lift to
the market. I'd run errands for my mother or pick up chess friends
from the airport when they came to town. It was a liberating sensation, being in such direct control of where I went and when. And
it didn't get old.

I also took up kickboxing around this time, training several
times a week with a former world champion at a gym in Budapest.
Although I never got very far with it, the feeling of self-possession
and resilience it gave me was undeniable. I started out afraid to fall

on the ground. After just a few sessions, I was displaying a degree of physical courage I didn't know I had.

That newfound sense of empowerment is probably what inspired me to travel alone for the first time for a tournament in San Francisco that March. To be twenty-one years old and alone in such a boisterous, faraway city was thrilling, but it was also terrifying. Just walking down the street near my hotel in Chinatown, I would begin to question if people could see how inexperienced or out of place I was. I normally had my parents and sisters around me, a bubble of familiarity I inhabited like a spacesuit to stay protected no matter how strange or hostile the environment. Now I was alone in a way I had never been before.

One of the tournament spectators actually professed his love to me during that trip, a young Filipino American man who drove some flashy sports car, a Porsche, I think. He came to the tournament just to meet me. One night, after I finished my game, he sat in the hotel lobby with his guitar and serenaded me with love songs. I had no intention of accepting his advances. But he was harmless, and I took his little act as a compliment. It also wasn't lost on me that had my family been there, they wouldn't have let this young man anywhere near me.

As I turned the corner to my hotel one afternoon, I saw that several police cars had gathered in a semicircle. A man was down on the ground being handcuffed by a shouting policeman, as at least a dozen officers pointed guns from behind their open car doors—all in broad daylight. My first thought was that I had wandered onto a movie set. This was California, after all. *But where are the cameras?* I thought. Then it dawned on me. This was really happening.

It was a jarring reminder of my own vulnerability and naïveté, my own obliviousness to the threats that lurk around every corner in the real world—in this case, literally. *How am I supposed to react to this situation,* I wondered. *Should I run? Look away? Get inside? Am I doing something wrong?* Normally, I would have looked to my father for some sign of what to do. Now there was nobody whose lead I could follow. I was alone.

I was alone each night in my hotel room and ate many of my meals alone at tables for one at nearby restaurants. In the morning, I'd prepare for each day's game by myself, without my sisters there to check my thinking or contribute ideas. International phone calls were rather expensive in those years, so I talked to my family only a couple of times during the trip, and just for a few minutes. There was nobody there to tamp down my anxieties or remind me that I was safe, protected, and cared for. I had known the word *lonely* before then. But until that trip to San Francisco it was merely an adjective.

Naturally, I took every opportunity to engage with a familiar face, one of whom was Mikhail Tal, who was playing in what would turn out to be one of his final tournaments (he would die a year later at the age of fifty-five). Spending time with Tal was easily my favorite part of the trip. He remembered me from our little blitz session back in Moscow when I was thirteen and would sometimes seek me out between rounds. As gregarious and lively as ever, he had what seemed like an endless collection of stories about his adventures around the world, recounting his time and games with Bobby Fischer and Pal Benko or Lajos Portisch, which I never tired of hearing. I managed to draw him in our one game at that tournament.

We talked late into the night at a reception in Berkeley after the tournament, a conversation that was punctuated by Tal's frequent trips to the bar for refills. He complimented me on my win against Larry Christiansen, which happened to get the tournament's brilliancy prize—the award given for the most beautiful game played during the event. I was beyond flattered. Getting acknowledged in this way by the "magician from Riga" himself is one of those things you grow up dreaming about.

Tal's overindulgence at the party caught up with him on the car ride back to the hotel. Sitting next to me in the back seat, he dozed off halfway through a story, resting his head on my shoulder. I couldn't help but find it charming.

I had a few days to myself following the tournament and decided to get in touch with Mr. Rooz, an old acquaintance who lived nearby. He was a Hungarian expat my father had met on a plane years earlier, and we had all kept in touch. I didn't realize how homesick I truly felt until I heard Rooz's voice on the other end of the phone speaking my mother tongue. My loneliness must have come through in my voice, because he quickly arranged for his daughter Jenny to show me around town that week.

Jenny was pretty and stylish and roughly my age. She spoke no Hungarian, having been raised in the United States, and knew nothing of chess. But she gave off a deep savviness of the sort I knew I lacked. After dinner, she asked me what I was in the mood for that night. I told her I felt like dancing. The dancing I knew took place at weddings and anniversary parties and bar mitzvahs. It was innocent and joyous. I never had any special gift for it, but I loved it all the same. And I had assumed it was the same everywhere.

My request took Jenny by surprise. She sat quietly for a moment. With cold objectivity, she looked me up and down, contemplating her next move.

"Are you sure?" she asked.

I got almost the exact same look from the large man at the door of the dance club we went to, "the bouncer," Jenny called him—a word I found oddly playful given how intimidating he seemed. I thought he was just thrown off by my Hungarian driver's license. Then I saw what I had gotten myself into.

The club was dark and smoky and crowded beyond what seemed reasonable or even legal, with music so loud that it actually numbed my ears. It was as if the environment was designed to assault every one of my senses simultaneously. Many of the people there were noticeably intoxicated, some in ways that were wholly unfamiliar to me. I didn't smoke or drink, and had never been around drugs before, so it was all a bit of a shock. Once the door closed behind us, the walls of the room seemed to vanish, creating a boundaryless space I struggled to navigate. I felt other people's sweat rub off onto me as we forced our way through the mass of bodies on the dance floor, which was lit up intermittently by a blighting flash of artificial light.

"Is this normal?" I asked Jenny, screaming into her ear as loud as I could, barely able to hear my own voice.

"It's usually busier," she shouted back. "We're a little early."

All I could think was: *People actually enjoy this?* We danced for a little while, but I had trouble enjoying myself. I was just beginning to discover my own likes and dislikes, how I fit into the adult world. I knew one thing for sure, though. This wasn't for me.

Becoming a grandmaster marked the beginning of a new period in my career. It also felt like the end of something. The days of making big leaps in ability and judgment were over. All I could work toward now was slow, grinding progress. There was a duality in how I saw myself as a player, two contradictory ideas that I could switch between but never embrace simultaneously. On the one hand, I was better than 99.9 percent of people who took chess seriously. Among the three hundred or so living grandmasters, though, I was the new kid. I had earned my way into the highest levels of professional competition. Yet at almost every tournament I would play in during this time, I was one of the weakest players.

I knew that, on a good day, there was almost nobody on the planet I couldn't hold my own against. From here on out, the tough part would be summoning my abilities when it counted. I learned that lesson the hard way in Munich that year in my second tournament as a grandmaster.

For the first few games I struggled to build momentum. I fell into a pattern, achieving a decent or even better position early on, only to let it slip away slowly. It happened to me against John Nunn and again in my game with the American grandmaster Larry Christiansen—both of whom were far more experienced and higher rated than I was. I squandered another good position against the Soviet grandmaster Alexander Beliavsky, ultimately losing to him despite having some winning chances.

It was a humbling reminder of how vanishingly small the margin for error was at this level. It's not enough to have the right idea about how to play a position. In critical moments, you need to find the truth, the single best move. It's not enough to lean on your strengths and hope they will outweigh your weaknesses. You need to have practically no weaknesses. It wasn't enough anymore for me to be precocious or promising or on my way to greatness. My play needed to be great.

Many of the people I was now up against played with an endurance and precision and intuition that was palpable from across the board. They could capitalize on my most minor inaccuracies, and they were willing to fight ferociously up until the very last move of every game, seemingly never breaking concentration or letting their emotions derail them. I had many of these traits myself, but not the way they did, not yet. If I wanted to knock them down, I'd need to play as close to perfectly as possible. And in these games, I just fell short.

I felt a lot better after playing Boris Gelfand, who was already one of my closest friends—although that game didn't start out well. I made a huge error in the first few moves, and eventually found myself down a rook for just one pawn in the endgame. It was a careless mistake, the kind that could have easily led to a complete collapse if I hadn't kept my head. He had an objectively winning position; we both knew it. But there were still enough pieces on the board for me to keep posing problems for him, making his life difficult, forcing him to play precisely in order to convert his advantage into an actual win.

Eventually, he found himself under time pressure. And by move 40, I had forced a position that made it impossible for him to win. The game ended in a draw. He was shaking his head during the postmortem, frustrated that he had let this win slip through his fingers. As for me, I was just proud to have shown some backbone while battling it out with one of the world's best players—and to have rescued a lost position instead of spoiling a good one.

I lost against Vishy when he outplayed me in a very complicated game. But I did find my way to a win against Leonid Yudasin. My sister Judit and I had this strange relationship with Yudasin and Vishy. Both of them were significantly higher rated than we were. Yet, for some reason, I always ended up beating Yudasin and could never manage to beat Vishy. For Judit, it was always the opposite. She consistently beat Vishy, but never Yudasin. Part of it was due to our particular styles. I was more of a solid, positional player, which served me well against Leonid, while Judit was more aggressive, attacking, and tactical, which, in her case, tended to give Vishy trouble in those years. I'm sure some of it was purely psychological, a self-fulfilling prophecy. Whatever the cause, we first noticed this strange pattern that May in Munich.

———— ◦•◦ ————

I'm not sure what I was thinking, traveling to Slovenia that summer. It was supposed to be a routine "Polgaria" match against three strong players: the Soviet grandmaster and future world champion Alexander Khalifman, the Slovenian Aljosa Grosar, and the Italian international master Ennio Arlandi. Things got a lot more complicated after Croatia declared its independence from Yugoslavia that

March, prompting one of the first conflicts in what would become
known as the Yugoslav wars. Slovenia fought its own war for independence that summer, not long before we were scheduled to visit.
Had I known what I would see on the car ride to the exhibition, I
don't know that I would have agreed to go.

There were miles-long stretches in which buildings had been
gouged by bombs or leveled completely, with mounds of rubble
piled alongside each road. There were bullet holes in the sides of car
doors and the blackened remnants of incinerated houses and store-
fronts. Occasionally you'd see a partial piece of clothing blowing in
the wind, or a mangled baby stroller lying sideways somewhere—
evidence that this used to be a place where people lived. This used
to be somebody's home, somebody's school, somebody's business.
It shook me up to realize just how quickly our whole society can
come apart. I was looking at the aftermath of human suffering on
a mass scale, and it was just a couple hours' drive from my own
home. Yugoslavs had a reputation in Hungary for being among the
kindest, friendliest people in the region. This was definitely true of
those I had met personally. How could they do this to each other?

My sisters were in the car with me. I wanted to tell them to
close their eyes. I wanted to protect them from this dark display
of human cruelty, to give them just a little more time to be innocent of hatred and brutality. Maybe I wanted that for myself, too.

Even with this somber backdrop, the actual match turned out
to be a high point for Polgaria. In fact, the final score of 12½ to 5½
turned out to be the most lopsided victory we'd ever achieved in
our team competitions against men.

NINETEEN

That year, I was invited to play in the Akiba Rubinstein Memorial, an exclusive tournament held each year in Polanica-Zdroj, Poland. It had been a dream of mine to play a tournament like this for as long as I could remember. Rubinstein was a giant of early twentieth-century chess, and the tournament had been held each year in his memory for more than a quarter century at that point. Vasily Smyslov had famously won the event several times. As the new kid, I acquitted myself well enough, finishing somewhere in the middle of the pack. The chess isn't what I remember most about Polanica-Zdroj, though.

I was there by myself, my first solo voyage since San Francisco. The loneliness that had followed me around that city months before was there to meet me in Poland. Only this time, there was none of the novelty associated with that first adventure. I felt a vague fear that I might never feel quite comfortable on my own, that whatever I might tell myself, I was merely feigning my adulthood, a child playing the part of a mature, self-possessed person.

I decided not to run away from that feeling but to reason my way around it. Growing up in a cramped apartment with two siblings, you stop noticing just how rarely you're actually by yourself. I just needed to get used to being alone. If it was an unfamiliar chess opening that was giving me anxiety, I would simply become an expert in it, confront my insecurity, desensitize myself to whatever I found so flummoxing about it. And so that's what I did. On my days off, when others were socializing, I would take long walks by myself along the river that ran through the center of town. Sometimes I'd disappear for a couple of hours into the woods for a hike, listening to my own breath, attending to my own solitude. My strategy was no cure-all. It only made that trip just a little more tolerable. But it was a move in the right direction—slow, grinding progress.

Coming home, it's often said, is one of the great pleasures of traveling. I never really understood that until I arrived back from Poland. I had never been so happy to see my family, to hear what they'd been up to, or to analyze my games with my sisters. It wasn't just the familiarity of it all that I found comforting. It was the shift in how my sisters saw me. I was now an adult in their eyes, an initiate into a world they were still years from experiencing for themselves. They didn't see my apprehensions and self-doubts, only a capable, worldly young woman, which is how I wanted so badly to see myself.

I wanted to keep that image alive in their minds as well as my own, which is why I volunteered to drive my sisters and mother to a tournament in the Czech city of Brno that October. For the first time, I wasn't a passenger in the Polgar caravan. I was its chief navigator, leading our crew on an adventure, demonstrating my competence and independence to the people who meant the most to me, yet still able to join in all kinds of frivolous fun with my sisters. One of my favorite family photos is from that trip. My mother snapped it while we were goofing around at a park near the tournament. I'm on the low end of a seesaw, hoisting Judit high off the ground on the other side. Sitting in between us a few feet back is Sofia, placed perfectly in the center of the frame. It's a beautiful day, and we're surrounded by sun-streaked green trees. We have this look of unselfconscious joy on our faces.

We were looking for something to do on our night off, and our friend, the grandmaster Pavel Blatny, suggested we stop by the Boby Center, a local entertainment complex with several floors of music venues, an arcade, and a bowling alley, and countless other amusements. The four of us spent the next few hours bowling and playing video games, taking breaks to snack on chocolate bars and popcorn. At the end, we stopped at the disco they had there, dancing and laughing and making fun of each other. I thought of all of those people packed into that dark San Francisco nightclub. They didn't know what they were missing.

———•◦•———

Not a year after I became the first woman to earn the grandmaster title, Judit made some history of her own at the Hungarian Championship, which was held at the Radisson Beke Hotel in Budapest. We had both qualified for the tournament. But given how strong the competition was, neither of us was favored to win. The event was actually dubbed the Super-Championship, since it brought together nearly every top Hungarian player—including the Olympiad champions Lajos Portisch, Gyula Sax, and Andras Adorjan. For Judit, though, there was more on the line than a championship trophy.

She had already secured the second of the three performance norms she'd need to earn her own grandmaster title. And there was a chance that if she played well enough, she could nail down her third norm right there in Budapest. That wouldn't just make her a grandmaster. At just fifteen years and a little under five months of age, it would make her the youngest grandmaster in the history of chess—a record that since 1958 had been held by none other than Bobby Fischer. I wanted it for her so badly; the whole family did. For her sake, though, my family and I avoided the subject for the duration of the competition. The best thing we could do to support her, we figured, was to treat this like just another chess tournament, and let Judit take it from there.

My little sister didn't disappoint. She held Portisch to a draw in a marathon second-round battle. She beat the grandmaster Attila Groszpeter and later won a critical game against Sax. Going into the final round, she faced what must have been one of the most difficult decisions of her life.

She was tied for first place—just a half point ahead of me. In many ways, she was in an enviable position. She would face Tibor Tolnai in her last game, who was lower-rated than she was at the time, but she would have to play with the black pieces. All she needed for her final GM norm was a draw in the last round. If she played solidly, there was a good chance she could find her way to a draw and guarantee herself a place in the history books. If she wanted to stay in contention for the championship, however, only a win would be enough.

We talked it over for hours that night. I had my own opinions about how she should handle it, but none of that mattered. Only she could make this call. I told her not to overthink it, to trust her gut, and to see where the game took her. I knew her better than anyone, and there was no doubt in my mind that she'd know what to do when the time came.

I spent a lot of time during my own final round game walking over to Judit's board, trying to stay out of her line of sight so as not to distract her. The more I could make this feel like just another game of chess for her, the better. It was obvious from her choice of opening—a wild Sicilian Defense—that there would be no draw. She was playing for the win. It was a gutsy move, but it paid off.

After a forty-eight-move slugfest, Tibor resigned. Judit was now the youngest grandmaster in history—as well as the Hungarian national champion. I remember being impressed by her reaction to this monumental achievement. She didn't rush away from the table to celebrate, the way most teenagers might. Instead, she remained at the board for a postmortem analysis with her opponent, not just out of respect for Tibor but also out of genuine interest. As her big sister, I was proud beyond words at what Judit had just done. But I was just as proud of the manner in which she had done it.

There was a formal banquet after the tournament, initially intended to celebrate the new national champion. But everybody there knew what we were really celebrating. Judit's unprecedented achievement wasn't just a career victory for my little sister. It was the greatest vindication to date of a project my parents had embarked on nearly two decades before—a project that everyone had told them was hopeless, misguided, offensive even. I'd never seen my parents so happy. And yet, the significance of what had just happened went well beyond our family. Until then, the very possibility that a woman could rise to the same heights as a man in the game of chess was still treated with skepticism in many parts of our community. Just a couple years earlier, in an interview in *Playboy* magazine, of all places, none other than Garry Kasparov remarked that "Some people don't like to hear this, but chess does not fit women properly. It's a fight, you know? A big fight. It's not for women. Sorry. She's helpless if she has men's opposition. I think this is very simple logic." I hated seeing the world champion disparage women players this way. I thought about all the young girls who might hear comments like this and decide that chess had no place for them. Thanks to Judit, that position was now a lot harder to support with a straight face. In a way, she had finished what I had started.

It was just a few weeks later that I headed back to Pamplona, the same tournament where I had won my own GM title a year earlier. I spotted the Peruvian player Julio Granda Zuniga before the first game. His eyes locked on mine when he saw me approaching, a wide smile on his face. He was pleased to learn that I was now fluent in Spanish. We headed off for a walk.

I had harbored a schoolgirl crush on Julio when I first spent time with him at the New York Open back in 1987. I have grown up a lot since then. Talking to Julio that afternoon, though, I felt like a swooning young girl again.

I had very little romantic experience at the time, and it took me a while to realize that his interest in me was more than merely friendly. He wanted to know about my recent travels and what life was like at home now that Judit had broken the record. He was twenty-four years old and handsome, with thick black hair. And he seemed completely at ease in every situation, even at the chess board. And the way he looked at me as I answered his questions in my best Spanish, it was as if there was nobody else in the world he'd rather be talking to. I started to feel that he wasn't just being polite. This charming young man actually liked me.

Sometime after the closing ceremony, as we were about to say our goodbyes, he surprised me with a passionate kiss. He told me he was going to Madrid for a few days on his way back to Peru, and that he'd like me to join him. I no longer cared if my parents were expecting me, or that I'd need to rearrange my travel, or that I'd barely gotten to know him. I just wanted to spend more time with him. When we finally parted ways a few days later, Julio was my boyfriend.

It wasn't uncommon for chess players to get involved romantically with other chess players in those years. Although, since males outnumbered females pretty substantially, women usually had a lot more choice. And Julio was who I chose.

After the tournament in Pamplona, he and I promised to keep in touch. We didn't realize just how complicated that would be. This was long before the days of email and cell phones. And Julio didn't even have a phone in his house. Yet somehow we made it work.

At a predetermined time about once a week, he would go to a public phone near his home in the small coastal town of Camana and call me. We'd chat for a few minutes over the staticky phone line, recounting what was happening in our lives and trading affectionate little jokes. At the end of our conversation, we'd make an appointment for our next call. It didn't always work so smoothly. There were times when he'd call hours after he said he would, or sometimes not at all. But especially in those early weeks of our relationship, I couldn't bring myself to be angry with him.

Back home, my sisters were the only ones who knew about Julio. They wanted to know everything about him, and I never got tired of telling them. My mother suspected I was romantically involved but never asked me about it directly, although I could tell she wanted to. My father, however, was completely in the dark.

I'm sure both my parents were secretly dreading the day when their oldest daughter would bring home her first serious boyfriend. And Julio was definitely not the kind of man that either of them had in mind for me—a Catholic Peruvian who barely spoke English, much less Hungarian. I wasn't rebelling against my parents, really— not consciously, at least. To be honest, I really just didn't care if they took issue with his background or not. I felt like this was a part of my life that didn't belong to them. It was mine.

At times, it was almost funny how little Julio and I shared in common, even in our approaches to chess. On the days we spent together before and after tournaments, I'd always want to break away for a few hours to work. My father had drilled into me and my sisters the belief that missing a single day of chess study would set us back ten days. It may have been an exaggeration, but it was also a powerful motivator. Julio had the completely opposite attitude. He would rarely study unless he was preparing for a specific opponent at a tournament, and even then he'd leave it until the last possible moment.

It was amazing how easily things came to him. Despite having next to no work ethic, he was more highly rated than I was. By the time we started dating, he was ranked twenty-fifth in the world. To a smitten twenty-two-year-old, this seemingly effortless skill just added to his charisma and made him seem mischievous and a little dangerous.

It wasn't until February 1992—not long after we started seeing each other—that I finally broke the news to my parents. Mr. van Oosterom had asked me to organize a tournament in Aruba, where he spent most of his time during the European winter. The idea was to do a short training camp there for me and my sisters, after which we'd hold a tournament.

"I think you'd be good at putting together something like this," he said. "And, naturally, I'd be willing to sponsor it."

I loved the idea of being put in charge of something with so many moving parts. And, of course, the freedom to invite which-ever players I wanted was too good to pass up. Not surprisingly, the first player I thought of was Julio.

I knew there would be no hiding my feelings toward Julio once my parents saw me with him, so I came clean to my mother before we left for the trip. It didn't go well. She was worried that Julio and I were too different for the relationship to last for very long, and that he'd end up breaking my heart. She also knew that it wasn't in her control to stop me from seeing him.

"If this is what you want," she said, "I won't stand in your way."

It wasn't the response I was hoping for, but it would have to be good enough. What I was really dreading was my father's reaction, so I asked my mother to give him the news once we arrived in Aruba.

I guess it was the chess player in me that prepared for the worst. I tried to anticipate all of my father's possible reasons for disliking Julio, devising a wide range of carefully worded replies, points, and counterpoints to use, depending on how the exchange developed. I was ready for a fight.

When it finally came time to talk to my dad about him, I saw a side of my father I didn't know he had.

"Do you love him?" he asked.

"I really do, Dad. Very much."

"That's all that matters to me, then."

I walked around in a state of bliss for the next few days of the tournament, dumbfounded at how perfectly my life was arranging itself before me. I was in a serious relationship with a brilliant, fascinating man. And now I had if not the blessings, then at least the acceptance of my parents. The tournament I had toiled anxiously for weeks to pull together went off flawlessly, filling me with a potent sense of competence, self-possession, and relief. As if that weren't enough, all of this was all happening in Aruba, the closest thing to a physical paradise I had ever known.

I knew this feeling couldn't last forever. But I had no idea it would leave so abruptly. It was the last day of the tournament, and Julio was nowhere to be found. I knocked on his hotel room door, but got no answer. I did a lap around the hotel, the café, the beach: nothing. It must have been hours I spent looking for him, finally ending up back outside his hotel room door, banging furiously on the off chance he had just fallen asleep. Still no answer.

For days, I had floated around, completely free of anxiety and self-doubt. Now, those feelings rushed back in. Had he just left without saying goodbye? No, he wouldn't do that. Would he? Had he been in an accident?

Then came the worst thought of all: What would I tell my parents? They had been so concerned about me. I didn't want them to be right. I could tell them Julio had a family emergency, and had flown back to Peru early that morning. Anything was better than the truth.

My desperation gave way to anger, at myself more than Julio. I had never misled my parents about something this big before. Now there I was, curled up in a hotel hallway, concocting fictions like a child. And all because of a boy. *How could I have let him do this to me?*

I got startled when his hotel room door opened. He walked out. "You were in there the entire time?!"

"Yes. I'm sorry. There's something I need to tell you, and I wasn't sure how to."

"You're leaving me," I said matter-of-factly, trying to protect my dignity by beating him to the punch.

"No! That's not it at all! Is that what you thought?"

"What is it, then?"

"I have a child. Back in Peru."

I asked if he had a wife. He insisted he did not. The baby was from a previous relationship, a girlfriend he had been with only briefly, he said. He hadn't intended to keep it from me for this long, but the time never seemed right. After meeting my parents, he felt he needed to come clean.

It wasn't good news. But it wasn't as bad as I had feared, either. I told him I understood, and that the lie had been so much worse than the truth. I had spent the last few hours doing battle with my own insecurities, grasping for ways to convince myself I wasn't mistaken about this man, that fundamentally, he was exactly who I thought he was. And his explanation provided something good enough. He had hidden this part of his life from me, yes. But only in a moment of weakness. His deception wasn't representative of his true character, I told myself. On top of all that, his decision to share his secret with me made me feel closer to him, like I had been granted special access.

"No more secrets," I said.

"Absolutely. No more secrets."

TWENTY

For much of my career, I made a conscious decision not to play in female-only events. I had made an exception for the Olympiad a couple of times, but those were special circumstances. They were also team events. It had been more than a decade since I had played in an individual women's competition. From my point of view, my experience playing against men put me in a more elite category than most other female players. Not everyone agreed. There was still a theory circulating that by staying away from women's chess, I had somehow given myself an unfair advantage. It was easier to earn rating points in men's events, the thinking went. Others thought that I was afraid to play against women.

By 1992, I was really tired of hearing these complaints. If people wanted me to test myself against other top female players, then fine. I'd show them how wrong they were. My father had been working on organizing a women's world championship for rapid and blitz chess in Budapest on behalf of the Hungarian Chess Federation. It seemed like as good a time as any to get back onto the female circuit.

With the help of Mr. van Oosterom and a few other Hungarian sponsors, my father had booked space at the Aquincum Hotel in Budapest for the blitz leg of the event, right outside the city center on the banks of the Danube—one of Hungary's most well-known spa hotels. The rapid tournament would be held not too far away at the Radisson Beke. Many of the top female players of the time had signed on, including Maya Chiburdanidze, Alisa Galliamova, and Alisa Maric. I really enjoyed faster chess, so if nothing else, I thought it would be a good time.

The first event on the schedule was the blitz championship, a one-day, twenty-seven-person round-robin in which players got five minutes each to make all of their moves. Since a great deal depends on how quickly you can physically move the pieces and punch the clock, fast chess has an athletic component, one that rewards precise hand-eye-coordination. This makes the atmosphere at blitz tournaments completely different from more sedate classical events. From the instant the first round begins, the playing hall fills with frenetic, adrenaline-fueled activity. Sharp, percussive chatter echoes through the room, the sound of colliding wooden pieces and that satisfying click that a chess clock makes when it's punched with a little more force than is necessary. It's like an atonal piece of music played with nothing but blocks of wood and mechanical switches.

Playing that first blitz game, I simply felt at home, utterly in my element. That feeling never went away. As the tournament's highest-rated player, Judit was the odds-on favorite to win. Nevertheless, I finished in the top spot, becoming the very first Women's World Blitz Chess Champion. It gave me a burst of momentum going into the rapid event, which I had no intention of wasting.

The thirty-minute per-player time control in rapid chess makes it a completely different game from blitz, one requiring a lot more depth and calculation. Try to play rapid chess with the same nervous energy you bring to blitz, and your impulses can get the best of you. I needed to switch gears, slow down, and contain myself a little.

I just remember feeling good during the rapid event—focused and energetic and sure of myself. My thinking felt crisp and natural, and the games seemed to unfold on my terms, at a pace I was determining. It was a fiercely contested event, with my sisters and I—as well as Maia Chiburdanidze—all in contention for gold until the very last round. But after my win in that final game, another world championship was mine.

Sofia also had a very good event, winning silver in the rapid. Judit was a little disappointed with her performance. She only managed second place in the blitz event, while taking fourth place in rapid. Nevertheless, of the six medals given out, my sisters and I won four of them.

I followed up those two championships with a string of very strong grandmaster tournaments, including one in Madrid that May. I was back in New York that July, in part to compete in the Reshevsky Memorial tournament, but also to spend time with Julio, who actually ended up winning the event. Watching the man I loved do well at something that was so close to my heart was special, in a kind of puppy-love "that's my boyfriend!" way, but also in the sense that our fates felt entwined, and his successes felt like they belonged to both of us.

That was the same summer that Mr. van Oosterom held his very first Ladies vs. Veterans tournament in Aruba. The competition pitted a team of the top female players in the world against a male team of well-known legends, most of whom were nearing the end of their careers. It was an inspired idea on Mr. van Oosterom's part, the aim of which was simultaneously to promote women's chess and to give some of the old-timers a chance to earn a little money and publicity. It was held in a different country each year, always in a luxurious hotel, the Aruba Hyatt, in this case. The tournament would take its name from some local dance—the Monaco tournament was dubbed the Palladienne, for instance. In Prague, it was called the Polka Tournament. In Aruba that year, it was called the Tumba. It was a coy reference to the "dance" that the men and women were having over the board, and also the playful spirit in which the events were held.

It was a lot of fun spending time with greats like Vasily Smyslov and Lev Polugaevsky. But the standout moment for me was my win against the two-time Soviet champion Efim Geller, which ended shortly after I trapped his queen early in the game.

I don't know that I would have even considered playing the classical Women's World Championship cycle in 1992 had I not won the rapid and blitz championships earlier in the year. But after sweeping those two events, the prospect of holding all three women's world titles—the triple crown, as it's now called—seemed too good to pass up. No player of any gender had ever been the reigning world champion in all three chess time controls. I had two of those under my belt already. Why wouldn't I try for a third?

The first hurdle I had to clear would be the Candidates Tournament, which took place that October in Shanghai. The top two finishers there would play a second match to determine who would go up against the current women's world champion at the time, the Chinese player Xie Jun. Mr. van Oosterom had hired the celebrated Danish grandmaster Bent Larsen to travel with me to China as my coach. Bent's wife, Laura Benedini, also made the trip—as well as Julio.

My father wasn't crazy about my decision to go after that particular championship. His fear was that anything but a first-place finish in the candidates would hurt my reputation. He'd rather I put my energies toward fighting the guys and stay out of women's events for good. We debated it up until the night before I left for China. He never came around. In fact, one of the last things he said to me as I was heading out to the airport was "It's not too late to back out." It was the only time I can remember when he showed anything other than complete support. If anything, his disapproval helped motivate me. I wanted to prove him wrong.

We all got to Beijing a few days before the tournament to recover from jet lag and do a little sightseeing. The weather was so painfully cold at the Great Wall that I was still shivering when we got back to our hotel. I was under the impression that Asia was supposed to be warm. But not this time of the year, at least not in Beijing.

Shanghai, thankfully, was completely different. Not only was the weather quite pleasant, but the playing conditions were of a quality I had only rarely seen at a chess tournament before. This came as a huge relief. Initially, I was a little apprehensive about playing in Shanghai. It's no secret that communist governments at times weren't above dirty tricks in professional competitions. I had heard countless stories about players developing sudden bouts of food poisoning before critical games. Now that I saw where we'd be playing, those fears fell away. The environment just felt welcoming and safe and professional.

This was around the time when China began taking women's chess very seriously, largely in response to Xie Jun's success. And the playing conditions were a reflection of that. The competition took place at a closed resort, which was normally reserved for Communist Party leaders and their guests. The playing hall was pristine and peaceful, with a healthy supply of delicious snacks and hot tea for the players. My favorite part was the beautifully manicured Asian gardens scattered throughout the resort, each one full of elaborately arranged trees, creeks, and walking bridges.

Unfortunately for me, this serene atmosphere stood in stark contrast to my emotional state leading up to the tournament. On the plane ride from Beijing to Shanghai, Julio had begun reading Gabriel García Márquez's great magical realist novel *One Hundred Years of Solitude*. It had a powerful effect on him. In the days leading up to the first game, he seemed distant and contemplative, unwilling to engage in anything but the most superficial way. He was hiding something from me, I could just tell. But I didn't know what. Needless to say, this isn't the best state of mind to be in on the eve of a big competition. I don't know what would have happened, had Bent's wife Laura not been there. She happened to be a trained psychologist. And at that moment, I needed a little help. That night, she pulled me aside and asked if I needed to talk about anything.

"Julio is acting strange," I explained. "It's hard to explain, but he feels so far away all of a sudden."

"This sort of thing happens when you're with someone for a while," she told me. "You just need to remember that Julio isn't the reason we're all here. It might work out with him, it might not. But right now, you need to focus on what you came here to do. Deal with Julio after."

Julio finally came around just a couple of hours before my first game, accompanying me into the playing hall and giving me a good-luck kiss. I wanted to be angry at him. Really I was just happy to have him back in my corner.

By the end of the first half of the event, I had won nine out of my ten games, with the only exception being a draw against the Serbian player Alisa Maric in the sixth round. I completed the tournament a full three points ahead of the second-place finisher, Nana Ioseliani, and without giving up even a single loss. But it wasn't nearly as easy as the results suggest.

If I'm honest, I didn't play especially well in Shanghai. All of that relationship drama must have worn me down, because I just felt off, like I was making too many mistakes or struggling to close out games that I should have won much more easily. The only thing that really kept me going was that I really wanted to prove something— to my critics, but also to my father. And, in the end, this fighting spirit made up for the inconsistency in my play.

My huge lead notwithstanding, the rules still dictated that Ioseliani and I play a match to determine who would advance to the World Championship. Once again, Mr. van Oosterom stepped in. He organized the event that February in Monaco and gave me every resource I needed to prepare. He also told me that should I advance to the Women's World Championship match, he'd sponsor a winning purse of $1 million, which even today would have made it the largest ever in chess history.

I had enjoyed Larsen's company on our trip to Shanghai, and his wife was an absolute lifesaver, but we never really clicked in terms of our chess work. I knew I needed to find someone to help me get in shape for Monaco. The first person who sprung to mind was my friend Boris Gulko.

Boris was one of these players I had grown up hearing about. A former Soviet champion, he was among the most prominent "refuseniks" in the chess world—the term used for Soviet Jews who had been denied the right to emigrate to Israel during the height of the communist regime. As part of his fight to leave the Soviet Union, he and his wife—the two-time Soviet women's champion Anna Akhsharumova—staged multiple hunger strikes, one of which lasted for thirty-seven days.

He was also known for being one of the few top players to have a positive score against Kasparov. I had experienced his mastery firsthand in competitive play and had a particular respect for his seemingly bottomless knowledge of openings as well as his deep general understanding of the game. And his cautiously attacking approach to the game complemented my own style quite well.

I invited him to come to Budapest for a few weeks before the match with Ioseliani. We'd sit in my apartment for hours each day, working on opening theory and trying out new lines in blitz matches. Although only in his forties, his thinning gray hair and relaxed attitude gave him a sagelike authority you'd expect from someone much older.

We knew that Ioseliani would be studying every game of mine she could find, looking for weaknesses in my play she could exploit or finding ways to lead me into unfamiliar territory. With that in mind, Boris had the idea that I should prepare a secret weapon, the Caro-Kann, an opening with the black pieces that I had never played before and that Ioseliani would never think to look at. I didn't end up using the opening in the match, but just having it in my back pocket, knowing I could surprise her whenever I wanted to, gave me a bit of a psychological edge—or at least it would have, were it not for another Julio-inflicted crisis of confidence.

Following my victory in Shanghai, everything with Julio and me seemed to have returned to normal. The haze that hung over him lifted, and for the weeks before Monaco, we felt like our old selves again. In fact, those few days we spent in Monte Carlo before the match got underway were like a fairy tale. I took him to one of my favorite places in the world, a magnificent thirteenth-century castle that sits on a hilltop in the French village of Eze, and at night we'd eat dinner on our balcony looking out over the Côte d'Azur.

The only even remotely tense moment from that week came while I was driving Boris and Julio around Monte Carlo and the beautiful French towns nearby in my Hertz rental car. I had forgotten just how curvy and steep the streets can get in that part of the world. I was driving uphill when we came to a roadblock. The street had been reduced to a single lane, and cars were lining up to be waved through. I flashed back to that day on the icy hill in Buda, when I struggled with my manual transmission to get the car moving. There was now a long line of cars waiting behind us. I knew that if I released the hand brake and lost control of the vehicle, I'd roll backward, crashing into the cars behind me and potentially send everyone plummeting off the side of the mountain. It was time to admit I was in over my head.

I got out of the car and asked one of the other motorists to drive my car to someplace flatter. It was a little humiliating, but I didn't really mind. I thought of the headlines that would appear in the next day's papers had something gone wrong, big block letters proclaiming the deaths of three of the world's top chess players—and naming me as the person behind the wheel. Embarrassment felt like a small price to pay. We were already laughing about it by the time we were down the mountain.

For the first five games of the match, I played solid, consistent chess, outclassing Ioseliani in almost every game, and racking up a full two-point lead. After that game is when Julio's whole attitude changed. It felt like an exact repeat of what happened in China. He became cold and standoffish. He refused to join me for meals. *What was this man doing to me!?* I thought. *Didn't he know I was playing for a world championship!?*

The few times I tried to address the situation, all I got was evasions and denials.

"Is everything okay with us?" I'd ask him.

"Yes, of course. Everything's fine. Why wouldn't it be?"

He could tell I was unconvinced, which only made him sink deeper into himself. Something was eating him—something that, for whatever reason, he didn't want me to know about. I felt angry and anxious and frustrated. I was sleep-deprived and emotionally exhausted, and it showed in my chess.

I gave Ioseliani too many chances in the last few games of the match. And, to her credit, she took advantage. I had a clear 100 rating points on her, and I had completely outperformed her at the Candidates Tournament a couple of months earlier. But you wouldn't have known it from the chess I was putting out in the second half of the match. I wasn't in control anymore. I was just trying to survive.

The match ended in a 4–4 tie. After a two-game playoff, we were still tied. My emotional state was deteriorating fast. I wasn't just worried about Julio anymore. I was also furious with myself. *Why can't I finish this woman off? Why can't I push through? I'm better than this!* The next two-game playoff ended in another 1–1 tie—as did the third. Never once in the entire match did Ioseliani lead. Even in the playoffs, it was always me who pulled ahead in the first game only to give it away in the second.

Now there was no more chess left to play. According to the rules, after fourteen games, the match would be decided by a drawing of lots. The players would be presented with two identical boxes—one containing a gold medal, the other containing silver. The winner of a coin flip would then have the option of choosing a box or letting her opponent choose one instead.

I always hated this way of deciding matches, and I had expressed my feelings to FIDE earlier in the event. They were sympathetic and even offered to let the playoffs continue indefinitely if both players agreed. But Ioseliani didn't like the idea. Later on FIDE did end up eliminating lot drawing, in part because of this match. For now, though, my fate would have to be decided by a game of chance.

Ioseliani won the coin flip and asked me to choose a box. I drew silver. My shot at the World Championship was officially over.

I slunk back to Budapest feeling shattered and inadequate in nearly every way. I was flying high just a few days before—basking in the glow of my picture-perfect relationship with Julio, coasting to an easy victory against Ioseliani, all on my way to a record-breaking $1 million championship match. I was going home alone and with none of these things. I had no idea where I stood with Julio. Even my chess—my most reliable source of self-esteem and stability—was faltering.

Days later, when I was offered a wildcard spot in the Zonal Tournament that was held in Budapest, I accepted on the spot. My self-confidence was at its lowest point in years, and part of me just wanted to sit alone in my apartment and lick my wounds for a few weeks. But I knew that the best way to get over both my relationship troubles and my collapse in Monaco was to stay busy. I played well enough, given how tired and unsure of myself I felt. I finished the event with a 50 percent score—respectable, but not great. I was just grateful for the distraction.

———— • ◦ • ————

After Monaco, Julio's mood swings became more frequent, and I could still sense he was hiding something from me, or that maybe he just didn't love me anymore. When he invited me to Peru for an exhibition match against him, I took it as a good sign. His plan was for us to play six rapid games over the course of a month, each in a different Peruvian city. His team would line up the sponsors and handle the logistics. There would even be a $5,000 prize fund. All I had to do was show up ready to play in a few weeks. He was talking like the old Julio again, telling me how much I would enjoy Peru and how he couldn't wait to introduce me to his father. I told him it sounded perfect.

As we got closer to the match, he started to get evasive. I'd ask him if the organizers had sent me my plane tickets yet, like he said they would, or about the hotel he said they'd booked, only to get some vague excuse about why they hadn't gotten to any of it yet. At one point he told me that the prize money had fallen through, and that we should probably cancel. Finally, I got tired of waiting for him to take care of things.

"I'm coming to Peru," I told him. "Match or no match. If the organizers want to pay for my plane tickets, that's fine. Otherwise, I'll just buy my own."

My plane tickets arrived a few days later.

I had this image in my mind that I'd step off the plane in Lima and Julio would be there to meet me at the baggage claim. We'd kiss and hug, and he'd lift me off the ground like at the end of some romantic comedy. I should have known better.

Julio didn't even bother to meet me at the airport. He sent his friend, someone I had never met, to pick me up and take me to my hotel.

"Where's Julio?" I asked.

"He's really sorry. He told me he'd meet you at the hotel later."

I waited for hours in my hotel room. There was no knock on the door. No phone call. I thought about what had happened back in Aruba, when he told me about his child for the first time. How he had stayed away from me so he wouldn't have to tell me. By the time he showed up, I was convinced he had another secret. It was so obvious. Why hadn't I seen it coming?

He could tell from the look on my face that I was in no mood for hugs and kisses—that moment had passed.

"Julio. What aren't you telling me?"

"Why don't we sit down."

He explained that he hadn't been entirely honest back in Aruba. He had a second child from the same mother as his first. He said that he loved me. But right now he needed to be with his kids. "I think we need to break up."

I had suspected this was coming. But even so, something just didn't add up. If he was willing to admit to having one child, why hide the second one? We spoke for a long time without really getting anywhere. Whatever Julio was hiding, he had no interest in telling me. As it turned out, he wouldn't have to.

Julio was still with me in my room at around three in the morning when the phone rang. I answered it.

"Hello?"

Silence.

"Hello? Can I help you?"

"What are you doing with my husband?"

Now it all made sense.

"Do you *know* that we have two children? Do you *know* I am pregnant with our third?"

I hung up the phone without saying another word. I was heartbroken.

Julio and I stayed up almost the entire night talking. He explained that he wasn't actually married to the mother of his two (soon to be three) children, and that he had no intention of marrying her. The situation was complicated, he went on, but he did want to be around to help raise the kids. I could barely look at him. I was so angry. But I did believe him.

My first impulse was to pack my bags and head straight home. But I knew it wasn't so simple. The first game of our match was just days away, and there was no backing out of it. A lot of time and expense had gone into our tour of Peru. I also didn't want to leave before I got the full story out of Julio, and I sensed there might be more he wasn't telling me. As hurt and disgusted and angry as I was by what this man had done, I couldn't be rid of him just yet. I took the next few days to pull myself together. *I've come all of this way*, I told myself. *Might as well make the best of it.*

We traveled to six cities over the course of the next month, playing rapid games before huge crowds at each stop. I hadn't realized just how big a national celebrity Julio had become. He wasn't just Peru's most famous chess player; he was one of their most famous athletes, period. Seeing so many people cheer for a man who had just betrayed me threw me off of my game.

It was no coincidence that one of our games took place in Arequipa, the city where his children lived with their mother. We were checking into our (separate) hotel rooms the night before the game when she appeared. She launched into a furious tirade in Spanish. Julio had made a fool of her. All of this time she had stayed home raising their children while Julio was out traveling the world with another woman. After a while, I joined in, thundering away about what he had done. How dare he humiliate me like this? And how dare he make me complicit in another woman's betrayal? Julio stood there like a little boy who had been caught stealing a candy bar from the corner store.

I ended up losing the match 4–2. But I did beat him in Arequipa.

It took some effort, but I did my best not to let the drama with Julio completely ruin my trip. It was a skill my mother had taught me from an early age, the ability to find something positive in even the most difficult situations. And it came in handy in Peru.

We visited Machu Picchu and toured archaeological sites in the city of Chan Chan. I still think about the sprawling, colorful markets in Cusco, and the ancient culture that still shapes daily life there. And the ceviche, which I had never even heard of before, was nothing short of sublime.

Julio still encouraged me to meet his father, who lived in the small town of Camana, where one of our games was played, and I obliged, mostly because I was curious what Julio's dad was like. I don't know if his father was aware of our situation. If he did know, it didn't seem to bother him. He was gracious and cordial and generous with his home.

Seeing his father's house made me realize just how little I knew about Julio. To me, Julio was a model of sophistication and worldliness. He wore well-tailored suits and crisply pressed shirts. His hair was always perfectly styled. I would have never guessed that he could have grown up in this doorless, windowless little home in a small Peruvian coastal town. At that moment, the man I had been so committed to for the last year and a half felt like a stranger.

TWENTY-ONE

I was twenty-four years old in 1993 when I packed up my VW Passat and headed for the border. My destination: a secret location in Yugoslavia. I had been summoned by an international criminal who was on the run from US authorities. But that's not how I saw him. To me, he was simply one of the greatest chess players in the history of the game. And if Bobby Fischer wanted to meet me, I wasn't going to say no.

Bobby was one of those towering historical figures I had grown up hearing about. I first heard his name as a little girl, a few months after he beat Boris Spassky for the World Championship in 1972. My father would tell me stories about him at some of our earliest chess lessons, recounting the adventures of the lone American genius who had single-handedly dismantled the Soviet chess machine. It was my first glimpse at how chess could be something more than a game, how it could be a political weapon, a means of challenging authority.

Bobby wasn't just the most famous chess player in the world in those years. During his brief reign as world champion, he was one of the most famous people alive. His match against Spassky was also treated in the press as a kind of Cold War proxy battle,

pitting the individualist American genius against the dehumaniz-
ing forces of communism and totalitarianism. And, in many ways,
Bobby was perfectly cast for the part. As a young man he was tall
and lean, with these dramatic, expressive features—Hollywood's
ideal of what a genius should look like. In interviews, he spoke with
a thick Brooklyn accent, which conveyed a degree of street smarts
as well as a powerful intellect.

Within the chess community, Bobby was known as far and
away the leading player of his generation. He came up in an era
when giants like Mikhail Tal and Bent Larsen were in their prime.
And yet, for those few months leading up to the 1972 match with
Spassky, Bobby made it undeniable that he was in a class by himself.
He played with this beautiful simplicity that struck the perfect
balance between the dry, positional style of Anatoly Karpov and
the pyrotechnic aggressiveness of Tal. He had this almost super-
human sense of when to attack, when to squeeze, when to defend.

And he brought a level of competitiveness to every game that is
rare even today. In an era where many grandmasters would agree
to early draws in roughly equal positions, Bobby would fight to the
bitter end, never running out of energy or focus.

Most impressive of all—to me, at least—was that he worked
almost entirely by himself. The great Soviet players of the time—
including Spassky—had an entire infrastructure of coaches and
researchers and trainers supporting them. Many had attended
specialized chess schools from an early age and, as adults, were paid
a salary by the government. Bobby had none of that. He studied in
seclusion, often in hotel rooms late at night, with little input from
even his closest friends. And yet he managed to surpass every player
on the planet.

Bobby was also instrumental in raising the public image of
chess, particularly in the United States. And he used his cultural
influence to demand better playing conditions and bigger prizes
for chess events.

Today, he's mostly remembered for having walked away from the sport at his peak. I remember how disappointed I was in 1975, when Bobby refused to defend his title and allowed Karpov to succeed him as world champion. It would have been such a great match. Not long after that, Bobby disappeared from public life altogether. For the next two decades, he was a ghost that haunted the world of chess. Only a handful of people knew where he was. He would never play another official game for the rest of his life. Yet the influence he exerted on the chess culture was so profound that it was impossible not to feel his presence. There was always speculation that he might be in deep study somewhere, plotting his return, developing ideas that would soon revolutionize the game. But as the years went by, the prospects for a Fischer comeback appeared less and less likely.

When he finally reappeared on the scene in 1992 in the Federal Republic of Yugoslavia for an exhibition match against his old rival Spassky, I for one was excited. It was obvious that the two were well past their primes. Fischer was forty-nine years old by then, and Spassky was fifty-five. But the chess world was still hungry to see Bobby Fischer play again, and we were finally going to get it.

It was no secret that both had been playing each other mainly for the money and the publicity, which was certainly understandable. The exhibition earned Bobby the lion's share of a $5 million purse—the largest in chess history. For his part, Spassky walked away with $2 million, which was absolutely life-changing for him. He had been living a relatively modest life in France at that point. So I was happy to see him doing so well financially.

Unfortunately for Bobby, the exhibition also prompted a US arrest warrant, since he had knowingly violated economic sanctions against Yugoslavia by playing in the match. In the run-up to the event, the US Treasury Department warned him in writing that his participation would be punishable by up to ten years in prison. At a press conference the day before the match, Bobby produced the letter from his briefcase and spat on it. "That's my answer," he said. The US government didn't appreciate the gesture.

And so, after a brief reappearance on the world stage the year before, Bobby was back in hiding—only this time it wasn't voluntary. He was holed up in a dingy hotel room in the small town of Kanjiza, Yugoslavia. And, of all people, he wanted to see me.

Bobby had reached out to my family through our mutual friend Janos Kubat early in the spring of 1993 to request a meeting. I was still touring Peru at the time, so my family visited him without me—which, of course, made me jealous to no end. I was flattered to learn how disappointed Bobby was that I hadn't joined them on that first trip. He had insisted that the whole family return once I was back in Europe so that he could finally meet me, and of course we agreed.

I'd be lying if I said I wasn't surprised by his invitation. I knew that Bobby held female chess players in very low regard. "They're all weak, all women," he remarked in a 1961 interview. "They're stupid compared to men. They shouldn't play chess, you know. They're like beginners. They lose every single game against a man." He even bragged that there wasn't a woman in the world that he couldn't beat, even after giving her knight odds.

I only hoped he had changed his views since then. If he hadn't, he certainly hid it well. From the instant my family and I stepped into his hotel room, Bobby showed us nothing but warmth and hospitality. Seated behind a table as we entered was Filipino grandmaster Eugene Torre, who I had gotten to know well since my victory over him in the 1986 New York Open. The only other person there was Bobby's bodyguard, a tall, well-built Yugoslav gentleman who greeted me with a polite nod and remained standing for my entire visit. I wasn't used to seeing private bodyguards. And his presence added an air of spy-novel intrigue to the meeting.

The room itself was a drab, run-down little space with nothing in it but some standard-issue motel furniture, most of which had clearly seen better days. Part of me was expecting some kind of luxurious hideaway with a private chef and an Olympic-sized swimming pool out back. This was Bobby Fischer, after all, a man who for years had dressed exclusively in bespoke suits commissioned from the finest European tailors, a man who would walk away from tournaments because he didn't like the chairs or the chess pieces or the lighting. And yet, here he was, living out of a suitcase in some low-end motor lodge on the outskirts of a war-torn country.

As Bobby pulled over a chair for me, I was struck by his sheer physical size. He was over six feet tall, with remarkably long arms and large hands. He had grown a beard—as well as a slight paunch—and his thick head of wavy hair had thinned quite a bit. Had I passed him on the street, I might not have recognized him.

He certainly knew who I was. "I hear you're just back from Peru. You were playing a match against Granda, am I right?" he asked. Bobby wanted to know all about the trip—and about my life in general. In fact, it seemed as if he only wanted to talk to me that afternoon. The rest of the room was there almost as an audience—a situation that might have otherwise been awkward, were it not for Bobby's disarmingly gentle demeanor.

Not only was he full of thoughtful questions and comments, but he was incredibly funny, often making humorous remarks and then bursting into a loud, awkward chuckle. I was immediately taken aback. This was not the Bobby I had read about—the ornery, mistrusting loner on the brink of insanity. No, this was a version of the man few ever got to see. And when I look back on our friendship, it's this Bobby—kind and charming, quick to laugh—that I remember most fondly; the Bobby I wish more people had gotten to meet.

Before long, we were sitting across from each other, a chess board between us, discussing ideas and analyzing positions, his long fingers moving the pieces around the board with speed and exactness, as if he were playing a musical instrument. He had been following my career for years and even had thoughts on some of my recent games. He showed me a new kind of chess clock he had invented, which added seconds to each player's time with every move—a technology that has since become standard in tournaments around the world. He was clearly ahead of his time. But his favorite creation, the one he never tired of discussing, was a new variant of chess he dubbed Fischer Random.

As Bobby saw it, high-level chess had become dominated by rote memorization. Many top players would prepare endless lines of moves and commit them to memory before sitting down at the board. In some cases, players could go twenty or thirty moves—or even an entire game—without ever having to make a decision for themselves. Fischer Random was Bobby's attempt to remove memorization from the equation. The variant keeps all of the rules of traditional chess the same but changes one important detail: Each side's back rank of pieces—that is, all of the pieces except the pawns—begin the game in a mixed-up position. Since neither opponent knows the arrangement of the pieces before the game starts, there is no way to prepare in advance. This forces players to find good moves and combinations in the moment.

The game appealed to me right away. For one thing, my playing style has always relied more on over-the-board calculation and inventiveness than on home preparation. But more important, Fischer Random spoke to my belief in chess as a great equalizer, as a sport in which one's age, gender, wealth, or background has no relevance. All that matters is that one finds the right moves and plays them at the right moment.

Bobby understood this more than most great players. Like me, he had come from modest means and spent his career battling a chess establishment that was committed to bringing him down, even if it meant breaking the rules. We were kindred spirits in this way, and we sensed it from our first conversation. He had triumphed in the face of overwhelming resistance and managed to change the game of chess more than anyone in modern history. I was attempting to do the same.

We played just one game of Fischer Random that afternoon. And although I was new to this strange chess variant, I played Bobby to a draw. As we were finishing up, there was one question I couldn't help but ask.

"So Bobby," I said, "do you still believe you can defeat any woman in the world, even giving knight odds?"

"Not anymore," he said.

I knew that would be his answer. I just needed to hear it with my own ears.

Of course, I hadn't come to Kanjiza to earn his approval or even his respect. I came mainly out of curiosity. I wanted to see for myself what had become of this great champion. And while I genuinely enjoyed his company, I was deeply saddened by his situation.

Bobby used to be held up as an American hero. Now he was a man without a country, stranded in a cramped hotel room thousands of miles from his home. I didn't know him well. But I got the sense that this place wouldn't be good for him. I had heard that Bobby could let his emotions get the best of him. And I feared that if left to stew in isolation, his paranoia and resentment would consume him, if they hadn't already. He needed a new environment, someplace more cosmopolitan, where he could socialize and move around freely. But most of all, Bobby needed a friend.

My first act of friendship, I decided, would be to help get this international fugitive over the border to my home city of Budapest. Bobby wasn't so sure about the idea. He thought the Hungarian authorities would arrest him as soon as he entered the country, which was certainly possible. So I did a little reconnaissance on my drive home that afternoon. During a passport check at the border as we entered Hungary, I asked the guard what might happen if a friend of mine named Robert James Fischer came to visit us in Budapest from Yugoslavia. "Would anybody care?"

"It depends. Does he have a valid passport?" was the guard's reply.

"He does."

"Then there shouldn't be a problem."

I got word to Bobby that evening through our friend Janos. It was all the reassurance he needed. Two weeks later, he drove across the border with his entourage and checked into the Gellert, one of Budapest's most luxurious classic spa hotels overlooking the Danube on the Buda side of town. He called me as soon as he arrived, and I rushed over right away to welcome him.

Over the next few months, I'd see him at least a couple of times a week. Since he didn't drive, he often needed me to shuttle him around Budapest. I'd pick him up at his hotel and take him to lunch, or go for walks in the park, almost always accompanied by his bodyguard and, at least early on, Torre. He fell in love with the city's spas, and we'd sometimes spend afternoons wading in the warm-water mineral baths, talking about chess. Many nights, we'd eat in a restaurant somewhere around town, whether alone or with local mutual friends like Pal Benko or Andor Lilienthal, two legendary Hungarian grandmasters who had both been advocates for me from early on in my career. We'd all cram into my Passat, and I'd drive us on little adventures. Seafood was Bobby's favorite. He'd always tell me that "fish makes you smart." We became regulars at Budapest's only Japanese restaurant, where Bobby would usually order the salmon. "The skin's the best part," he'd used to say.

Most of the time Bobby was an amazingly pleasant person to be around. But he also had his dark side. Without warning, he would launch into some hateful diatribe about a global Jewish conspiracy.

Even for me, who was used to shrugging off the small-minded beliefs of arrogant men, these ideas were difficult to hear. As a Jew—and a granddaughter of Holocaust survivors—I found his views both appalling and, at the same time, utterly mystifying. Not only was Bobby highly intelligent, but he was also Jewish. What's more, many of those closest to Bobby were Jewish. Yet he seemed to exempt us from his hatred. "I'm not talking about you and your family," he would say. "You're obviously an exception."

I tried to disabuse Bobby of his toxic beliefs, and especially his antisemitism. But it was no use. In chess, the absolute best moves—"the truth" as chess players sometimes call it—is all one needs to win. When it comes to defeating bigotry and delusion, the truth is rarely enough.

Eventually he just stopped discussing these topics around me and my family. To the extent that Bobby indulged in conspiracy theorizing, it was to accuse the Soviet Union of fixing top chess events, and specifically the first World Championship match between Karpov and Kasparov. He was convinced that the two players had colluded, a conclusion he had reached not just by analyzing their games, but also from his experiences with the Soviet world.

One night at our apartment, he put a position from one of the Karpov-Kasparov games on my chess board. It was the position that had been reached just before the game was adjourned and both players retired for the evening. Each side's team would have had all night to analyze the adjourned position and come up with the best ways to continue the game the next day. Yet, as Bobby saw it, the moves that followed the adjournment were so inaccurate that the game's outcome had to be prearranged.

"How could two men like Kasparov and Karpov play this poorly?" he asked. "They had all night to find the right continuations, and this is what they found? I don't buy it. This was a setup. It had to be."

People often get the wrong impression about Bobby's obsession with the Karpov-Kasparov match. They think he had a grudge against these players, that he thought they were frauds and only succeeded by cheating. But really, his theory was based on his utmost respect for both of them. He just couldn't believe that players of that caliber could miss ideas that seemed obvious to him. I'd often argue back at him, doing my best to be diplomatic.

"I see what you're saying, Bobby. I do. But of all people you know what it feels like to play in one of these matches. Isn't it possible that the pressure got to them? You made a few mistakes in your games against Spassky. You let him trap your bishop in the first game. Nobody ever accused you two of colluding."

He wouldn't budge. Once he had an idea in his head, there was no changing his mind. The inexhaustible fighting spirit that served him so well over the chess board could also make him impervious to persuasion.

It didn't take long for Bobby to become part of the family. He'd come by my parents' apartment a few nights a week with some caviar he'd buy from a nearby street vendor (one of his favorite foods in those years), and he'd analyze games with me and my sisters while my mother cooked dinner. Bobby had this Polaroid camera he'd carry with him, and he was constantly snapping photos of me and my family. Some he would keep; others he'd give to us. I guess it made him feel good to finally be in an environment where he didn't need to hide, where he could feel at home. It was only after Bobby's death in 2008 that I learned that his biological father, the physicist Paul Nemenyi, was also a Hungarian Jew. So, really, it makes sense that Bobby fit in so well with our family. We were connected by something deeper than chess, even if Bobby would have never admitted it at the time.

At least once, Spassky came to Budapest to visit with us all. It was a surreal experience. Even though I had known Spassky for years by then, having both him and Bobby sitting at my parents' dining room table discussing chess wasn't something that seemed possible. They might have been seen as archrivals, but they had long since become good buddies and were incredibly great company when together, always laughing and playfully arguing.

In most of these get-togethers with Bobby, the subject would eventually turn to Fischer Random. The version of the game Bobby first showed to me was a bit different from the one played today.

The initial idea was to have each side start with only a row of pawns on the board across the second and seventh ranks—just as in

ABOVE: At the New York Mayor's Cup with Rudy Giuliani in 2001. Seated are thirteen-year-old Hikaru Nakamura and GM Leonid Yudasin.

BELOW: 2004 Dream Team cake celebration, with Anna Zatonskih, Irina Krush, and Jennifer Shahade. *All photos by Paul Truong unless otherwise noted.*

TOP: 2004 Olympiad in Calvia, Spain before my game against Xie Jun.

ABOVE: 2004 Olympiad in Calvia, during my game against Maia Chiburdanidze—one of my all-time favorite games.

BELOW: 2004 Olympiad in Calvia, final round match against Vietnam.

TOP: Shortly after the start of the world record simul in Palm Beach Gardens in 2005.

ABOVE: Late Soviet president Mikhail Gorbachev preparing my tea at the press conference for the Chess for Peace event in 2006.

RIGHT: My World Cup trophy in Dresden, Germany, in 2006.

BELOW: Chess for Peace exhibition match against former world champion Anatoly Karpov in the Battle of the Sexes in Lindsborg, Kansas, in 2006.

TOP: In Central Park with my kids Leeam and Tom in 2006 during the filming of Nat Geo's *My Brilliant Brain* documentary.

ABOVE: In Budapest at the Szecsenyi Bath in 2006 during filming of Nat Geo's *My Brilliant Brain* documentary.

LEFT: A proud mom, after Tom just won his first national title in 2006.

ABOVE: Paul and me on our wedding day in December 2006. *Photo from the Polgar family album.*

BELOW LEFT: At the opening of Texas Tech's Chess Park in 2009. The bench has the engraving of my motto: "Win with grace, lose with dignity."

BELOW RIGHT: During our first official visit to Webster University in the spring of 2012, receiving my jersey from President Stroble.

ABOVE: Celebrating our first Final Four victory with Webster University at the Fourth of July parade in 2013

LEFT: Winning the Final Four with my Webster team in New York City in 2017.

BELOW: At the Webster SPICE headquarters in 2020.

FIDE

GENS UNA SUMUS

FÉDÉRATION INTERNATIONALE DES ÉCHECS

Recognized by the International Olympic Committee (1999)

54 Avenue de Rhodanie, 1007 Lausanne, Switzerland

☎ (+41) 216010039 ✉ office@fide.com 🌐 http://www.fide.com

21 January 2021   N.01-06-2021
Moscow

GM Susan Polgar

Dear Susan,

Allow me to express my sincere admiration for your sport achievements and congratulate you on your 30th anniversary of gaining the title of International Grandmaster!

Beyond all doubt, you are one of the strongest female chess players in the world.

Your name is a highlight in the annals of chess history – the eighth World Women Chess Champion, you became the first female player to be awarded the title of Grandmaster after completing the norms and achieving the necessary rating.

The key to your success is an outstanding talent, multiplied by the character of a true champion, many hours of hard work, and the highest level of self-discipline.

Taking part in prestigious international competitions you have demonstrated brilliant play, superb preparation, and excellent skills. You put in an outstanding performance time and again bringing moments of joy to your family, friends, mentors, and fans. Upon completion of your playing career you have reached new heights as an organizer and coach.

I wish you every success, good health to you and your relatives, and all the best!

Respectfully,

Arkady Dvorkovich
FIDE President

ABOVE: Congratulatory letter by FIDE president Arkady Dvorkovich in January 2021.
BELOW: Celebration time with my husband in 2022.

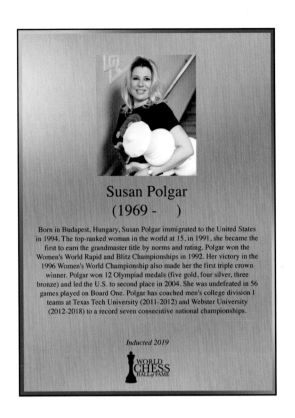

Susan Polgar
(1969 -   )

Born in Budapest, Hungary, Susan Polgar immigrated to the United States in 1994. The top-ranked woman in the world at 15, in 1991, she became the first to earn the grandmaster title by norms and rating. Polgar won the Women's World Rapid and Blitz Championships in 1992. Her victory in the 1996 Women's World Championship also made her the first triple crown winner. Polgar won 12 Olympiad medals (five gold, four silver, three bronze) and led the U.S. to second place in 2004. She was undefeated in 56 games played on Board One. Polgar has coached men's college division I teams at Texas Tech University (2011-2012) and Webster University (2012-2018) to a record seven consecutive national championships.

Inducted 2019

WORLD
CHESS
HALL*of*FAME

LEFT: My World Chess Hall of Fame induction plaque in 2023. *Photo from the Chess Hall of Fame.*

ABOVE: Back in my hometown after receiving the "best female coach in history" award by FIDE in 2024.

BELOW: Family photo with my sisters (Sofia on the left and Judit on the right) and my parents in Budapest in 2024.

regular chess. Instead of making a first move, white would choose a piece—a knight, say, or even the king—and place it anywhere they wished on the back rank. Then black would do the same. The only rule was that the bishops had to start on opposite-color squares. After eight turns, each side would have a jumbled arrangement of pieces on their back ranks. Only then would the players get to make their opening moves.

It was an interesting game. But we both agreed that it was too dissimilar from regular chess. All of this strategy at the beginning about where to place your pieces seemed contrived. And it meant that each side would start with two completely different setups. Wouldn't it be better, we thought, if each side had the same random arrangement at the beginning? The only restrictions would be that each bishop must start on a different color square, and that the king must be placed somewhere between the two rooks, to allow players to castle.

After many months of experimentation, this is the version of Fischer Random that we ultimately landed on, which remains popular today. He consulted a mathematician to figure out how many such arrangements were possible. The answer was 960—which, as far as he was concerned, was enough to prevent players from planning their opening moves in advance. Today, the game is sometimes referred to as Chess960 for precisely this reason (although many still prefer to call it Fischer Random). We'd play countless games of Fischer Random during our time together, with neither of us ever really dominating (I believe our lifetime score against each other was around 50/50, in fact).

Bobby was always looking over his shoulder whenever we were in public together, which I suppose was understandable, since he was technically a fugitive from the United States government. We had just sat down for lunch with Benko one afternoon when we saw a camera flash coming from the back of the restaurant. Bobby panicked. "We need to go!" he said, rushing us out of the restaurant and toward my car. It was like something out of a 1970s crime movie.

Once in the car he held his giant hand up against the passenger-side window to block any more photos, and, as we drove away, he kept shouting "Get me out of here! Turn here! Now turn here! We need to lose them!" I found it all a little ridiculous but wouldn't dare laugh in front of him. I just tried to keep my eyes on the road.

There was a similar incident that summer. Bobby had joined my family at a country home we had purchased in the town of Nagymaros, along with Torre and Bobby's bodyguard. I still have a distinct memory of Bobby in the kitchen chopping mushrooms for dinner one night. We were lounging outside one day when we saw a paparazzo in the distance filming us with a video camera. Again, Bobby panicked, instructing his bodyguard to go confiscate the tape. I can only imagine what the bodyguard said to the cameraman, but within a few minutes, we had the tape—which Bobby quickly destroyed, smashing it with a hammer right there in our kitchen.

During these fits of paranoia, he was completely different from the warmhearted Bobby we saw most of the time. He could really be quite gentle. When a stray cat wandered into the summer house one day, he picked it up and started playing with it without even thinking. The two were inseparable for the rest of the trip. In fact, in photos from that summer, he almost always has the cat nestled in his long arms.

By the fall of 1994, though, his antisemitic views had become harder for him to suppress, even around me. I had ignored this part of him as best I could during the year and a half we spent together in Budapest, mostly out of respect for him and what he had accomplished. Now I had had enough. I would never stop caring about him and considered him a friend for the rest of his life, but I needed to get some distance.

TWENTY-TWO

Were it not for Bobby, 1993 would have been a very dark year for me. My run of bad luck in the World Championship semifinals and my breakup with Julio were two of the most painful episodes in my life, and they came right on the heels of one another. I was at a low point, both professionally and personally, and I wasn't quite sure how to move forward. I'd play in another Ladies vs. Veterans event in Vienna. And I'd return to Brno for the same tournament I had won two years before. But the classical chess tournaments that had defined my career up until that point started to feel unsatisfying, repetitive even. So I began to seek out different formats and new challenges. Maybe this was Bobby's influence. I started to understand his disdain for traditional chess and his obsession with new alternatives to the game, like Fischer Random.

Lucky for me, this happened to be the year when rapid and blitz chess tournaments began to take off in a serious way. I played in four such events over the course of a few months, which would have been unthinkable just two years earlier. The first was the Melody Amber tournament, the combination rapid-blindfold event that Mr. van Oosterom had named after his little girl. It was the strongest tournament I had ever competed in.

I ended up exceeding expectations in the rapid portion, draw-ing Karpov and Vishy and beating both Ivanchuk and the British grandmaster Nigel Short. I also finished ahead of Karpov, which was a particular point of pride.

But the blindfold portion of the event was by far the most fun. Blindfold normally refers to any form of chess in which players can't see what's happening on the board. Instead of moving physi-cal pieces, each side either calls out their moves or transmits them through a computer, keeping track of the game's progression in their heads. The white side might start by saying "d4," after which black might say "knight f6," and so on. If two players are proficient at blindfold, they can literally play a game while sitting on a park bench or in a dentist waiting room, simply by speaking moves back and forth to one another.

It's a skill I started developing at a very early age. My sisters and I would hold our own blindfold tournaments at home. I can still picture myself sitting across from an eight-year-old Judit, playing blindfold blitz games with nothing but a chess clock between us. I'd call out a move and hit the clock, and she'd do the same, while my father and Sofia sat out of view, tracking the game on a physi-cal board to make sure neither of us slipped up and made an illegal move. Sometimes we'd even wear actual blindfolds.

You might think that blindfold chess requires players to visu-alize the board and pieces in their minds and maintain a perfect image of the game as it unfolds, as if we were watching it on a computer screen in our heads. But the actual experience of playing blindfold is so much stranger and harder to describe than that, at least for me. I don't see a board or pieces. I simply know where the pieces are and understand how each piece relates to the others. I'm not seeing so much as grasping, comprehending, navigating. I've been told it's similar to what a musician experiences when playing a complicated piece without the sheet music in front of them. At times, the experience can feel transcendent, like you're communing with the game as it truly exists in some platonic realm, freed from the confines of time and space. What's strange is that, when you lose track of the position in a blindfold game, it's never completely gone. You can always just replay the game from the beginning in your head until the pieces are back where they ought to be.

I also played in the inaugural Tal Memorial, a blitz tournament celebrating my old friend and hero Mikhail Tal, who had passed away in June 1992. It was a fitting tribute to a man whose appetite for blitz chess was notoriously insatiable. And I was honored to be invited.

This was my first time back in Moscow since the fall of the Soviet Union, and it was strange to me how little had seemed to change since I first visited back in the 1980s. There were nicer cars on the street, and the stores were better stocked, but it still felt like the same old Moscow.

Throughout the tournament, I kept thinking back to my first meeting with Tal when I was thirteen—which was also in Moscow—and he cut short his tournament game just to play me in blitz. Professional chess was already starting to lose some of its shine for me. And the thought that I would never run into Tal at a tournament again—never hear one of his stories or challenge him to a late-night blitz game—only added to my sense of disenchantment.

Sometimes I'd travel with one of my sisters to a tournament, just to get out of Budapest for a while and meet new people. That summer, in fact, I went with Sofia to Israel, where she was playing in the chess portion of the Maccabiah Games, a sort of "Jewish Olympics" which brought together thousands of athletes from nearly fifty different nations in dozens of different events. The whole event had this positive sense of community that I had never felt before at a sporting event. I came along mostly to provide my sister with moral support and keep her company. But, shortly before the games got underway, someone from Hungary's table tennis team approached me.

I had gotten to know a lot of the top table tennis players, since my sisters and I often played at the same facility in Budapest as them. The player explained to me that his teammate had dropped out of the event at the last minute, and he suggested that I take her place. I couldn't turn him down. I had been training at table tennis for five to ten hours a week for three years at that point, so I knew I could at least hold my own. Before I knew it, I was wearing a uniform and representing my nation in mixed doubles table tennis. We did pretty well, considering the circumstances, making it all the way to the quarterfinals before getting knocked out. It remains my proudest moment as a table tennis player.

This was the year when Kasparov and Nigel Short broke from FIDE and set up a rival organizing body called the Professional Chess Association. For the next few years, the chess world would have two separate world champions—one crowned by FIDE, and the other by the PCA. I never much cared for the arrangement. I thought we owed it to chess fans to have just one champion at a time. But I didn't feel strongly enough to boycott the PCA altogether. I was willing to see where the experiment led.

As number 56 in the world in the PCA rankings, I was invited to compete in the Interzonal Tournament in Groningen, Holland, that winter. The event was the first of several competitions set up to choose the first PCA World Championship challenger. Julio happened to be playing as well. Seeing him after so much time was so much harder than I expected. We kept our exchanges very cordial. But just being in the same room with the man was uncomfortable for me. I'd spent the last few months dealing with the emotional fallout from what he had done to me, swinging back and forth between being angry at him and missing him. I really thought I was past all of that. Seeing him in Groningen, though, I could feel those emotions flare up inside me again, and I hated it.

To be fair to Julio, when we ran into each other at the 2003 US Open championship in Los Angeles, he apologized for how badly he handled our relationship. I told him I forgave him, and for me that chapter is officially closed.

Groningen was also where I first became friends with Gata Kamsky. Gata is a Soviet-born grandmaster who is just a few years younger than me. And he had been living in New York for several years. I didn't know it at the time, but my friendship with Gata would have serious consequences on the trajectory of my life.

Gata did very well in that Interzonal, advancing to the next stage of competition—a quarterfinal match against the Dutch grandmaster Paul van der Sterren. And he asked Judit and me to help him prepare. I think I was mainly interested in a new experience. Neither Judit nor I had ever worked closely with someone who wasn't related to us. And this seemed like as good a time as any to try our hand at helping out another top player.

Gata came to Budapest that January for the first leg of our training, which went pretty smoothly. The following month, my mother, Judit, and I headed to New York to stay with Gata and his family and continue his preparation. I was happy for a chance to spend time in one of my favorite cities without having to abide by the rigid schedule of a chess tournament.

One of the people I met on that trip was Jacob Shutzman, or Cobi, as we called him. He was an Israeli-born software developer whose brother was a master chess player and a good friend of Gata's. I remember Cobi took a liking to me right away. And pretty soon, we were spending a lot of time together. We'd had dinner together several times and even took a short trip to Atlantic City. I was a little apprehensive about getting involved with him, not least because he was almost ten years older than I was. But he was very nice to be around. I liked how grown-up and competent he seemed, and that he had a solid career that had nothing to do with chess. He also knew his way around New York as if it were his hometown, which only added to the air of worldliness he gave off—all of which I found intriguing.

When Cobi suggested that we keep in touch after I was back in Budapest, I was genuinely thrilled. It seems funny to think about now, but we mainly communicated through faxes. We'd handwrite little notes to each other, or print them out on computer paper, and send them back and forth across the phone lines. He came to visit me in Budapest that May. He was clearly taken with me, which felt good. As for me, I was just happy to let it all unfold on its own accord and see where it led. I had no idea things would progress as quickly as they did.

We had only known each other for about three months when I got a fax from him proposing marriage. I was completely stunned. I knew I wanted a husband one day, but not right then. The more I thought about it, though, the more the idea started to appeal to me.

Unlike Julio, who came from a completely different culture and background than I had, Cobi was from a traditional Jewish family. I also liked that he had a life outside of chess and that he was passionate about physical fitness. Then there was the prospect of living in New York, where I already had a lot of friends. For me, New York represented excitement and possibility more than any other place I had ever been to. And at that moment in my life, I craved adventure.

I was twenty-five years old, and already my life had started to feel routine, like a chess opening I had played thousands of times before, the same fifteen moves resulting in the same familiar positions. I was tired of living out of a suitcase for half the year, shuttling from one hotel to the next. I played in another Melody Amber tournament that spring, and another Ladies vs. Veterans event. In the fall, I was scheduled to play in another Olympiad. But some of the joy I used to derive from these events was gone. Whereas I used to take comfort in familiarity, now I wanted something new. I just didn't know what, exactly.

Marrying Cobi wasn't an obvious choice for me, or even an easy one, but that's what I liked about it. I had no idea where it would take me, but I knew it wouldn't be boring. Cobi was offering me a chance to write a new story, to live a different life. All I had to do was say yes. So I did.

That July, on a trip to New York for a big PCA rapid tournament, I accepted his proposal. By September, I had moved in with Cobi in his apartment in Rego Park, Queens. My relocation marked the biggest change in my personal life up until that point. And it wasn't exactly a smooth transition. My parents and sisters were understandably disappointed that I would move so far away, and so suddenly. Judit was especially broken up about it. I don't blame them. The move was a lot easier for me than it was for them. I would have felt the same way had it been Judit or Sofia who had left Budapest first.

It was also a major professional shift. New York also gave me a little distance to think about my career and figure out what I really wanted to do with my life. I hadn't fallen out of love with chess—not even close. But playing in tournaments was no longer enough by itself.

I wanted to have a larger influence on the game and how it was perceived. I dreamed of doing something comparable to what Bobby had done—to give chess a new image and get it the respect it deserved, not just in places like Eastern Europe and Russia, but in my new home of the United States.

I was fed up with how little respect and notoriety chess players received in the wider culture. We worked just as hard as the top players in tennis and basketball and soccer, but with none of the respect—and only a small fraction of the pay. Growing up, I had accepted this situation as simply the way things were. But that didn't work for me anymore. It was time for me to do my part to change things.

TWENTY-THREE

I didn't exactly have a plan for how I would help revitalize chess in mainstream culture. But I knew that winning the Women's World Championship would be an important first step. The title would give me a louder voice in the cultural conversation. So I decided to focus on that goal and figure out the rest later.

As a semifinalist in the last championship cycle, I had already earned a spot in that year's Candidates Tournament—an event I was determined to win. Now I needed to assemble a team. The first person I thought of was the Soviet Israeli grandmaster Lev Psakhis.

Lev was yet another of the many grandmasters who was held back by the regime, despite being one of the greatest players of his generation. He was a two-time Soviet champion, and might have even become the world champion, if he had gotten the chance in his prime. His experience came through in his play, which exhibited a kind of higher-order judgment that only comes from a life of experience at the board.

I first met Lev in the mid-1980s, at a major blitz tournament in Pilsen. And I had gotten to know him when we had gotten along well at the 1990 OHRA tournament in Amsterdam. And he joined my sisters and me for a training camp in Aruba in 1992. Since then, he had served as Judit's second in a match she played (and won) against Spassky, so he already felt like part of the Polgar family in many ways. I met up with Lev during a visit to Israel with Cobi in the summer of 1994. We clicked from our very first training session.

I soon realized that if I was going to be in good fighting shape for the World Championship cycle, I'd need to find some sparring partners who lived nearby. I called up everybody I knew I thought could give me a good game, and most of them were happy to pitch in—people like Joel Benjamin, Max Dlugy, and Maurice Ashley. I'd invite them over to our apartment a few times a week for some practice games—blitz and rapid, mostly—or we'd meet at the Manhattan Chess Club or the Marshall Chess Club.

I missed my sisters a lot after moving to New York. Both were having a spectacular year. Judit took first place at an elite tournament in Madrid, finishing well ahead of the pack. And Sofia won a silver medal in that year's World Junior Under-21, where she competed against the boys. I wanted to be there to cheer them on and analyze games and celebrate with them—just like in the old days. It was sad to admit, but the era of "Polgaria" was over.

As we got closer to the Candidates, I could feel my motivation growing stronger. The previous time, I had entered the World Championship cycle to prove my critics wrong. This time, I had a broader purpose as well. The title was no longer an end in itself, but a stepping stone to a larger project, one I hoped would define the next stage of my career.

By the time the tournament rolled around in September of that year in Tilburg, Holland, I felt like I was in peak form. It was obvious from very early on that my toughest competition would be the Georgian Maia Chiburdanidze, who had held the women's world champion title from 1978 until 1991. Playing her in the very first round, she found her way to an objectively better position. But I kept pushing. Eventually, she got into trouble on the clock and made a decisive blunder, opening a path to victory for me, which I took.

I really found my stride after my mother and Judit arrived sometime in the middle of the tournament. Almost automatically, we fell back into our old rhythms. Judit and I would analyze my games after each round, the same way we had hundreds of times over the years. My mom was there to provide that unwavering moral support that I had secretly missed since moving away. Lev was also on hand to work on openings with me each morning before my games. It was a perfect team.

The event went fairly well, although Maia did get her revenge later in the tournament, beating me with the white pieces—her only victory against me to this day. We finished the event tied at 10.5 points each. Thanks to the tiebreaker, I was named the event's winner. We would both move on to a semifinal match to decide who would play the reigning champion Xie Jun for the title.

That November, Cobi and I married under a chuppah in a traditional Jewish wedding in Israel. It was a huge party with nearly 250 guests. I didn't have nearly as big a family as Cobi, so only about a dozen of the guests were from my side, which felt a little odd. We had just a few days for a honeymoon before I headed off to Moscow for the Women's Olympiad. It was the first time that Judit wasn't part of our team, since she had decided to play in the men's section that year. Her absence definitely hurt us at the Olympiad. Nevertheless, our team managed to walk away with a silver medal, and I kept up my Olympiad streak, scoring 11 out of 14 without ever losing a game.

Sometime near the end of that tournament, I was woken up by a knock on my hotel room door in the middle of the night. I assumed the worst. People don't wake you up the night before a crucial game to tell you good news, after all. I opened the door, but nobody was there. It didn't take me long to realize what was happening. One of the rival teams was playing a dirty trick, although it's impossible to know which one. We were in Moscow, after all, and back in the communist era, the Soviets were famous for their foul play.

Whoever it was, I would have expected something a little more imaginative. *Is this all you've got?* I thought. *Ring and run?* I struggled to get back to sleep for the next half hour. And I was finally dozing off when the phone rang. It was the front desk. The hotel had just received an important fax for me. I told them I'd get it in the morning.

Even as I played in Moscow, FIDE had yet to work out the details of my match against Maia. I mentioned this to my friend Zurab Azmaiparashvili, who was playing in Moscow alongside us.

Right there and then, he worked something out with some Russian officials, who agreed to host the match. Not long after that, it was announced that I would play Maia that February in St. Petersburg. I headed back to New York to continue my preparations with Lev. And, within a couple of months, I was back to Russia for the match.

Lev, Judit, my mother, and Cobi were all with me as well. And when time came to play my first game, I felt rested, focused, and ready to get to work. The weather hadn't warmed any since the Olympiad. But the playing facilities almost made up for that. It was a beautiful theater, with six hundred or so seats, the kind of venue that makes you want to put on a show, which is exactly what we did. Both Maia and I came out swinging in the first two games—both of which were draws. By the fifth game, I had secured a significant lead of 3.5 to 1.5. It gave me enough confidence to relax a little on the rest day that followed and accompany my sister, mother, and Cobi to a performance of *Madame Butterfly*.

After that, my chess seemed to flow naturally. Intuition, calculation, time-management—all of these elements came together. I swept the next two games, winning the match with three games to spare. I was now on my way to the World Championship final.

We all went out to celebrate at a Chinese restaurant, and spent the next few days taking in the city—the Hermitage Museum, Nevsky Prospect, the Winter Palace. It made me nostalgic for all those trips my family and I had gone on together, one inseparable unit touring the world together.

According to FIDE regulations, my title fight with Xie had to occur within six months of the St. Petersburg event. Unfortunately for me, FIDE wasn't in a hurry to set a date. I'd check in with the higher-ups there periodically to see if there had been any progress, only to hear that they were struggling to find a venue or that there weren't enough sponsors. There were plans to hold the event in Yugoslavia or Paris or Hungary, all of which fell through. The truth was, a match between two women just wasn't a priority for FIDE. After a few months, it started to feel like it would never happen.

The challenge for me was staying in top chess form for however long it took to schedule the match. If you don't play in actual tournaments for a while, you can start to lose your touch. So I did my best to stay active, playing in a handful of events. One of them was a blitz tournament in Israel, which allowed me to reunite with my sisters. After the event, a charming Israeli grandmaster named Yona Kosashvili asked Sofia out for dinner. The two of them had chemistry from that first meeting. They remain married to this day.

Back home in New York, I continued to work with Lev to get ready for the championship match, during his occasional visits to the city. I also enlisted the help of Zurab, who, as a fellow Georgian, had actually worked on Maia's team in St. Petersburg. Now that she was out of the running, he had no problem coming over to my team.

Working with Zurab in New York, it quickly became obvious why he had the reputation he did as an opening maestro. It didn't take him long to propose a strategy for me designed specifically to exploit Xie's weaknesses. What he came up with was both completely unexpected and absolutely brilliant.

Zurab had noticed that Xie struggled to find the best moves in certain continuations of the Scotch Game—a king's pawn opening for white. I was strictly a queen's pawn player, so a switch this dramatic would almost surely put Xie on her back foot. Over the next few months, Zurab would help me develop a range of ideas in the Scotch, as well as a few other king's pawn openings. I also got occasional help from Judit and a few other friends. But the majority of my time I spent working alone.

I also started taking physical fitness very seriously after moving to New York, in no small part thanks to Cobi, who was fanatical about exercise and bodybuilding. It didn't matter if he worked late or we had a busy day, he would still be at the gym until midnight rather than missing a workout. In the run-up to the World Championship, I was at the gym with Cobi for at least ninety minutes a day. I'd also go on runs several times a week in Flushing Meadows Park with my good friend from the neighborhood, Andy, who was preparing for that year's New York City Marathon. The results I saw were so dramatic that I kicked myself for not having started sooner.

All of a sudden, I had more mental and physical endurance, which enabled me to work at chess longer and harder than I ever had. It gave me confidence and composure and emotional stability that served me amazingly well at the chess board.

It was just by coincidence that my new hometown was the site of the World Championship match between Garry Kasparov and my old friend Vishy Anand that fall. Despite being involved in professional chess for nearly my entire life, I had never actually attended a World Championship match before. I would have never guessed that my first one would be in America. Vishy had made huge strides since our time together back in Budapest years before. And I was proud to see him making a run for the championship. I wished him luck before the match got underway and spent a lot of the event watching alongside Vishy's second, the American grandmaster Patrick Wolff.

It was the most spectacular setting for a chess match I had ever seen. Garry and Vishy played on the 107th floor of the World Trade Center, and there were these stunning publicity photos of them playing chess on the roof of the tower, with New York City stretching on for miles in the distance. Instead of sitting on a stage in some theater, they played in this giant soundproof glass box, so that journalists and spectators and commentators could get close to the games while still being able to make as much noise as they wanted. It looked pretty claustrophobic behind that glass. But I also appreciated what the organizers were trying to do, which was to make chess more dramatic, more newsworthy, more of a spectator sport.

There was seating for more than a hundred people and a snack bar serving pizza and hamburgers. My frequent sparring partner Maurice Ashley was on hand to provide move-by-move commentary—which he did with such intensity and speed that you felt like you were watching a prizefight or a basketball game. Mayor Rudy Giuliani even showed up to make the honorary first move.

I could hardly believe my eyes the next morning when I saw a picture of Garry and Vishy in their little glass booth on the front page of *The New York Times*. The whole production just reaffirmed my belief that if handled properly, chess could get the attention and respect that it genuinely deserved.

And then there were the actual games. I remember the excitement that Patrick and I shared when Vishy took the lead after game 9. My old friend was closing in on the biggest title in professional chess, and it felt absolutely electric. In the end, Garry fought back well, winning the match in just eighteen games to retain the championship. I for one was crestfallen, even though I knew this was just a bump in the road for Vishy. The way he played, it was clear that we hadn't heard the last from him. He was just getting started.

Of course, watching that match made me even more impatient for my own championship bout. So when FIDE reached out to me and asked me for help finding sponsors for the match, I agreed to do what I could. I got very close to a deal for the Swiss bank UBS to sponsor a championship match in the United States, but that plan ultimately fell apart.

In the end, it was a chess journalist from Yugoslavia named Dimitrije Bjelica who found us our sponsor. He got in touch with the Spanish businessman Luis Rentero, the longtime supporter and organizer of the Linares International Chess Tournament, a cele-brated event that had been going on since the late 1970s. Rentero said he'd be willing to sponsor the Women's World Championship, so long as it took place in Jaen, Spain, which suited me just fine.

Rentero scheduled the match for just two months later, in January 1996, and set the prize fund at $200,000. It would be a best-of-sixteen taking place over nearly a month, with a few rest days. Nearly a year had passed since my match against Maia in St. Peters-burg, and I was tired of waiting. But at that point, I was just glad it was actually happening.

It was a heady experience, that first day in Jaen, seeing giant posters advertising our match all over town, at bus stops and in store windows. A few weeks earlier, I was struggling just to get the match scheduled. Now, we were the hottest ticket in town.

Xie and I arrived at the hotel at the same time. I couldn't believe just how massive an entourage she had brought—nearly twenty people, including several chess coaches, a chess computer specialist, a psychologist, a medical doctor, and a personal chef. I don't know if it was an intimidation tactic, a way of signaling her superiority, but I wasn't going to let it bother me. I might have had the smaller group—only my mother, Judit, Lev, and Cobi were with me for the match—but they were all I needed. I told myself that, if anything, Xie's travel detail would get in the way, a classic case of too many cooks in the kitchen (one of whom was an actual cook, in Xie's case).

There was a crowded opening ceremony, where a group of tradi-tional Spanish dancers performed, followed by a big dinner with hundreds of guests. The match took place in a medieval castle high up on a hill overlooking the city that now operated as a hotel, where we also stayed. It was all so picturesque. But, I knew that, once all the pomp and circumstance was finished with, I'd be sitting down with the reigning world champion. I had nothing against Xie—I actually liked her. But that didn't change the fact that I had come to Spain to take something precious from her, something she had no intention of giving up.

I tried to steel myself for the battle ahead, but by the time the first move was on the board, I was still on edge. I could feel the gravity of the situation in the pit of my stomach and on every inch of my skin. It was a kind of nervousness I had never experienced before. By the drawing of lots I got the white pieces. I didn't want to deploy my secret weapon, the Scotch, too early in the match. So I opted for a king's fianchetto opening, using my first two moves to position my light-squared bishop on the board's long diagonal, something I had worked on with Lev.

It didn't go well. Somewhere along the way, my anxiety got to me and I lost the thread, which Xie gradually punished me for. Her play wasn't perfect, either. Even near the end there was a chance for me to get back in the game and pull out a draw, but I let it pass me by. The first game went to Xie.

The psychology of playing in a match is very different from that of normal round-robin tournaments. You're facing the same opponent, game after game—someone you've spent months studying and analyzing and speculating about. And you know she's done the same with you. There's also a special power imbalance that can develop in matches. When you win, you don't just earn points; you take away confidence from your opponent. If you lose, it can be harder to recover. I needed to wake up the morning after and sit down across from the person who had just beat me. It's one of the hardest things to do in chess.

Lev could tell I was affected by the loss and did what he could to calm me down. He advised me to play for two results in the next game—to cautiously pursue a win, without burning any bridges, in case a draw was all I could hope for. This would give me time to settle my nerves. It turned out to be sound advice.

In the second game, I went for a variation of the Sicilian Defense I had never played before in competition, and it worked beautifully. Xie offered a draw relatively early on, and I accepted, although in retrospect I had a slightly better position.

Finally, in game 3, I reached for my secret weapon, the Scotch, which I had prepared with Zurab. I could tell right away that Xie was surprised. Unfortunately, she handled the situation very well and managed to equalize fairly quickly. We agreed to a draw after just nineteen moves.

Just as I was starting to feel steady, circumstances conspired to knock me off balance yet again. Against my strong objections, Cobi had invited his parents to join us in Jaen. They arrived sometime around my third game. And, just as I had feared, their presence was a big distraction I would have rather done without.

But it didn't stop there. When I arrived back at my hotel that evening, I found a letter from Rentero. It seems he wasn't pleased with the early draws in the second and third games, and he insisted that Xie and I each pay a fine of $25,000 as punishment. It was an outrageous demand. It's true that, at Linares, the tournament he had sponsored for years, players usually signed a contract stating that they would not offer draws before the fortieth move. But neither FIDE nor the match regulations stipulated such a rule in this event. I ran into Xie in the hallway of our hotel right after receiving the letter. She was as baffled as I was. We didn't know whether to laugh or cry or scream about it. We briefly discussed the possibility of abandoning the match in protest, but we both knew that wasn't wise. Eventually, FIDE president Kirsan Ilyumzhinov personally assured us that he'd take care of the matter. But things remained tense between me and Rentero for the remainder of the match.

Game 4 was a wild opposite-side castle slugfest in which Xie and I each threw our pawns up the board as quickly as possible, racing to be the first to corner the other's king. In the end, I was able to deliver the decisive blow, trapping her queen and forcing Xie to resign. It was a huge relief. A loss in that game would have made a comeback so much harder for me. Now that the score was equal, I regained self-confidence and could relax a little.

I won the fifth game, using a slightly improved version of my opening from game 3, which Lev and Judit had helped me prepare. After a draw with the black pieces in game 6, I once more unleashed the Scotch in the seventh game. This time Xie was prepared. For a while, I felt like she was seizing the initiative. She developed her pieces quickly and was playing with a palpable confidence. By the time she sacrificed her knight on move 15, her attack looked very scary. *Don't panic*, I told myself. *Just take your time.* I went into a long think, trying to see where this position actually led. What I found was that nine moves out, her seemingly dangerous attack would actually fall to pieces. I was betting she hadn't looked this deeply into the position—she wouldn't have sacrificed her piece if she had. And I was right. Not only did I successfully refute her attack, but I won some material in the process. It was enough to decide the game in my favor.

Game 8 was probably the most critical game. It was Xie's last real opportunity to claw her way back into the match. Playing with the black pieces, I used the same opening I had in the sixth game. Xie had anticipated I might do this and was ready with a reply. She uncorked a dangerous assault on my king that forced me to defend fiercely for much of the middlegame. It was a real battle. But Xie missed a golden opportunity to convert, allowing me to neutralize her attack. By move 40, I had a clear advantage. Xie knew how important this game was and showed some amazing fight in that game. After another twenty moves, though, her situation was pretty hopeless, and she reluctantly resigned. My lead in the match—5½ to 2½—was now nearly unsurmountable. Xie got another win in game 12, outplaying me in a Ruy Lopez. But by that point, I was just one win away from the title.

It's tricky to keep your head about you when you're that close to something as big as a world championship. For a year, I had devoted most of my waking hours to a goal that I was inches from achieving. But, at this point, I couldn't think about any of that. I couldn't let myself imagine what it would feel like when I actually won, because I hadn't won yet. And if I relaxed for even a moment, it could all slip away from me. I was still haunted by my world championship qualifier match against Ioseliani a few years before, where I had given up a sizable lead and ultimately failed to win.

I would not let that happen again, I told myself. The night before game 13, I settled on a strategy for how I would close out the match. All I needed was one more point in the next four games—which I could secure with either two draws or one win. I had the white pieces, and I badly wanted to play for a win and finish off Xie right then and there, but I stopped myself. Xie needed a win much more than I did. And I was sure she'd play something sharp to try to convert with the black pieces. The smart move, I decided, was to play for two results. Better to let Xie take the risks.

I showed up to the board the next day more exhausted than I had ever been, operating purely on nervous energy. I took a deep breath and said to myself, *This is just another game.* Then I made my opening move. I expected something new from Xie, a King's Indian Defense maybe. But that's not what I got. Instead, she went with the same Grunfeld she had played two games before. That's when I knew I had her. Lev, Judit, and I had prepared something for exactly this line, something I hadn't gotten the chance to use yet. I just needed to stay calm.

Pieces started flying off the board very early on, and by the fifteenth move, I got Xie into an endgame in which I was clearly better. I found a tricky tactic on move 20, which earned me a piece. After that, there was nothing left for Xie to do. She played only four more moves before throwing in the towel. I knew how difficult it must have been for her, and I was impressed with how well she handled her defeat. "Congratulations," she said, like a real class act. "You are now the world champion." *World champion*—nothing had ever sounded so sweet. I politely thanked her, holding my emotions back for just a few more seconds before finally, at long last, letting loose that torrent of emotions submerge me. I felt tears well up in my eyes and an uncontrollable smile take over my entire face. It was fulfillment and joy in its purest form, and it made everything that came before—all the disappointment and sacrifice—seem so endlessly worth it.

Everything happened quickly after that—faster than I could even process. The playing hall, which had been pin-drop silent for hours, exploded with cheers and applause. My father—who had only just arrived in Spain—ran onto the stage to hug me and swing me around. Within seconds, I was rushed out into a lobby full of television cameras and flashbulbs and microphones, answering questions in multiple languages and shaking hands and posing for pictures.

It wasn't until I saw the wreath that the magnitude of what was happening really hit me. It's tradition that world chess champions receive a large laurel wreath to commemorate their victory. Having a wreath of my own had been a dream of mine since I was a little girl, looking at pictures of Botvinnik and Tal and Fischer flush with victory wearing that giant ring of foliage around their necks. Standing there as FIDE's president lowered that beautiful wreath over my head, a fusillade of camera flashes igniting the room in light, it occurred to me that I was now one of those champions, and that soon it would be my picture that some young dreamer would be looking at with awe and envy.

In Jaen, I reached the summit of my playing career. I'd shown up all of those critics who thought I couldn't hack it in female-only competitions. And I did it in historic fashion, becoming the first Hungarian of either gender to win a classical World Chess Championship and the first person to ever achieve the "triple crown," holding the blitz, rapid, and classical world championship titles at the same time.

I spent the next few days in a kind of trance, celebrating with my parents, Judit, Lev, and Cobi in Jaen. But once that initial euphoria tapered off, a feeling of vague uncertainty crept in. I knew that once the party was over, my family and I would go our separate ways, and I'd head back to New York to confront a question I wasn't sure how to answer: What now?

TWENTY-FOUR

For the first time in my life, I had nothing concrete to work toward, nothing on the horizon to keep me focused and organize my days. I was no longer a striving chess player chasing a championship. I was the world champion. And it would be years before I would have to defend my title. At first, it felt freeing. There was finally time to pursue projects I had been putting off for years. I was teaching myself to cook Indonesian food and some of my other favorite cuisines, and learning to speak Hebrew at an Ulpan in Manhattan—my seventh language at the time. Often on weekends, Cobi and I would go dancing at one of the Russian restaurants and clubs in Brooklyn, like Rasputin or Odessa. And we'd take regular trips to Israel and Hungary. We also traveled to Cancun, which was the first real vacation I had ever taken in my life.

But before long, the lack of routine became disorienting and, at times, unfulfilling. On a typical day, Cobi would go off to work, and I'd find myself alone in the apartment with only our cat, Buba, to keep me company.

It's not like I didn't have goals I wanted to achieve. I was as determined as ever to raise the profile of professional chess in some way, but I had no real strategy for getting there. I didn't even know where to start. Cobi and I were also trying to start a family, which was proving more challenging than we had imagined. My first pregnancy ended in a miscarriage. And we struggled to conceive for a while after that.

By the time Maurice Ashley called that summer, I was hungry for a new project to sink my teeth into. Maurice was one of the most funny and outgoing people on the New York chess scene. And I had held him in very high regard for years. He was one of America's most recognizable chess players, and had gained some much-deserved notoriety for his high-energy style of chess commentary. I also really admired the work he had done in the New York City public school system. At that time, he was overseeing the Dark Knights at Mott Hall School in Harlem, a middle school team that he had founded years earlier and that he would lead to multiple national championships during his tenure.

He called me that day to ask me to join him at Mott Hall. The school was looking for someone to teach chess and critical thinking to fourth and fifth graders, and he thought I'd be a perfect fit. It was one of those aha moments for me. I had wanted to make an impact on the larger culture of American chess. It hadn't really dawned on me how much could be achieved by engaging with young people at the community level. Seeing what Maurice had done at this underprivileged upper-Manhattan school—the way he had changed the lives of so many young people and welcomed them into the chess world—was an inspiration.

All of a sudden, ideas and aspirations that had been developing in mind for years came into focus. I had enjoyed teaching chess ever since I started coaching my sisters when they were children back in Budapest. I saw it as the family business in certain ways, since both my parents were educators who had spent careers working with disadvantaged kids. My father had instilled in me a deep belief that any healthy child could achieve greatness, if given the right guidance and support and opportunities. I had been the beneficiary of that philosophy since I was a little girl. Now I had my chance to pass on that same gift. I accepted the position sometime that summer, and started reading up on critical thinking. By the fall of 1996, I was teaching two classes three days a week, and doing some after-school sessions as well.

Most, if not all, of the kids were from disadvantaged minority communities, and although some of them had learned how chess pieces move, most didn't know how to play. They were in the same situation I was as a three-year-old sitting at our dining room table for my first chess lesson with my dad. And with a few modifications, I used the same techniques to teach them the game as he had used on me. We started with king against king. Then we played pawn wars. And within a few weeks, they were playing chess.

It was a completely new situation for me, standing in front of a room full of kids, teaching in English, finding ways to hold their attention and keep them motivated. But I was surprised at how naturally it came to me. Occasionally, I'd call my father and ask for advice, but for the most part I knew what to do. Watching him and my mother homeschool my sisters, and being homeschooled myself, I had absorbed so much of their technique without realizing it. And by the time I was teaching a class of my own, my instincts were fairly sharp.

It may not have been easy work, but it was so incredibly energizing. Initiating these kids—many of them young girls—into the world of chess and seeing the sense of mastery and self-worth it gave them was deeply meaningful for me. And I knew that, for the rest of their lives, their first memories of chess would be of the female grandmaster who taught them the rules. It wasn't about upsetting gender stereotypes anymore. I was preventing those stereotypes from taking hold in the first place, one class at a time.

I got the sense early on that I was doing a decent job with the kids, at least for a first-year teacher. But I had no idea just how quickly they were progressing until that December. The school's other middle school chess instructor and I decided to host a friendly match—his students against mine. We'd been assigned our students randomly, and most of them had started the school year knowing nothing about chess, so I was curious to see how our classes stacked up against each other. I was surprised that the results weren't even close. My kids won 27–2.

It was the first time I realized that education might be a vocation, something that I'm meant to do. As a girl, I used to have actual dreams about the chess school I would open one day and the classes of young pupils I would teach. I had forgotten about those dreams somewhere along the way, but it all came rushing back to me that year at Mott Hall. By the end of the school year, I knew that my next project would be to open up my own chess center.

I asked friends in the neighborhood, to see if they'd be interested in chess lessons for their kids. That's when I got a call from Mr. Musheyev, an older Uzbeki man whose daughter and six-year-old granddaughter, Elina Kats, lived near me in Rego Park. He had heard about my plan for a chess school, and he promised to find me at least a dozen students, starting with Elina.

With his help, I rented a space in a nearby Georgian synagogue. And by February 1997, I was teaching two dozen or so kids, most of them ages five to seven, every Sunday. I set up two classes, one for absolute beginners and one for kids who knew a little something already. I assumed it would be just a slightly different version of what I'd been doing at Mott Hall. I hadn't anticipated that teaching a group of children this young requires its own specific skills, the most important of which was patience. Repeating things multiple times, making sure everybody is following along, or just keeping the room's attention—all of it could be trying. And I left some of those early classes frustrated that I hadn't achieved more, or that I let a few troublemakers derail the lesson a bit.

I had been so successful at my job for so long that feeling like a novice at something—and especially something as hard as teaching young children—wasn't easy. Never once did I feel discouraged, though. It took a few months, but I eventually got the hang of it, and once that happened, going to those classes each week was something I looked forward to.

One of the biggest things I learned in those early classes was how to lead kids toward the right answer by asking the right questions—as opposed to simply showing them where they went wrong. This is something I had heard my father talk about for years, but it didn't really sink in until I had students of my own. It's amazing how a simple question like "Where do knights like to be?" or "What's the only piece that doesn't move backward?" can get someone's thinking headed in a completely new direction. And that look on a student's face at that moment of epiphany, when their eyes widen and a smile creeps across their mouth— it's one of the best parts of teaching.

I began to see chess through the eyes of a beginner again, and I couldn't believe how much I discovered. Before I started teaching, I would never have thought to describe the queen as a combination of a rook and a bishop—which is how it was often explained in the beginner books I was now reading. I imagine it's similar to what a native language speaker experiences when teaching her mother tongue to nonspeakers for the first time.

What I really hadn't anticipated was the amount of time I'd be devoting to parent management—something I had never been responsible for at Mott Hall. After each class, many of the parents would rush up to me, wanting to know how their child was progressing or whether they had talent or simply to check in. Most of them were perfectly nice; it simply wasn't an aspect of the job I had planned for, and just like teaching itself, it required a kind of patience and open-mindedness I was only starting to develop.

That May, New York hosted yet another historic chess event—
one that captured the world's attention even more than the match
at the World Trade Center. That's when Kasparov sat down for
a rematch with IBM's supercomputer Deep Blue—the strongest
chess computer in the world at the time. Computers still hadn't
measured up to the best humans, a fact Kasparov made clear the
year before, when he defeated an earlier version of Deep Blue. But
the computer he faced in New York that spring was considerably
stronger. And the event, which took place in a midtown skyscraper,
was covered in the press as the ultimate showdown between human
and computer—which it was.

My old friend Frederic Friedel was working as a consultant for
Kasparov during the match, and he invited me to come and watch
it all unfold.

I was genuinely curious about what was about to happen. There
were still skeptics in the chess world who believed that computers would never have the capacity to beat humans in chess. But I
wasn't one of them. I just couldn't be sure if this version of Deep
Blue had made the leap, and I was as excited as anyone to find out.
Before the match was underway, Frederic gave me a quick peek of
the room where they were housing Deep Blue, which felt like being
backstage at a big rock concert. It was a giant machine, housed in
these two black rectangular cabinets that were about as tall as I was.

Kasparov played in a closed room across from a technician who
would make Deep Blue's moves on a physical board after reading
them from a computer screen. And there was a separate theater,
where an audience could follow the games on video screens.

I happened to be there for the infamous game 6 in which
Kasparov stormed away from the board after losing. It was a power-
ful moment. The world champion played a risky variation of the
Caro-Kann Defense that he believed would trip the computer up.
Refuting this particular line would require the Deep Blue to offer
a knight sacrifice—the kind of intuitive, feel-based move that, at

the time, was believed to be outside the capacity of cold, calculating computers. To the amazement of many—Kasparov included—the computer found the right move. Garry was forced to resign after just nineteen moves, and Deep Blue was declared the winner.

To many of us at the time, it looked like Kasparov had simply blundered or forgot the opening theory. I'm even quoted in the *New York Times* story as believing he didn't try his best. But in retrospect, it's clear he simply underestimated what the computer was capable of and paid a steep price. For a long while after that, he insisted that some sort of human interference was at work in Deep Blue's play, which caused quite a controversy. From that day on, the debate over whether computers could eclipse humans in the game of chess was over, and I was glad that I had the closest thing to a front-row seat.

By the fall of 1997, I had enough interest in my classes to open the Polgar Chess Center in a dedicated full-time space on Saunders Street, just south of Queens Boulevard in Rego Park, where I lived. More than just a venue for my classes, the center was a meeting place for chess players, where anybody could come to play a casual game with friends or simply hang out and analyze. We'd hold our own tournaments—some with as many as sixty players—and we practically never took a day off.

Watching my childhood dream take shape right before my eyes was exhilarating. But it wasn't without its own share of stresses. After all, I wasn't just teaching; I was running a business, paying rent and utilities and a part-time receptionist. I had to worry about the fire code and accounting and marketing. I spent as much as I could afford on advertising, buying space in magazines like *Chess Life*, as well as some of the city's Hungarian and Chinese and Russian publications. We even opened a store within the chess center, where we'd sell things like chess sets and books and clocks. Between the prize money I had earned from the world championship and Cobi's salary, I knew we had enough of a financial cushion to get the enterprise up and running. After that, it was anyone's guess if we'd succeed. I knew I'd never get rich doing this. This was a passion project, pure and simple. But I at least wanted it to sustain itself.

Even as I worked furiously to get the chess center off the ground, I had my next championship match in the back of my mind. Xie Jun had clinched the challenger spot that year, setting up a rematch between the two of us. Technically, FIDE should have notified us by that summer about when and where I would have to defend my title. But, as usual, it was behind schedule, struggling to find sponsors, and not doing all that much to speed things along. It was a story I'd heard before. I decided to go on with my life, continue to work on my business, and bide my time while FIDE got its affairs in order.

Walking to the chess center one afternoon, I bumped into my old friend Paul Truong on the street. I had gotten to know him back at the New York Open in the 1980s, and we always liked spending time with each other. He had retired from competitive chess years before. Seeing him again after all of this time made me nostalgic. I was pleased to find that he was his same exuberant self, always smiling and laughing and full of energy. As it turned out, he was living just a subway stop away from me in Forest Hills. We exchanged numbers, and I encouraged him to come visit the chess center, which he did a few times. Then he just stopped showing up. I called him once or twice to check in on him, but he never answered. I tried not to take it personally, but I missed having him around.

Cobi and I hadn't given up on starting a family. And in the summer of 1998, I finally became pregnant. In many ways, it made everything very simple. All of a sudden, championship titles and playing venues and prize funds seemed less important. I had one job above all others, and nothing else even came close. I really enjoyed being pregnant, becoming a vessel for another life, nurturing a new human being into existence—it all felt miraculous. I had heard about all of the ways pregnancy can be uncomfortable and exhausting, the morning sickness and backaches and so on, but I felt almost none of that, or at least not enough to really mind. I was just happy. It helped that I was in the best physical shape of my life. In fact, I maintained a pretty strenuous workout regimen well into my pregnancy.

I also kept up a hectic schedule at the chess center, teaching classes and running tournaments, while still making time to prepare for the match. Lev came to New York that winter to train with me at our apartment, and I'd play practice games with Maurice or Joel or one of my other local sparring partners, reaching past my growing round belly to make my moves. For those first few months of pregnancy, it felt like everything I had ever dreamed about had come to me all at once. I was busy with work I cared about deeply, preparing to defend one of my three world championship titles, and overcome with gratitude and excitement for the child growing inside me.

It was not long after that when FIDE finally came knocking with some news of their own—none of it good. I had been waiting to hear about three specific issues: the location of the world championship match, the amount of the prize, and the date. On all three counts, FIDE had managed to break its own rules and put me in a serious bind.

First there was the timeframe. After dragging its feet for almost a year, FIDE wanted me to play in late March or early April, just a few months away, and around the time I was expected to give birth. Championship matches are also supposed to occur in a neutral country, which, in our case, should have excluded Hungary, China, and, one could have argued, the United States. Yet FIDE had chosen a venue in China—where Xie was both a national celebrity and a darling of the communist establishment. And then there was the prize money—$100,000—which was only half of the minimum required by the regulations.

I was livid. Did the higher-ups at FIDE expect me to agree to these conditions? This wasn't just a flagrant violation of the rules and norms of championship chess; it was an insult—to me and to all of the women in my profession. The implication was that the Women's World Championship is so unimportant that I should be happy it was occurring at all. That they weren't willing to make any allowances for my pregnancy added a new dimension to it all. Did they really expect me to put my life on hold indefinitely until they finally got around to doing their jobs and scheduling my match? Would they have liked me to ask permission before trying to start a family?

These were the thoughts that raced through my mind when I first heard the news. When that initial wave of anger subsided, though, I started figuring out how to push back. I had learned enough during my first year as a small business owner to know that there was always room for negotiation. I'd be willing to compromise on the prize fund and, if push came to shove, maybe even the venue. But there was no way I could agree to a match so close to my baby's birth.

FIDE wasn't interested in negotiating. As they saw it, having a baby was my choice, and if it got in the way of playing in a championship match, then that was my problem. I wasn't asking for special treatment. FIDE had already broken the rules by failing to schedule the match in a timely manner. It was clear they weren't in a rush. So why insist on holding the event during the few weeks when it was impossible for me to play? They pretended they were giving me a choice, but it was no choice at all. They were stripping me of the title that was rightfully mine by any interpretation of the rules, and they were using my pregnancy to do it.

At some point, I just had to stop fighting and accept my fate. I was out of options. I did end up taking FIDE to court and winning, so at least their misdeeds were on record. But by then, my world championship title was long gone. I had had enough of professional chess.

———•◦•———

Everyone tells you that your first baby will be life-changing. But there's no preparing for what it actually feels like. More than any other event in my life, Tom's birth in March 1999 marked the beginning of a completely new chapter. From that day on, I was a parent. And everything that came before it felt like another life. Especially in those early months, this beautiful baby boy was the object of nearly every thought, every feeling, every worry, everything. It all felt so natural, even when it was difficult—and it could be difficult. I was used to having complete control over my days, the goals I pursued, the things I did. Now he was in charge. And he liked getting his way, particularly when he was hungry, which was often. The first couple of months, I was nursing up to ten times a day. Despite how daunting and unforgiving those times could be, I still look back at them with great joy.

My mother came over from Budapest to stay with us for the first month. I don't know what I would have done without her. Half the time, I felt like I was guessing at what to do and hoping I wasn't inflicting any lasting damage. Watching my mother change him, rock him to sleep, or simply sit with me as I fed him or bathed him assured me everything was going to be okay.

A month after I stopped nursing Tommy, I was pregnant again. I remember how lucky we felt. It took so much trying and disappointment before I became pregnant with Tommy, and now it was happening again, without us even having to think about it. It was a gift.

When Leeam was born the following November, I already felt like a natural. All of the anxiety I had with Tommy was gone. It amazed me how quickly I adapted to my new circumstances. Just two years before, my life was a serious, adult affair. I was spending so much of my time in silent rooms, engaged in quiet intellectual dramas over the chess board. Now I spent my days surrounded by my own young children and the students at the chess center. Life was a lot messier and louder and more emotionally draining, but also so much richer. None of it seemed like work. Being a parent, being a teacher, running a business—these were labors of love in the truest sense, and there was nothing else in the world I'd rather be doing.

TWENTY-FIVE

I always saw the Chess Center as part of a larger project. I wanted to raise the game's profile in the United States, and getting more kids—and especially girls—interested in chess at an early age was a way of advancing that goal. I knew it was a long-game strategy. But I was confident that if I reached enough kids, some of them would carry their passion for chess into adulthood, and potentially help bring the game into the mainstream. I could see that something similar was happening with soccer in those years, a sport that was slowly gaining in popularity in the United States thanks mostly to the growing number of kids taking it up. There was no reason why something similar couldn't happen with chess.

This was only part of the strategy, though. I also wanted to get people talking about chess right away—not years down the road. I had seen how Kasparov's matches with Anand and Deep Blue had been covered as front-page news. My idea was to put together a big event somewhere in the city in the hopes of generating some buzz. Elite invitational tournaments didn't exist in New York at that time. And as someone who had played in more than my fair share of these events—and had at least some experience organizing them—I felt I needed to do my part to fill the void. When I told this to my friend Gabriel Erem, the founder of *Lifestyles* magazine, he quickly arranged an introduction for me with the city's sports commissioner, Ken Podziba.

Ken got on board almost immediately. And within a few days, he had secured the backing of Mayor Rudy Giuliani, who agreed to make an appearance during the tournament's final round to award medals to the top finishers. That's how the first Mayor's Cup came into existence.

The nine-day event would take place in the summer of 2001 at the Elmhurst Hospital auditorium in Queens. Of course, it's not like I had a lot of time on my hands. When the Mayor's Cup started to take shape in early 2001, Tommy was about to turn two, and I was still nursing Leeam, who was just a few months old. I also had a chess center to run. So there was no way I was going to pull the tournament together on my own.

For some reason, I thought of Paul Truong. He had been in the back of my mind since our serendipitous run-in on the street in Queens a few years before, and especially since he disappeared mysteriously not long after. I remembered that he ran his own corporate marketing business. And as a veteran of big tournaments himself, he seemed like someone who could help me get the Mayor's Cup off the ground. He hadn't picked up the last few times I had called him. But I figured it was worth another try. If nothing else, I might find out what happened to him.

This time, he answered the phone. I made it clear there were no hard feelings for his disappearing act, and that I missed having him around at the chess center. He apologized for losing touch. He told me he had been going through a divorce. His wife and two children now lived in Florida, and he was spending as much time as he could down there with them, while still running a business in New York. Given how hectic his life had become, I didn't think he'd have any interest in helping me with the Mayor's Cup. As it turned out, he loved the idea. "Anything you need, just name it," he said with characteristic enthusiasm. "I'll make the time."

Paul and I worked well together right from the start. I loved how much energy and positivity he brought to everything we did, even when things weren't going as planned. He was thirty-five, just four years older than me. And his time in corporate America had made him adept at bringing complex projects to completion, on time and on budget, while still having fun. He is also a parent and knew the demands of having two young children at home to take care of, which was a godsend, especially as we got closer to the tournament.

What I liked most about him was that we understood each other and, even more important, trusted each other. When I told him about my long-term vision for changing the face of chess, he got it immediately and started firing off ideas for how to get us there. I should be doing simultaneous exhibitions and publicity matches and hosting girls-only tournaments all across the country, he told me. The way he saw it, I was the only former world chess champion living in the United States, and I could use that status to become an ambassador for the game.

From that moment on, I knew I'd found a visionary partner, someone who shared my ambitions and had the know-how and temperament to help me achieve them. He was what had been missing from so many of my endeavors since coming to the United States. I had spent years maneuvering my pieces onto the right squares, but I still didn't have a plan—and Paul did. He knew how to make things successful, and how to tell a good idea from a bad idea. And he believed in my vision just as much as I did.

There are several things I'm very proud of concerning the Mayor's Cup. First, it made the New York commissioner of sports, Ken Podziba, start to take chess seriously as a game that could do good things for the city. There was also the publicity it garnered, earning coverage in *The New York Times* and *The Washington Post*, among other places. But the results of the tournament are what stand out most to me.

Tied for first place with the Ukrainian grandmaster Igor Novikov was a talented seventeen-year-old young woman from Brooklyn named Irina Krush. I didn't know Irina that well before the tournament, but watching her battle her way through a field that included multiple grandmasters, I knew she was special. Best of all, Irina's performance in that tournament made her the first American woman to achieve a grandmaster norm. It was almost too good to be true. I had become the first woman in the world to earn the GM title a decade earlier. And now, in an event I had organized, I was helping the next generation climb that same mountain.

Playing alongside Irina was a promising young American named Hikaru Nakamura, who, at thirteen years of age, showed an impressive understanding of the game. Hikaru's stepfather, Sunil Weeramantry—who Paul and I had known for years—was also there. Irina and Hikaru were exactly the sorts of players I was hoping the Mayor's Cup might elevate.

The event also reignited Paul's excitement for organized chess and marked the beginning of one of the most important relationships in my life. He visited the US Open chess tournament in Massachusetts not long after that, just to hang out with Sunil and also to reacquaint himself with the US chess scene. At the very last minute, Hikaru coaxed Paul into playing in the US Open Blitz Championship. Paul hadn't touched a chess piece in almost a decade, and mainly signed up on a lark. I only wish I could have seen the look on everyone's face when Paul actually won the event. After that, Paul's passion for the game was back at full force, which only added momentum to the projects we were undertaking together.

Paul and I were scheduled to meet with a potential sponsor near the World Trade Center that September. We thought nothing of it when, the night before, our contact called to push our nine o'clock meeting a couple of hours. I happened to be working out at my local gym when I saw the news on television. A plane had crashed into the North Tower. Like everybody else, I just assumed it had been a horrible accident, that some inexperienced pilot had lost control of his plane. The first thing I did was rush home and call Cobi. He was working in an office in Brooklyn, commuting from Queens on a subway that took him into Manhattan and under the World Trade Center. And, before my mind could even consider the idea of my children's father dying suddenly, he answered the phone. Fortunately, he had gotten to work before the first plane hit. Then I called Paul. I told him to turn on the television.

"What channel?"

"Any channel."

He got to a television just in time to see the second plane hit. We stayed on the line together, watching silently, unable to comprehend what had just happened. "We were supposed to be there this morning," Paul reminded me. For some reason, that thought hadn't crossed my mind until then. The phone lines went down a little while after that, crippled by the volume of calls coming into and out of the city.

The World Trade Center had been a special place for me since moving to the United States, a symbol of the city's grandeur and ambition and scale that never failed to impress me. Cobi used to work in one of the towers during our first few years of marriage, and I'd often meet him for lunch just so I could gaze up at those two miraculous structures. Getting to spend time at the top of the South Tower during the Kasparov-Anand match (a match that, coincidentally, began on September 11, 1995) is still one of my favorite New York memories, just as watching both buildings smolder and collapse that day remains one of my worst.

I got word to my family back in Budapest by email, letting them know that the kids and I were safe, and sat by the television for the rest of the day, waiting for Cobi to come home. It wasn't until another plane hit the Pentagon that the gravity of the situation set in. Like most people in New York that day, I felt like another attack could come at any moment. I knew Cobi may have to walk back from Brooklyn, and I tried not to think of all the things that might happen to him on the way. When he arrived a few hours later, I rushed to the door to hug him. From what he had seen on the streets, he knew that leaving the city wasn't an option. We'd have to wait it out in our home and pray that the worst of the attacks was over.

Bobby Fischer's remarks that day added a sad new dimension to an already horrific episode. He and I had drifted apart a little since our time together in Budapest. But we were still on good terms. Every now and then, I'd get a phone call from him, which was always a pleasant surprise. He had been completely gone from public life for years at that point. Then, on September 11, just hours after the attacks, he phoned a Filipino radio station to share his thoughts on what was happening. "This is all wonderful news," he told the interviewer. "It is time to finish off the US once and for all." He said he was happy about the attacks, and that it "just shows, what goes around comes around, even to the US." He ranted against the Jews and Israel, all with a note of cruel satisfaction in his voice.

It wasn't until December that the Western media learned of these remarks and released a recording. When I heard it, my heart sank. *Oh no, Bobby,* I thought. *What did you do?* I wanted to be angry at him, but mostly I was just worried for my friend. I had seen the early signs of his mania years before. I could see now that his demons had gotten the better of him, and I was afraid of what might happen to him. The American authorities were still after Bobby for flouting US law by playing in Yugoslavia back in 1992. He had managed to stay out of trouble by remaining underground.

Now he had stuck his neck out, announced where he was living, and effectively dared the United States to come and get him. Months later, I got a visit from the FBI. They asked if I had any idea where Bobby might be hiding, or where he kept his money. I didn't know anything, though.

Spreading poisonous, bigoted ideas at a time of national tragedy was bad enough. But Bobby also disgraced the game of chess. Here I was, trying my best to give chess a more positive image, to bring a more diverse range of people to the game. And now the most famous player on the planet has brought chess back into the public conversation in the worst possible way. It was a mess.

My relationship with Cobi also started to suffer. We had been dealing with a number of issues in the marriage for some time but were committed to making it work for the sake of the kids. I saw things differently after the attacks. Coming that close to death, and seeing with my own eyes how quickly it could all be over, filled me with a new sense of resolve. I started to envision my life without Cobi. A divorce would be hard on the kids, I knew. But it would only get harder as they got older. Better to make a clean break now.

We separated the following January, with every intention of getting divorced. Divorce in New York can be a complicated, drawn-out process even in the best of circumstances. That the city was reeling from the worst attacks in modern history didn't help matters. Cobi insisted on fighting tooth and nail over every point, particularly when it came to our finances and custody of the kids. It would be years before we were officially divorced.

The events of 9/11 were also a turning point for Paul. Up until then, he had been working with me during his spare time while still running his marketing business. He had long since fallen out of love with his day job, though. And after the attacks, he was determined to do something about it. That winter, he liquidated his business and became my full-time pro bono business manager. Reinvigorating chess in the United States was what he was meant to be doing, he told me. And for us to succeed, it would require all of his energies.

I was finally adjusting to life as a single mom in the summer of 2002 when I got a call from the executive director of the United States Chess Federation, Frank Niro. Frank had gone over the USCF's membership numbers, and was concerned with the lack of women and girls. Only a tiny percentage of the organization's members were female, he said. He wanted to change that, and felt that I could play a key role. I told him that he had come to the right place. We quickly set up a meeting, where Paul and I shared the plans we were hatching for attracting more girls to the game. Frank had a bigger idea.

As he saw it, however influential I could be as a former women's world champion, there was a limit to what I could do as a retired player. The next Olympiad was scheduled to take place in Calvia, Spain, in 2004. He suggested that I come out of retirement to lead the US women's team. No American team in history had ever won a medal at a Women's Olympiad.

And he wanted me to break that streak. I would have total freedom to recruit and train a team, and he'd provide whatever resources he could to support the project. I didn't know what to say.

It had been over six years since I had played an official classical chess game. And there was no guarantee that I could get myself back in playing shape—especially now that I was raising two toddlers on my own while running a business. If I couldn't get my chess to where it needed to be, I could end up doing more harm than good for the perception of women's chess. I also ran the risk of spoiling an otherwise stellar record in Olympiad play and ending my career with a very public disappointment.

Still, I couldn't deny that it was an inspired idea. Just a few years before, Mia Hamm had helped revitalize America's soccer culture by leading the US team to a legendary victory in the Women's World Cup. Medaling at the Olympiad could do something similar for chess, while also giving the sports world the thing it loves most: A comeback story.

I told Frank I'd have to think about it.

I spent the next couple of weeks turning the idea over in my mind and discussing it at length with Paul. We kept arriving back at the same thought: This might be the best opportunity we ever get to change how young women see chess in the United States. I'd be assuming a lot of personal risk, but the potential rewards were more than worth it. It was also perfect timing. Had Frank approached me before Paul had come back into my life, there was no way I would have said yes. Having Paul in the picture—someone whose judgment I trusted and who had a deep understanding of the chess world—made all the difference.

We went back to Frank with a detailed plan. I would agree to play, I told him, but only if Paul served as the team's captain and business manager. We weren't interested in a one-off project, either. We wanted to create the basis for a sustained, yearslong effort to help young women succeed in chess. To that end, we pitched him on a nonprofit, the Susan Polgar Foundation. We'd use the new organization to oversee the team's training operations and launch future projects for supporting female players around the country. As a career hospital administrator with an accounting background, Frank saw the value of the idea right away. He even offered to set up the foundation for us and help run it with us.

Once that was settled, Paul and I got to work finding the team. Our plan was to invite four players to a series of training camps in and around New York. Unfortunately, since nations were allowed to bring only four players to the Olympiad in those days—and since my participation wasn't in question—this meant one of our recruits would end up staying home. But that decision would come later.

Frank provided us with a list of the top-rated female players in the country. Naturally, the first name that jumped out at us was Irina Krush. I had gotten to know her well since the Mayor's Cup and had become even more convinced that she was a unique talent. We also tapped the woman grandmaster Anna Zatonskih—who had just come to the United States from Ukraine earlier that year—and the reigning US women's champion Jennifer Shahade.

The big surprise, however, was a Georgian-born player named Rusudan "Rusa" Goletiani. Despite being a woman grandmaster, Rusa wasn't on the USCF's top women's list, which seemed inexplicable to us. When we called Rusa, she explained that it was a clerical error she had been struggling to get fixed. Whoever entered her into the USCF system didn't recognize Rusudan as a female name. On paper, she was a man, as far as the federation was concerned. What's amazing is that it didn't take us long to find her. It's just that nobody had done a serious search for the best female talent until we came along—which was precisely the error we were trying to correct. Once we had our initial list of players, we scheduled our training camps and got to work.

In his capacity as a board member of the Susan Polgar Foundation as well as the Olympiad team captain, Paul headed up the marketing effort, putting together a whole array of promotional materials, including a "Dream Team" calendar with all five of us on the cover. One of his biggest successes was getting IBM on board. He had reached out to a friend of his who worked there and ended up convincing the company to donate six state-of-the-art laptops custom built for chess analysis and study. Our friends at Chess-Base agreed to provide us with their latest software and database.

I also took advantage of recent advances in online chess as part of my training program. My friend Marty Grund was running the Internet Chess Club at the time, one of the early online chess hubs, and graciously offered to create an anonymous account for me to play practice games online. The ability to play at any time, without leaving my living room, completely changed how I trained. I used to have to find players to spar against and schedule a time for us to be in the same physical location. Now I could hop online and play a quick ten-minute game while the kids were napping or while the oven was heating up, and try out a new opening idea without anybody knowing it was me.

One of the other projects we pitched to Frank was the creation of the first-ever national invitational tournament aimed specifically at young women. We modeled the event on the famous Denker Tournament, which was held each year in conjunction with the US Open. Founded by the grandmaster Arnold Denker, the tournament has brought together the best high school players from each state to compete for a single championship title each year since the 1980s. We wanted to do the same, but with only the top girls from each state—an idea that Arnold fully supported. The Denker's longtime organizer, Dewain Barber, also agreed to help, suggesting that we call our girls event "the Polgar," and that, unlike the Denker, we open it up to all female players age eighteen and under (provided they hadn't yet enrolled in college).

With the two of them on board and Frank in our corner, we didn't think it would be a tough sell. But before we could move forward, we needed the backing of the USCF's executive board, as well as the federation's delegates—most of whom were men, and few of whom warmed to the idea. In fact, most rejected it out of hand. The prevailing opinion was that girls didn't need their own tournaments. If they were good, they'd succeed on their own merits. Why should they get special treatment? More than a few board members pointed to my own career as proof of this position. After all, I had deliberately shunned female events for years, and yet it didn't slow down my career one bit.

It wasn't the first time I had heard this argument. But, as I tried to explain, the fact that I had chosen not to play in female-only tournaments didn't mean that these competitions weren't valuable. They were incredibly valuable, and I always thought so. They just happened not to suit my own personal career goals. Now my main goal was to bring more girls into chess, and on that front, female-only tournaments were a powerful tool. In fact, one of the main reasons there were more female players where I grew up was the existence of female-only tournaments. A lot of young girls wouldn't have pursued the game if it meant being one of the few females in a room full of young men. If the USCF was serious about increasing the number of girls taking up chess, creating venues where they felt more comfortable and accepted was crucial.

The federation also wanted to make the US competitive at the Women's Olympiad. Here too, events for young girls were an essential part of achieving that goal—if not immediately, then over the long term. If you boost the number of girls playing, I argued, you'll vastly increase the odds of finding the kind of elite talent that can medal at an Olympiad.

Again, I wasn't saying that women and girls should be limited to gender-specific tournaments—nothing of the sort. If they'd rather compete against boys, as I did, they should be free too. But by not giving them the option, we were creating a significant barrier to girls getting interested in chess and sticking with it throughout their lives.

The more I made my case, the more I understood that most of the people objecting to my idea weren't making a philosophical point. They just weren't interested in attracting more girls to chess. They liked things the way they were.

I honestly couldn't believe I was getting so much pushback. I had grown up in a place where gender bias and arbitrary oppression were part of everyday life. I had always assumed America was different, more committed to equality, more open-minded. I suppose they expected me to go away after that. But I didn't. And after months of intensive lobbying, the USCF finally agreed to let me move forward with the tournament. The annual Susan Polgar National Invitational for Girls officially became the first all-girls championship in the United States to be approved by the USCF.

Back in Queens, the Chess Center was having its best year to date in 2003, thanks almost entirely to Paul's help. I had been supplementing the business' finances with my own money since it opened its doors. With a divorce underway, that was no longer feasible. Paul's suggestion to implement a membership model changed everything. Instead of charging for individual classes or collecting one-off tournament fees, players could now buy one of several tiered memberships—either monthly or annually—the same as they would in a gym. It was one of those brilliant ideas that seems obvious in retrospect. But it took Paul's enthusiasm and organizational skills to make it happen. And within a few months, we were turning a small profit.

Paul also alerted me to the importance of location. When the chess center opened, we operated out of a basement in a building on a quiet street. We moved a couple of years later to a more central location, although we were still tucked away behind a veterinarian's office. Now that our membership model was generating some extra money, we could finally afford a more visible spot. And soon, we moved into a storefront, right next to the subway on Queens Boulevard. To capitalize on the pedestrian and motorist traffic, Paul slapped a coat of bright yellow paint on our front door and painted a giant chess queen. To people driving by, there was now no question what was going on behind that door. I can't tell you how many people walked in, shocked to learn that there had been a chess center right here in Queens this whole time—and that it was run by a former world champion.

As word got out, the quality of players that walked through our doors also improved. I recall a young man who stopped by for one of the super-blitz tournaments we used to host. When I looked at his paperwork, I saw that he had written down a rating of over 2600—which, if accurate, would have made him among the top players in the country. He was only around twenty years old, so I just assumed he was confused or maybe playing a joke. That's how I first met the Polish grandmaster Kamil Miton.

Future World Championship challenger Fabiano Caruana played his very first tournaments at the center when he was around six years old. And on weekends, a young Levy Rozman—who would go on to be one of the top chess influencers on the planet, better known today as GothamChess—would come by with his father to play in our tournaments.

I'd be lying if I said I knew which kids would go on to do great things in chess. But really, I didn't. Fabi, for instance, was a better-than-average player for his age, but by no means the best six-year-old I had seen. Other kids showed amazing intuition and focus as young children, but never did much with the game after high school. I remember Levy as a funny, energetic kid, but I wouldn't have guessed that he would emerge as one of the nation's biggest popularizers of the game.

What I hoped, however, was that by creating a place where kids could explore chess and get some experience in competition, and by fostering a community of young chess enthusiasts, I might be planting the seeds for a new generation of chess talent that could continue the work of bringing the game to more people. And on that count, I'm glad I was proven right.

TWENTY-SIX

The Olympiad team got a big morale boost after Garry Kasparov got involved. The head of the Kasparov Foundation, Michael Khodarkovsky, had caught wind of what we were up to and wanted to do what he could to help us succeed. Garry had made some negative comments about women in chess years before, and I think he wanted to show the world how much his thinking had changed since then.

The Kasparov Foundation provided some financial support, and Garry even participated in a couple of our training camps. He also liked our idea of creating a Denker-style event. To show how committed he was to the cause, he offered to arrange his own separate open event for girls. Not surprisingly, that event didn't meet with so much resistance from the USCF board—although it did take a little convincing. We used that momentum to pitch a third tournament, the Susan Polgar National Open for Girls and Boys, with the condition that, for the first year, it would be open exclusively to girls. Once again, we got the green light.

As we got closer to the Olympiad, it became obvious to me that I needed at least one practice event to get my sea legs under me. During the US Open that year in Los Angeles, Paul struck up a conversation with a major chess sponsor, the banker Frank K. Berry, who agreed to put together a special tournament for me and my teammates in his hometown of Stillwater, Oklahoma.

For someone who had spent years playing in illustrious cities like New York, Moscow, Paris, and Monte Carlo, Stillwater took some getting used to. I can remember driving past acres and acres of farmland on our way to the hotel from the airport, and the overwhelming stench of manure that filled my nostrils. I was a long way from Monaco, that was for sure.

A lot had changed in that time I played in an official competition, most notably the way games were timed. Throughout most of my career, we played with mechanical chess clocks, which gave each player a set amount of time to make all of their moves.

By 2003, many of the top official tournaments used digital clocks, which provided an increment with each move. Players would start with ninety minutes. And every time you punched your clock after a move, you'd have thirty seconds added to your time. This required an entirely new approach to time management than I was used to. Oddly enough, this was the very same technology that Bobby had shown me when I met him in Yugoslavia. So I was technically one of the first players to ever experiment with the device, mostly in blitz games with Bobby. But I had never used one in a serious classical event before. And it took me the better part of my first game to find the right rhythm.

After I got that first game behind me, I started to get comfortable. Really, it was like I had never stopped playing. Parts of my brain that I hadn't used in years seemed to switch back on. My concentration, my willingness to fight, my positional judgment— all of it was right there where I had left it. I won the tournament by a substantial margin.

We still hadn't decided which of us would be traveling to Spain later that year. The US Women's Championship, which was held that summer, would serve as a kind of qualifier. All four of my teammates entered the event, with the understanding that the player with the worst performance would have to sit out the Olympiad. Based purely on ratings points, Irina was the favorite going into the championship. But, to her credit, Jenn had one of the great tournaments of her life and walked away with her second US Championship title. Irina was close behind in second place, followed by Anna.

Rusa's fifth-place finish meant that she wouldn't be joining us in Calvia. It was a heartbreaking result. But she accepted it with grace and professionalism. She would continue to train with us all the way up to the Olympiad, on the off chance that someone got sick or injured. But barring that, she wouldn't be playing for the team. Rusa didn't let this setback slow her down one bit. She would go on to win the US Women's Championship the very next year, and eventually earned two medals for the United States at the Olympiad in Dresden a few years after that and became an IM.

———

Even after my win in Stillwater, there was still a lot of debate in the chess community as to whether I could stage a successful comeback. Paul kept a close eye on what top players were saying in the press and on the internet, and more than a few people thought that I was setting myself up for failure.

Lucky for me, I thrive on that kind of opposition. I'd go so far as to say that proving my critics wrong is my greatest source of motivation. I took all of that negative feedback and used it. And by the time we arrived in Spain, I was playing some of the best chess of my life.

Before we shipped off, though, Paul arranged for a publicity match between me and Karpov, modeled on the infamous "Battle of the Sexes" tennis match between Billie Jean King and Bobby Riggs. The event took place in Lindsborg, Kansas—"Little Sweden" as it's known—a town so small that it made Stillwater seem like a metropolis. We kicked things off with a huge parade, which the entire town came out to see. The format—two blitz games, two classical games, and two Fischer Random games—was designed for entertainment value more than anything. The final score was three to three, which, given who I was up against, gave me a pleasant surge of confidence going into the Olympiad.

Just a couple of weeks later, my teammates and I landed in Calvia and settled in for what would be nearly three weeks of intensive play against the strongest Women's Olympiad field in the event's history. Paul would arrive a few days later, due to some problems with his visa.

The day before my first game, I ran into a Hungarian chess fan at the hotel who I recognized from previous Olympiads. It wasn't a pleasant reunion. He told me how disappointed he was that I had decided to play for the Americans. I had betrayed my home country, he said, and I should be ashamed of myself. When I tried to brush him off, it only enraged him further. "You better hope you don't get paired with Hungary," he said. "If you sit down across from any Hungarian player, I promise, you won't live to see another day." Then he stormed off.

I had experienced nearly every form of harassment the chess world could muster by that point in my life. But I had never received a death threat before. I didn't know what to do. There was no way of knowing if he was serious or not. My first instinct was to report him to the tournament organizers. But I feared that raising a fuss would distract my team from the task at hand, which was to win the United States its first Women's Olympiad medal. There was also the chance that the US and Hungary wouldn't even face each other.

So I let it go. I turned my focus to chess and let everything else fade into the background, the same way I had done so many times before.

I struggled a little with the time control in my first game against Venezuela, just as I had in Stillwater. Complicating matters further was that the only bathrooms available to players were in the lobby of the casino where the event was being held. And with hundreds of women competing that year, there was often a line. When you're playing under such tight time restrictions, having to strategize about bathroom breaks can be a huge distraction.

Winning that game gave me some momentum. My official return to international competition had started with a victory. But it still took me a little while before I finally felt fully comfortable at the board. The next four games ended in draws—not an ideal result, but enough to keep our team in the running for a medal. My breakout moment came in game 6.

I was paired against my old rival, the Georgian Maia Chiburdanidze. Few people were as familiar with my playing style as Maia at that point. And I wanted to do something to shock her early in the game. Paul had the brilliant idea of playing the English, an opening that I had never used before in an official competition. Together, we found an aggressive variation we were confident Maia had never seen.

After eight moves, Maia and I had reached a fairly equal position. That's when I started advancing my g-pawn up the board toward her castled king. It was an unprincipled move, and not at all in line with my normal, positional style. But I could tell it unsettled Maia a little. The pivotal moment, however, came on move 14. I had found a very risky-looking combination that I believed would leave me better off, and it began with a knight sacrifice. What followed was an absolutely wild series of moves. After thinking for more than thirty minutes, Maia not only declined to take my knight, but she offered her own knight in return—a move she believed refuted my attack. I had anticipated this reply. And if my calculations were correct, I still had a path to victory. I continued my attack over the course of the next few moves, allowing Maia to capture my queen and several minor pieces as I bombarded her kingside, throwing caution to the wind in the hopes that my plan was better than hers. When the smoke finally cleared, most of our major and minor pieces had vanished from the board—and Maia's position was hopeless. She resigned on move 36. My play might not have been perfect. In fact, I made a slight inaccuracy near the end, failing to find the quickest way to victory. But I still look back on it as one of my most beautiful games.

Winning that game in such spectacular fashion was the clearest proof yet that I still had it, that all these years away from competition hadn't taken away the vision and toughness and instincts that made me successful in my twenties. Irina also won her game against Georgia—her third win out of the four games she had played so far. Anna happened to lose in that round. But she had already racked up four wins and one draw in her previous five games. From that point on, the US started to look like a medal contender for the first time.

I played with a lot of confidence after that, winning two more games over the next few rounds—one against Poland and another against Slovakia—and putting the US near the top of the standings with just three games to play. And as fate would have it, our next game would be against Hungary, where I would face my former Olympiad teammate Ildiko Madl.

Paul and the rest of the team already knew about the death threat I'd received. Like me, they had all spent the entire tournament hoping that we wouldn't play Hungary. Now that a face-off was inevitable, I had a serious dilemma on my hands.

First, I had my team to think about. Even before arriving in Spain, we had discussed the possibility that I might sit out my game against Hungary, provided it was an early round. I knew the game would rub a lot of people the wrong way. And, honestly, I had mixed feelings about playing against Ildiko. But this wasn't an early round. We were deep into the tournament now. And although China had an imposing lead, the US was still within striking distance of a medal. If I sat out the next game, we'd forfeit our best chance at achieving that dream.

This was also a matter of personal pride for me. In all my years playing in the Olympiad, I had never once missed a single game. To do so now, in response to the bullying remarks of some ignorant fan, was painful to even consider.

But I had more than myself and my team to consider. I had two young children at home who I was raising by myself. And there was a real chance, however small, that should I play in the next round, they'd be forced to grow up without a mother. This is not to mention the fact that my parents and Judit—all of whom lived in Hungary—might be in danger too. It was an impossible decision.

I called my parents and sisters and filled them in. They all had strong opinions of their own. My father, I remember, firmly believed I should play. But not everyone agreed. After discussing it for a couple of hours, I asked the four of them to vote yes or no. Should I play tomorrow, or sit the game out? They split 2–2. It was up to me.

I gathered my team members and Paul and announced that I would play—and that my decision was final. I told them to go get a good night's sleep and be ready to fight tomorrow.

That's when Paul pulled me aside. He expressed how proud he was of my decision, and that he wasn't going to let anything happen to me. "If they try to come for you," he said, "they'll need to go through me first." That night, he sat by himself on a chair outside my hotel room door, staying awake until the next morning just to make sure nobody tried anything. I was deeply touched but also completely unsurprised. Over the previous two years, Paul's selflessness and devotion to me had changed my life in so many ways. At every turn, he had put my interests before his own. And what he did that night reminded me how lucky I was to have him in my life. It wasn't just a gesture from a team captain or business partner. It was an act of love, and I knew it.

Nobody showed up that night. And there was no retaliation after I won my game against Ildiko the next day. My teammates showed amazing strength and focus in that round. Irina drew her game, and Anna won hers, keeping us in contention to win the US its first Women's Olympiad medal.

China still had a sizable lead going into the final round. But there was still a chance for us to close the gap and take silver if things broke our way. For that to happen, we'd need to score as many points as possible against our last opponent, Vietnam. Paul was especially pleased with the pairing. As a young boy growing up in Saigon, he had lived through the communist takeover. He and his family were forced into hiding to avoid persecution by the new regime. And he and his father only narrowly escaped by sea on a tiny wooden boat crammed with hundreds of passengers. He lived for more than six months in refugee camps, first in Malaysia and then in Indonesia, enduring the most abject conditions imaginable, and nearly dying of thirst and starvation before finally making his way with his father to the United States, where his aunt had sponsored them. For Paul, the chance to triumph over the country that had inflicted so much suffering on his family—and to do so on behalf of his adopted homeland—was profoundly meaningful.

We were by far the higher-rated team, so it should have been a relatively easy round, at least on paper. Yet somehow, Irina, Anna, and I each found ourselves in difficult positions after the opening phase of our games. Our situations were far from hopeless, but winning the round would be an uphill climb.

That's when the captain of the Vietnamese team approached Paul with a proposition. Vietnam offered a draw in all three games, a chance to finish the tournament right then and there. The tactic, known as a "package draw," was common in Olympiad chess during that era. And as captain, it was entirely Paul's decision. Given how our games were shaping up, it would have been reasonable for him to accept the offer and avoid what might have been a lackluster finish to the tournament. Several other members of the US delegation strongly urged Paul to do exactly that. But Paul wasn't interested.

He spoke in Vietnamese, so I only learned later what he actually said. "We didn't come here to play chicken chess" was the gist. "We will fight to the end." He said this loud enough for the Vietnamese players to hear, and they were visibly rattled by the remark. All of a sudden, I felt like I was in control of my own fate. I started to grind away, improving my position little by little until, eventually, victory was in sight. Both Anna and I won our games, which, together with Irina's second-board draw, gave us just enough points for a silver medal. For the first time in history, the United States was on the podium at a Women's Olympiad.

My own personal performance earned me two individual gold medals, one for best overall rating performance and the other for the most points scored on board 1. And, for the fourth time in my life, I played every game on board 1, all fifty-six of them, without giving up a single loss. I had gone years thinking that my life as a professional player was over. And I had risked not only my reputation but also my life to make this win happen. After all of that struggle and drama, it was a gutsy decision by Paul in the very last round that put us over the edge.

But there was another significant consequence of our Olympiad coup, one that I couldn't have possibly anticipated. Judit had gotten married several years earlier and was taking a break from competitive chess while she started a family of her own. As a result, after my Olympiad performance, I was once again the world's highest-rated active female player—and, most important, I had kept it in the family.

TWENTY-SEVEN

Days after my team members and I stood on that podium in Spain, the USCF informed me that the Women's Olympiad training program had been canceled. There would be no parade or party or even a press conference—just an unceremonious dismissal. The federation had gotten a little chilly toward us since Frank Niro stepped down as executive director the year before due to a medical emergency. Still, I expected our triumph at the Olympiad to at least buy us a honeymoon period.

The only reason I had even considered coming out of retirement was to help Frank fulfill his vision of getting more girls excited about chess. The federation's new guard didn't seem very interested in that vision. Some of the top brass would congratulate the team in public, sure. But their message to us was clear: *Don't do it again. There's no place for you here.*

As an added thumb in the eye, the USCF called off the cross-country publicity tour Paul had planned for the team in the months following the Olympiad.

If chess had taught me anything, it's that so much depends on timing. You can have the strongest position in the world, but if you don't strike when the iron is hot—if you delay your attack by even a single move—then everything you've worked for can slip away. Our silver-medal performance had made it clear to the world that American women can be a force in international chess. What is more, for the first time in history the world's top active female player called the American chess federation her home. If I didn't capitalize on all of this right away, then the moment would pass us by.

And so, Paul and I decided to organize our own tour. I would spend much of 2005 crisscrossing the country beating the drum for chess, and women's chess specifically. Paul's marketing acumen really had a chance to shine that year. We both knew that chess had a perception problem, that it was seen by many as a quiet board game. So we went looking for ways to present it as a big, eye-catching spectacle.

To date, the greatest solution to this problem has been the simultaneous exhibition, or "simul." Even people who have never played the game have probably seen images of some high-level chess player strolling around a circle of a dozen or more opponents, stopping at each board to make a single move over the course of two to four hours—one person, fighting off a room of people single-handedly, like a scene in a Bruce Lee movie. Contrary to what people might think, playing a simul doesn't require you to memorize every game and keep them separate in your head. It's really about finding the best move in each specific position as quickly as possible—almost like doing a series of one-move puzzles.

I did a few simuls that year, including a big one-hundred-board event with my sisters in Las Vegas, which brought the old Polgaria team back together. That July, I was back in Mexico City for a forty-five-board simul at the famous Casa del Lago in Chapultepec park. I remember how surreal it felt, seeing my image on these giant banners promoting the event—and in the very same park that my sisters and I had giggled about all those years before.

But Paul wanted to go bigger. If dozens of opponents are fun to watch, he figured, why not hundreds? In fact, why not take on the most players ever before attempted? The previous year, British IM Andrew Martin had set the record for most games of chess played simultaneously—321 in all. In the summer of 2005, I would attempt to break that record.

I loved the idea of displaying the athletic side of chess in such a dramatic fashion. It's an aspect of the game that's too often overlooked. In fact, the chess part wasn't what I was worried about. I had done hundreds of simuls since the time I was five years old. And I knew that, based purely on chess ability, I could easily manage at least 350 games against amateur players—even serious amateurs—without giving up too many losses or draws. But breaking the record wouldn't just come down to chess ability. First and foremost, it would be an act of physical endurance. I would need to be in peak physical condition just to stay on my feet for almost an entire day. And that's without factoring in the mental energy I'd be expending finding good moves over and over again. Luckily, I had been exercising pretty seriously for years at that point. And I figured all of those hours on the treadmill would serve me well.

The simul, which would take place at the high-end Gardens Mall in Palm Beach Gardens, Florida—and which was generously funded by the city—required months of careful planning and logistical problem solving. We would have to cordon off a large segment of the mall during prime shopping hours and would need teams of security officers to stand guard as the games continued into the small hours of the next morning. Paul and I worked with the organizers to scientifically figure out the optimal arrangement for the chess tables, to minimize the amount of walking I'd have to do. And we made sure to seat the players in order of strength as best we could, so that the games furthest away from me would be the most likely to end early, cutting down on the amount of ground I'd need to cover as the exhibition stretched on and the number of opponents slowly dwindled.

The simul wasn't the only item on my agenda that week. I spent the days leading up to it at a local network news studio filming one in a series of fourteen chess DVDs I was making with Paul Azzurro for his company ChessDVDs.com. This particular DVD was aimed at young beginners. We worked with an animation studio to turn the pieces into cartoon characters, each with their own unique personalities reflecting their role in a game of chess. The production would be the most expensive chess instructional DVD ever made, in no small part because of our animation and voice-actor costs. But the investment paid off. The DVD became a bestseller. It was also a huge hit with my boys, who for months would insist on watching it as entertainment every night before bed.

I happened to mention my world-record attempt to one of the news producers at the studio where we were filming. That chance run-in led to several segments about the exhibition on the next day's local news, which we were grateful for. Our biggest worry as the simul approached was that we wouldn't attract enough players to break the record. We had already spread the word around the chess community. But a little extra publicity was more than welcome.

I got to the mall at seven that morning just to sign autographs and greet players as they lined up to register. After 326 players had signed up, we decided to close registration and let the games begin. I made my first move at ten in the morning, and don't remember much of what happened after that. I took only three fifteen-minute breaks to eat a quick snack, use the bathroom, and drink some freshly squeezed fruit juice from one of the vendors. But other than that, the entire day went by as a series of chess moves. When the last game finally ended sometime after 3 a.m., the dozens of people who had stayed up with us erupted in applause. I had been so consumed by tunnel vision that I remember asking myself, *Where did all of these people come from?*

Just completing all of my games was enough to earn me the record for the largest simul. But that wasn't the only history I made that day. My 309 wins (I drew fourteen games and lost only three) set its own record, as did my overall score in those first 326 games of 96.93. Since we kept replacing players who finished early, I also got the record for most consecutive games played, which was 1,131—a record which was previously held by another female chess player, the Greek WGM Anna-Maria Botsari.

By the time it was all over, I had walked more than nine miles. My legs were numb and I could barely see straight. I still stuck around for a little while to pose for pictures and hand out the commemorative T-shirts the city had made for all of the participants. But by that point, all I could really think about was my bed. Paul, however, was up well into the next afternoon fielding press inquiries. And in the days after, major media outlets from *The New York Times* to *Sports Illustrated* were trumpeting my new records.

———•◦•———

That year, I would play another match against Karpov in Lindsborg, Kansas, as part of a Chess for Peace event, which included former Soviet president Mikhail Gorbachev as the honored guest. As with the previous Karpov match, the whole town (and then some) flooded onto the main road for a massive parade with a marching band and all kinds of elaborate floats—precisely the sort of big, eye-catching spectacle I had always dreamed of for bringing more attention to chess.

All three of us sat for a press conference after the parade, during which Gorbachev fielded questions about chess and global politics. I had never witnessed such a display of raw political talent up close like that. Even though his remarks had to be translated from Russian for the rest of the audience (he and I spoke only in Russian to each other), his ability to speak extemporaneously and answer questions with grace and humor was a sight to see. The city had worked with Gorbachev's people for weeks to get ready for his arrival, and the local tea house even prepared the former president's favorite blend, which they served in a unique teacup chosen especially for the occasion. At one point during the press conference, after noticing that neither I nor Karpov had been served any tea, Gorbachev kindly offered me his. The gesture got a chuckle from the press, but it put me in a tough spot. Although he didn't know it at the time, this was no ordinary beverage. It was presidential tea, a single cup prepared at great trouble to Gorbachev's exact specifications. To take it from him risked insulting my hosts. But Gorbachev kept insisting.

That's when Karpov, as quick as ever, chimed in with a chess joke. "You're in zugzwang, Susan," he said, referring to a position in which all possible moves leave you worse off. He was right. I accepted Gorbachev's tea, and the organizers quickly procured additional teacups before the press conference ended. In the weeks that followed, the photo Paul had snapped of this historic statesman serving me tea appeared in publications across the country, and even made the cover of *Chess Life*.

When a reporter asked me about my impression of Gorbachev as a person, I described him honestly as warm, considerate, and friendly—a comment that provoked him to kiss me on both cheeks in front of the press pool. As I pulled away, he corrected me that, in Russia, it's customary to kiss three times. Another roar of laughter came over the room.

Gorbachev got in one last laugh at the first game. Karpov had the white pieces. And as the event's honored guest, Gorbachev had agreed to make the first move—a tradition not unlike the ceremonial first pitch at a baseball game. "I'm going to make life difficult for you," he said to Karpov, as he played 1. g4, which is generally considered one of the worst opening moves in all of chess. Karpov laughed it off and started to put the piece back to its original square so that he could start the game in earnest. But Gorbachev intervened, reminding Karpov that in chess, there are no takebacks. As much as I dislike dirty tricks—especially from the Soviets—this one was at least in good fun.

As he was driven down the street after the match, Gorbachev spotted a bar and couldn't help himself from going in and meeting some of the locals—much to the chagrin of his security detail. He spent the better part of the next hour shaking hands and making jokes, like he was campaigning for office again, as his team of bodyguards, all in classic "men in black" attire, stood by nervously and waited for him to finish up.

Outside of big events like Chess for Peace, I was experimenting with new ways of bringing chess to a broader public. In addition to the instructional DVDs we were making, I was in the process of filming a documentary for the NatGeo cable network, which used my own life story career to explore the power of the brain. The project would take me back to Budapest to visit my family's old home and the local chess club, both of which are still there to this day. It eventually aired in more than a hundred countries in multiple languages. While touring the Amazon rainforest years later, Paul and I stopped in a small gift shop so that I could buy a pair of flip-flops. The woman behind the counter jumped from her seat the second she saw me, shouting my name: "Susan Polgar!" I was floored that a store clerk in the middle of a tropical wilderness had even heard of me. When I asked if she was a chess player, she told me no. But she had just seen my documentary on NatGeo.

———◦◦◦———

I looked at Paul differently after we got back from Spain. His chivalrous gesture at the Olympiad, standing guard outside my hotel room door that night, confirmed for me that our relationship was something very special. I had never been so close to anybody who wasn't my own blood. But he was more than my best friend. I saw him as my knight in shining armor—not just because of what he had done in Spain, but because of the way he swept into my life without warning and made me feel safe and appreciated. He was the one person other than my boys who I never tired of being around. I had been so distracted by all the battles we were fighting that it took me too long to see the obvious.

One afternoon, I invited Paul on a walk around Flushing Meadows Park. It was one of those picturesque early-autumn days when the leaves are just starting to change and the oppressive New York summer has given way to a vitalizing chill. I told Paul that I felt like a new chapter of my life was just beginning. My divorce from Cobi had just recently been finalized after years of legal squabbling. And for the first time in a while, I was excited about the future, and I wanted Paul to be a part of it. I could tell he knew exactly what I was getting at. Without saying a word, he stopped walking and turned to me. For just an instant, we locked eyes in a way we never had before, both of us smiling uncontrollably. Paul wrapped his arms around me in a great warm hug and kissed me.

"Of course I want to be with you," he told me. "I love you."

I really did feel like the protagonist in one of those romantic comedies my sisters and I used to watch in our hotel rooms as teenagers. The person I was meant to be with had dropped into my life at exactly the right moment, and after a series of adventures together as platonic friends and business partners, we both realized we were meant to be together all along. Within a few weeks, Paul and I were living together in his apartment just off of Queens Boulevard.

By the time the next Olympiad rolled around in 2006, it was clear I wouldn't be on the team. The USCF didn't exactly close the door on me, but they did ask that I qualify, which I took as an insult. If my rating—not to mention my performance at the previous Olympiad—wasn't proof enough that I belonged on the team, then I

didn't see the need to prove myself. Nevertheless, until their decision was official, I continued to train, making a conscious effort
to work on new opening ideas, keep my endgame skills sharp, and
stay abreast of what other top players were doing.

Once I knew for sure I was off the team, I didn't want all of
that work to go to waste. That was a major motivation for my playing in the 2006 Mayor's Cup. Once again, Paul and I organized
the tournament with the help of New York City sports commissioner Ken Podziba, who was by then serving under a new mayor,
Michael Bloomberg. And the prestigious New York Athletic Club,
where Paul and I were members, generously offered to host the
competition that June.

I invited some of the very best American players of the time,
including several members of the previous men's Olympiad team.
This made it the highest-rated double-round-robin tournament in
American history at the time. It also meant that I was the lowest-
rated player in the group.

Still, I went into the event with a lot of confidence, and
determined to show my strength, which is exactly what I did. By the
time Gata Kamsky and I sat down across from each other in round
8, we were tied for first. He was the highest-rated American player
at the time. I saw that game as my best chance to pull ahead and
win the tournament. So when I got a somewhat draw-ish position
with the white pieces, I kept pushing, eventually opening myself
up to a fatal attack. I finished the tournament in second place, only
half a point behind Gata. And as much as I would have preferred
to win, my strong showing sent a message that I could still go
toe-to-toe with the nation's best players, which was exactly what
I had intended.

My last event as a professional player was the Women's World
Cup in Dresden that July. I can't explain why, but it just seemed like
the right time to step back. I had achieved everything I had set out
to achieve. Continuing to train and travel and compete just didn't

make sense anymore. The tournament adopted an unusual knock-out format modeled on the World Cup in soccer, which was also being played in Germany that year. And it would include female players from thirty-two countries.

Playing against opponents like Germany's former women's champion Elizabeth Paehtz and Olympiad gold medalist and future women's world champion Anna Ushenina of Ukraine, I dominated the knockout event, winning six of my eight games without giving up a single loss.

My final game against Elizabeth—which would turn out to be my last game as a professional—was a real test of my mettle. The competition was held in the food court of a large shopping mall. And just minutes before the game started, a German reporter asked me for a quick interview, which I agreed to. I stepped away from the board very briefly and answered a few questions. When I returned, the computer bag I had under my chair had been stolen. To this day, I don't know if it was another player's team who did it or just a common thief. Regardless, nobody seemed to see where it went. It was one of the strangest experiences I've had at a chess tournament. And I went into that last game a little flustered. But after my first move, I snapped into a completely different mode. I became mono-maniacally focused on the task in front of me. It was a skill I had slowly developed over the course of decades, and could now summon so reliably that not even the robbery could knock me off-balance.

I won that last game, earning the United States its first World Cup trophy, a small soccer ball on top of a short wooden stand, in reference to the other World Cup, which was already under-way. Sadly, though, my brand-new laptop—and the thousands of files of chess research I had compiled over the years—was gone, as was Paul's passport, which was also in the bag. We were able to make arrangements with the consulate for Paul to get back into the United States.

But the process wasn't without some tense moments. When we arrived at customs back in New York, a number of officers pulled Paul into a room for questioning. It seemed that whoever stole his passport had used it to enter the United States a few days earlier. For years after that, Paul would routinely be stopped when entering the United States from abroad.

———•◦•———

The topic of marriage came up very early in my relationship with Paul. But neither of us saw any real need. We had both gone through divorces, although his was much less acrimonious than mine (I actually knew his ex-wife and got along with her quite well). We both knew we were committed to each other; we could feel it. A big wedding with a reception and a band just felt unnecessary, like we would be doing it for other people.

It wasn't until a meeting with my lawyer sometime in late 2006 that our view started to change. As we learned, getting married would make life a lot less complicated in many ways, especially when it came to my boys. Paul deeply wanted to be a full partner in raising Tommy and Leeam. That would be a lot simpler, from a legal standpoint, if he was my husband and not just my boyfriend. A few days later, at my lawyer's urging, we headed to the Queens courthouse to get our marriage certificate. My friend Andy served as our only witness.

Even though our "engagement" lasted just one weekend, Paul still found time to buy the perfect ring. It had a large diamond in its center, surrounded by thirty-two smaller diamonds, signifying the thirty-two pieces on the chess board. "That's you in the middle," he told me. "Commanding the pieces like a queen."

We celebrated with a small reception and photo shoot at my friend Jacqui's apartment in Manhattan, followed by a carriage ride through Central Park with the boys. It might not have been the most elaborate wedding, but to me it was perfect.

Back in Queens, the chess center continued to do a good business. Tommy and Leeam were taking an interest in chess by then and would come to work with me many afternoons. Tommy in particular was showing real promise, which of course made me proud. I first taught him the game when he was three, and he took a liking to it right from the start. By the time he started playing serious scholastic chess, he had developed a good sense for tactics. He also had a surprising amount of patience in endgames, which isn't common for young players.

I definitely wanted both of my kids to share my passion for the game, but I never forced the issue. It was good enough for me that they gave it a serious try. If they lost interest, that would have been fine—so long as they were interested in *something*. I might have considered homeschooling them or applying some of my father's pedagogical techniques if I had the chance. But it was never really an option. By the time Tommy and Leeam were school age, I was already sharing custody with Cobi. Between that and the demands of running a business, it simply wouldn't have been practical.

I will say that Tommy's early success with the game stirred up a new kind of pride in my chest, something wholly different from what I felt for my sisters or my students. He made it to the K–2 national championship at the end of 2006 in Orlando, which took place just days after Paul and I were married. It was just by coincidence that the NatGeo documentary crew was there on the tournament's last day to capture Tommy's amazing performance. For a lot of kids, having a film crew interviewing you between rounds and monitoring your progress would have been debilitating. But not Tommy. He won that tournament and gave the documentary a storybook ending.

Parenting is a messy business, and you can never be sure if you're giving your kids what they need to get on in life or if you're making some disastrous mistake. As I watched my firstborn child commit himself the way he did in that tournament and manage the pressures and emotions of competition, it felt like I had passed on one of the best parts of myself.

———◦•◦———

Where on Earth is Lubbock, Texas? That was my first thought after getting a call from Texas Tech University. One of the professors there, a geologist named Hal Karlsson, was a chess fan. And he wanted me to visit the campus for a simul and maybe a lecture. Lubbock is a small, remote college town. On the short ride from the airport to the university, there were cotton fields as far as the eye could see—long rows of fluff-topped bushes stretching endlessly off into the horizon.

The campus itself was absolutely beautiful, and everybody we met there was incredibly welcoming. But aside from the historic bed and breakfast where we stayed, I didn't get to see much of the place. In my mind, it was just a work trip like any other. And once I had finished up in Lubbock, I returned to New York with little expectation that I would ever come back.

I had mostly forgotten about the trip when I got a call from Hal. The university had done some market research, he explained, which revealed that my appearance there had left a strong impression. With the exception of the school's legendary football coach, Mike Leach, I was among the most popular people on campus. I was of course honored, but I sensed he hadn't called just to stroke my ego. I was right.

At Hal's urging, the administration had decided to start a chess program, and they wanted me to help build it from scratch. I flashed on that conversation with Frank Niro from a few years before, when he pitched his own "crazy" idea to me. This felt even crazier. I told Hal how flattered I was, and that I would have to think about it. I loved my life in New York. And even if I hadn't, the thought of uprooting my kids, my new husband—to say nothing of my business—to move to a college town in West Texas seemed far too radical to consider seriously. My kids were born-and-raised New Yorkers, and my life with Paul was just getting started.

Of course, the chess player in me knew that just because a move seems crazy on its face doesn't mean it isn't right. And after the initial surprise of the offer subsided, I started to give it some serious thought. Paul's reaction was a bit more positive than mine. We would spend the next week or so considering the possibilities and getting used to the idea of this fantastically different possible future.

The more research I did, the better the prospect seemed. I learned, for instance, that college chess was dominated by just a small handful of schools, with the University of Maryland, Baltimore County (UMBC) and the University of Texas at Dallas (UTD) at the top of the list. There was plenty of room for a newcomer to shake up the league, I thought. And if Texas Tech could pull off a rags-to-riches story, we could breathe new life into Division 1 chess, and maybe even inspire more schools to take the game as seriously as other sports.

Then I had a thought that broke everything wide open for me. I had been working for years to help bring chess into the mainstream—mostly by trying to ignite a passion for the game in students who were high school age and younger. And while I definitely moved the needle, I kept seeing promising young players give up on the game early in life. The problem, in almost every instance, was a lack of opportunity to keep going. At some point, kids must make a decision about whether to pursue chess seriously as a professional or go to college and start a career in some other field. Given how hard it is to make a living as a chess professional in America—or anywhere, for that matter—school and a job usually won out. Many of the best young players face this decision just as they're approaching the peak of their abilities, and even for them, continuing to devote the time needed to excel at chess simply isn't an option.

Paul experienced all of this firsthand as a top-ten junior player. He stepped away from the game after high school. But if he had been given a way to go to college *and* pursue a chess career at the same time, he would have done so without hesitating. And once we saw the Texas Tech offer as a chance to give young players a chance he never had, we were both on board completely.

Access to a serious college chess program could do for chess what NCAA sports had done for football, basketball, baseball, track: Give the best young players a place to go after their high school careers end. And where better to start such a chess program than at a school like Texas Tech, home to a well-known Division 1 football team, not to mention a basketball team led by one of the most legendary coaches in the sport, Bobby Knight? This was a place that took college athletics seriously and valued high-level coaching. And they were offering to put their resources and institutional knowledge toward creating a chess dynasty.

After that, the idea took on a life of its own in my mind. In America, it's common for top players in football or basketball or baseball to get a college education while still continuing to grow and compete at the highest levels. Why not open up a similar path for chess players? I could recruit some of the top young talents and provide them with top-flight chess training while also offering them a university education. In the process, I could help usher in a new generation of professional-level talent and nudge the game that much closer to the mainstream.

When I explained my reasoning to Paul, he knew I was onto something big.

"I guess we're moving to Lubbock," he said.

"I guess so!"

TWENTY-EIGHT

The move wasn't easy. Relocating Tommy and Leeam required another lengthy court battle with my ex-husband—and not long after my divorce had finally come through. Back in Queens, Cobi and I lived within a few blocks of one another, which made it fairly simple to share custody. Now that I was taking the job in Texas, I would have to get permission from the court. Thankfully, both of my boys were excited about the move. Honestly, I think they had gotten tired of shuttling back and forth between me and my ex.

Then there was the matter of finding a school for them and a house to live in. I would need to hand off most of the responsibilities at my chess center and find a way to manage the business from nearly two thousand miles away.

The one thing Paul and I had going for us was that we were wanted in Lubbock. Some of the faculty members went out of their way to ease our transition, advising us on where to live and helping us find a school for the boys. For their part, the university's administration assured us we'd have everything we needed to get the program up and running. The president at the time, Jon Whitmore—as well as provost William Marcy and senior vice provost James Brink—promised us several generous scholarships for recruiting young players. And all three collaborated with Paul and me in setting up a new institute within the university that would serve as the basis for the chess program.

I would helm the institute as director, in addition to my role as head coach of the Texas Tech chess team, with Paul running marketing and PR for the program. And to help ease our transition, Brink assigned us his longtime assistant, Peggy Flores. Early on, the administration took to calling the new organization the "Susan Polgar Institute for Chess" as a kind of working title. It was Paul who recognized the name's unfortunate acronym during a discussion with Hal Karlsson, the university chess club's faculty advisor. We added the word *Excellence*. And, with that, SPICE was born.

I was under no illusions about how long it would take to build a top university chess team. The school's existing team consisted of several amateur players, none of whom were even close to Division 1 ready. To qualify for Division 1 status, the average team rating had to be master level or higher. By the time I agreed to join the school, it was already too late to recruit any top-caliber talent for that academic year. Thankfully, our friends in the administration showed every sign that they were in this for the long haul, and they could tell we were as well. To demonstrate how serious we were about winning, Paul explicitly promised that we would make Texas Tech national champions within five years. And as a show of good faith, both he and I accepted lower salaries in our written agreement, under the condition that we'd be paid substantial bonuses should we win championships.

So yes, moving to Texas was a complicated, time-consuming ordeal. But the outpouring of support we got from the community removed any doubt that we had made the right decision. To help with my court relocation proceedings, a number of faculty and administrators gladly provided references on my behalf. The city of Lubbock embraced its new identity as a chess town, eventually installing a giant chess set at the city's airport next to a tourism poster boasting "You'll love our *knight* life." And the university built a beautiful chess park on campus, which featured stone chess tables and benches engraved with quotations from famous players— including my contribution: "Win with grace, lose with dignity."

To announce my arrival at the school and the creation of SPICE, President Whitmore presented me with a doctorate of humane letters and invited me to speak at the 2007 commencement ceremony. I never considered myself a shy person, but speaking in front of that many people proved to be one of the scariest moments in my career. The commencement audience was so large—over twenty-five thousand people in all—that TTU had to hold two separate ceremonies to accommodate the crowd. This meant I had to give my address twice in front of a packed house— once in the morning and again in the afternoon. To top it all off, the cable channel C-SPAN asked to televise my address—an opportunity that TTU and I couldn't turn down. The network chose only seven commencement addresses to air that year, including speeches by Oprah Winfrey and former president Bill Clinton. I was honored to have made the cut. Fearful that I'd sound too stiff if I read from a teleprompter, I instead worked from a list of bullet points. I opened with an obvious question I knew the audience was asking. "You may wonder," I said, "why did Texas Tech invite a chess champion to talk to you this morning?" Then I shared with them how, for me, chess is more than a game. It is a source of wisdom that informed so much of my life. And it is a vehicle for advancing the cause of equality. "It doesn't matter if you are a man or a woman. It doesn't matter what your skin color is. It doesn't matter what your religion is. It doesn't matter what your height, size, strength, or speed may be. When we play chess, there are two opponents, facing each other, each having eight pieces and eight pawns on a sixty-four-square chess board. How more equal can it be than that?"

After I finished, several reporters asked for a copy of my speech, and were shocked that I hadn't used one. They had to transcribe it from the video.

Looking back at the footage, I'm surprised I looked as calm as I did up there at the podium. The truth is, I was petrified. In fact, I still get nervous just thinking about it.

Perhaps the biggest surprise was just how much Paul and I fell in love with Lubbock, having spent so much of our lives in big cities. The four of us moved into a spacious two-story house at the end of a cul-de-sac not far from the campus, with a giant backyard—something we could have never afforded back in New York. It wasn't long before a new member of the family—Paul's fifteen-year-old son, Paul Jr.—joined us.

Really, it was an ideal environment for raising a family. There was a small-town country charm to the place, like something out of a Hallmark movie—a kind of quaint politeness in how people conducted themselves. Everybody seemed to know each other, from the mayor of the city on down to shop owners and groundskeepers. We ended up adopting several dogs—at one point we had five. Lubbock's famous drive-in movie theaters became a favorite weekend destination for me, Paul, and the boys. And after work, the five of us would often ride our bikes to a small lake near our house. Even the restaurants were good, which came as a pleasant surprise. A sworn pescatarian for years, I soon developed a taste for steak and BBQ, and it didn't disappoint (this was cattle country, after all). At night, a great blanket of stars would wrap itself across the sky, and the place would go dead silent, with none of the distant sirens and honking car horns we had grown used to in New York. I couldn't have chosen a better place to start over again with my new husband and our three boys.

The campus itself was beautiful and sprawling, with some of the nicest facilities I had ever seen at a college. As someone who likes to spend time at the gym, I was blown away by the outrageously elaborate athletic complex, which had every kind of machine you could imagine, and featured an enormous "lazy river" you'd expect to see at a water park.

Work was a different story. Not only had I never had a boss before or worked a regular full-time job, but I had never been part of a large organization, and certainly not at a public institution like Texas Tech. All of a sudden, my days were filled with meetings and budgets and formal proposals on university letterhead. For most of my adult life I had made my own decisions and put them into action at whatever pace I pleased. Now every idea and public statement, no matter how minor, had to be filtered through layers of bureaucracy. Even small tasks like renting a car or booking a hotel room required official approval. I understood why this was necessary, of course. This was mostly taxpayer money we were spending, and I was technically working for the state of Texas. But that didn't make the transition any easier. I've never been good at sitting still, especially when I have a job to do. It was our assistant Peggy who showed me that navigating the ins and outs of campus politics was now a big part of my job. Her institutional knowledge proved invaluable, especially that first year, when we were still learning the rules of the game.

We were starting from scratch that year. In fact, one of my first official acts was to order some chess boards and sets, since we didn't have any. Upon our arrival, the university set us up in a two-room office above a neighborhood bank while they found us something more permanent on campus. And once we were settled, Paul and I went to work hashing out a recruitment strategy. It was too late to bring on any new titled players for that coming year, that much we knew going in. But we were looking further ahead. As Paul and I saw it, convincing elite players to move to Lubbock would be a heavy lift, even with me running the program. But if we could secure just one top college-age player, we could turn a few heads and create a name for Texas Tech within the chess community. Our plan, of course, was based on the assumption that the university would guarantee at least a few scholarships for the coming years, so that we could offer any potential player up to four full years of funding.

It was sometime in our second semester when we got the bad news that Jon Whitmore would be stepping down as the university's president, and that William Marcy and James Brink—two of our biggest allies—might soon be sidelined in the new administration. Their commitment to the chess program was one of the main reasons we had come to Texas Tech in the first place. And there was no way of knowing if the incoming administration would give us anything close to the support they had. There was talk that our scholarship money was in danger, which would make it next to impossible to recruit players. But that didn't stop me from trying.

I had accepted a number of invitations to chess events across the country and all over the world, which I saw as an opportunity to spread the word about SPICE and scout players. It was a good way to leverage my celebrity status to help build up the program. And since my travel and expenses were usually covered by the organizers at these events, my trips came at little to no cost to the university.

In September 2007, I had traveled to Mexico City as the guest of honor at the World Championship. Jorge Saggiante—who had also put together my big simul at Chapultepec park not long before—also asked me to provide commentary at the event alongside my old friend Leontxo García. This would be a first for me, doing play-by-play in Spanish. But sitting up onstage with Leontxo, trading analyses and stories, was like a master class in chess journalism—not to mention the history of the game. A bald, burly man in his early fifties, Leontxo was a pioneer of chess commentary in his native Spain, where he covered the game regularly in the mainstream press. I can only describe him as some intoxicating combination of a learned professor and a European soccer announcer.

Leontxo could move effortlessly between serious analysis of opening positions and long, detailed yarns about Paul Morphy or

Mikhail Botvinnik or William Steinitz, full of colorful turns of phrase and insightful sports analogies. During especially exciting games, he would swell with enthusiasm, taking genuine joy in the possibilities and surprises, turns of fate and shocking brilliancies we were witnessing. Covering long classical games, day in and day out, can sometimes be exhausting and even tedious. But not with Leontxo. He made every game feel thrilling and operatic, and I savored every minute of our time together.

The more I traveled around to chess events, talking to prospective players about joining Texas Tech, the more I realized that I'd need more than a good elevator pitch to get players interested. That's where the idea for the SPICE Cup was born. An elite tournament on the Texas Tech campus would give serious players a reason to visit and could double as a recruitment camp for the team. I might not have had much experience as a college chess scout, I figured. But I certainly knew how to organize a chess tournament.

That event almost didn't happen. Less than two weeks before it was scheduled to begin, in November 2007, our main sponsor backed out. I spent the days leading up to the opening ceremony frantically working the phones, soliciting contributions through the Susan Polgar Foundation. The money came through with little time to spare. When the first annual SPICE Cup finally got underway it featured one of the most accomplished international fields of any invitational tournament the United States had seen in a long time—with American grandmasters Boris Gulko, Julio Becerra, and the eventual winner, Eugene Perelshteyn, among them. And by the time the curtain came down on the tournament's closing ceremony, serious players all over the world knew the names Lubbock and Texas Tech University.

I continued my foray into serious chess journalism the next year at the Olympiad in Dresden, where I served as the head of English-language media for the event. I would host press conferences several times a day with the players and VIPs, while also publishing a daily broadsheet news bulletin, which was unusual for chess tournaments in those days. Mainly, though, I was on the hunt for young players who might consider coming to Lubbock. In fact, a communications officer from Texas Tech made the trip with me and set up a small recruitment kiosk at the event. It didn't take long for a German grandmaster named Georg Meier to catch my eye.

The twenty-one-year-old was playing first board for Germany's B team. And he was blazing a path through one of the strongest fields in Olympiad history. He finished the tournament with the fifth-best individual score, outperforming far higher-rated players like the Armenian Levon Aronian, former world champion Vladimir Kramnik, and a young Norwegian talent named Magnus Carlsen.

Georg didn't exactly jump at the chance to spend his college years in a place he had never heard of. I told him that he needed to see it for himself, that if he only spent some time there he'd feel differently, just as I had. He definitely wasn't sold, but we agreed to keep the conversation going.

It would prove to be one of the few bright spots in an otherwise trying year. As I had feared, the chess program didn't find many supporters in the new administration. And those scholarships we had been promised no longer seemed like a sure thing. Luckily, the program wasn't entirely destitute. Early on in our tenure, the administration had helped us secure a $320,000 gift from an anonymous donor—just barely enough for four full scholarships. It was the years after that we were worried about, though. What we needed was a guarantee from the administration that any player who came to Texas Tech would be taken care of for four years, or however long it took to complete their degree. And it wasn't clear that we'd ever get one.

In the meantime, we used the money we had from our anonymous donor to recruit our first titled player, the Hungarian IM

Gergely Antal, in 2008. Within weeks of arriving in Lubbock, Antal did us proud, winning the national individual collegiate champi-onship that fall and giving SPICE its very first major title.

The next year, we got word that one of the players from UTD, the Croatian international master Davorin Kuljasevic, was look-ing to get his master's degree somewhere that would enable him to continue his collegiate chess career. Paul and I had watched Davorin for years at that point, and what we saw in him was impressive—not just his chess ability, which was considerable, but his discipline and professionalism on and off the board. When he sat down to play, you could tell he was there to work. That's not always the case in college chess, even with the best players. We could also see that he had yet to reach his full potential, which is something Paul and I always looked for in a recruit—someone who was coachable.

Thanks to our anonymous benefactor, we had just enough funds for one master's student scholarship. Davorin wasn't the only student we considered for that spot. In fact, a well-known and much higher-rated grandmaster had also expressed interest in coming to Texas Tech to pursue his master's degree. But given what we knew about Davorin and his character and work ethic, there was never any question that he would be our pick.

Our addition of international master Gabor Papp from Hungary proved to be yet another pivotal decision that season. Gabor was a huge source of team morale, always beaming with positivity and encouragement for his teammates. And rounding out the team was Chase Watters, who had been the school chess club's best player before the days of SPICE and quickly became a cherished member of the team.

Chess is unique among college sports in that championships are determined by just two major events. The first is a tournament known as the Pan-American, a six-round event held over four days and open to any four-player college team. The Pan-Am usually attracts anywhere from several dozen to over a hundred teams, with the top four finishers advancing to the President's Cup—often referred to as the "College Chess Final Four"—the winner of which earns the title of national champion. To call Texas Tech an underdog that year would have been an understatement. In the entire history of the Final Four up until then, only two teams had ever won: UTD and UMBC. Both of these dynasties had vastly deeper pockets than our chess program did, not to mention the fierce support of their administrations. They lavished scholarships on the top prospects and they had used that money to beat out Texas Tech for more than a few recruits over the years.

Going to work every day not sure if or when your funding will run dry—I don't wish it on anyone. But there was also a lot of joy in that period as well. I had a team of incredible people at my side. Chess and family have always been closely linked for me. And I knew no other way of leading that group than to treat them like my own blood. At times, I would cook dinners for them at my home and drive them to the doctor or dentist or take them shopping. There were birthday parties and trivia nights and table tennis tournaments at our house, long tailgate parties before Texas Tech football games, and apple-picking trips in the fall. If someone on the team was having relationship problems or a crisis in their family, I was often the one they turned to for advice or comfort.

It was a completely new role for me, guiding these young people through the ups and downs of early adult life. But I was shocked by how easily it came to me. In those moments, mentoring and hosting these players, I could feel my mother's influence more strongly than I ever had. I kept thinking back to the way she would welcome players into our little apartment back in Budapest, and the warmth and acceptance she'd show them. I wasn't following some list of lessons she had taught me so much as channeling her attitude, her capacity to somehow remain optimistic, while still seeing things straight and speaking her mind. I may not have been quite as good at this as she is. But that disposition, that way of meeting the world—I could feel it was a part of me, that she had given me some of her gifts.

Among my favorite memories from those first few years is from 2009, when the team organized a blitz tournament at Carlsbad Cavern in New Mexico. The site had captivated me since I first visited not long before then. It's a sprawling underground space full of little passageways and rooms and even a bottomless pit. The games, which took place more than eight hundred feet below the earth's surface, were played on little tables in the cavern's Big Room, each board only dimly lit by small miner's lanterns. Just getting down there took the better part of an hour. Once the games got underway, all you could hear was the sound of clacking chess pieces and clock punches echoing through this ancient place. After the games finished, we were treated to one of the site's famous bat flights—a wave of hundreds of thousands of bats barreling out of the cave into the open air at dusk. There was no real rhyme or reason behind the event other than to have a little fun, build some camaraderie, and capture some publicity for the team. But it ended up being the one of the most magical chess tournaments I had ever been a part of—and it set a world record for the chess tournament held at the lowest elevation.

From its inception, though, SPICE was about more than building a winning university chess team. It was a vehicle for making chess a bigger part of the local community, especially for kids. In this way, it was a continuation of the work I had started back in Queens with my chess center. Our players and I would give frequent lessons at public schools in the area and teach "Super Saturday" classes on campus for kids who wanted additional instruction. We would host chess summer camps, as well as a regular "Get Smart! Play Chess!" scholastic chess tournament series. Soon we moved the Girls' Invitational to Lubbock, where it continued to flourish, growing into something more like an annual camp or convention, in addition to a major competition.

But I'm particularly proud of the work Paul and I did with the state's University Interscholastic League (UIL). The program, which has been around for more than a century, invites public school students from across the state to compete against each other in a range of contests in subjects like music, debate, and math. Paul and I realized that if we could get chess added as one of the UIL contests, it would unlock a new stream of funding for chess instruction in public schools—not just in Lubbock, but throughout the state. We had heard that the UIL committee had rejected previous attempts to add chess to the mix. So Paul came up with a pitch that would be hard for them to refuse. Instead of asking the committee to purchase hundreds of chess sets and organize actual in-person chess competitions—which would have been a tall order—we proposed a statewide chess-puzzle-solving competition, which could be put in place at very little cost to the program. Paul and I even agreed to supply the chess puzzles. The committee greenlit a twenty-school pilot program. And today, hundreds of schools throughout Texas participate.

TWENTY-NINE

It wasn't until 2010 that the team really started to come into its own. One of our big recruits that year was the Brazilian grandmaster Andre Diamant, whose progress I had been charting since he came to Lubbock for one of the early SPICE Cups. He wasn't a conventional choice by any means. For one, he had a wife and child back in Sao Paulo. And, when we first started talking, he wasn't even sure he was interested in going to college. It was my friend Davy, who had known Andre since he was a little boy, who really encouraged me to bring Andre on board.

Over the years, Davy had become something of a mentor to Andre. And, as he explained it to me, Andre had the makings of a great chess player, if only he could find a little more discipline. Davy thought that some time in my program would be the best thing for Andre, because if there's one thing I demand from my players, it's discipline. It had become a bedrock principle in our program that players were expected to carry a full course load and perform well academically if they were to remain on the team. I think Andre recognized that what we were offering was exactly what he needed at that time in his life, and he agreed to join us that fall, along with his wife and young son.

The next piece of the puzzle was a grandmaster from Israel named Anatoly Bykhovsky. He had just completed his mandatory three-year service in the Israeli military, and he was looking to start a new chapter in his life. He was a bit apprehensive about leaving Israel for an American university—afraid that leaving his family would be too difficult. I gave him my word that I'd do everything in my power to make this transition as smooth as possible, and that he'd have a fellow immigrant—and a Jewish immigrant at that—in his corner. I went on about the town's Jewish community, and the synagogue. It was enough to get him to take the leap.

Rounding out the team was the international master Istvan Sipos, from my native Hungary. He had already completed several years of college and was interested in seeing a little more of the world. Right from our earliest interactions, he was humble and thankful for the opportunity. He would be the lowest-rated player of our top four. But rating was never the biggest thing Paul and I looked for in a player. More than anything, we judged them by their character, and on that front, Sipos was a good fit.

Although we ended up with an impressive group, there were a few disappointments in the recruitment process. Paul and I had been courting two other grandmasters, both of whom ultimately backed out. One of those players chose to attend a university in his home country instead of moving to Texas, and we wished him well. The other had already promised us in writing that he would be attending Texas Tech in the fall, only to renege on the agreement in order to negotiate a more generous offer from a rival team. The bait-and-switch occurred so close to the beginning of the season that we had no time to find a replacement, which left the whole team feeling more than a little bit betrayed.

We started talking to Georg Meier again not long after the semester started. He was by then Germany's number two player, and he agreed to visit Lubbock for the first time to compete in the SPICE Cup, an event he ended up winning. Georg left Lubbock with an open mind about returning the following fall as a student, which is exactly what I had hoped would happen. He promised to let us know his decision by April 1, 2011. It wasn't lost on us that he had named April Fool's as the day he'd give us his answer, and at first we couldn't be sure he wasn't making a joke. But we took him at his word and left the rest to fate.

It had taken three years, but we had finally put together a Division 1 team with at least an outside chance of winning a national title. Once the fall 2010 semester was underway, though, I could feel that this was the year that we might break out. Our team was far from the highest rated in the league. But we were definitely the hungriest. Most important, we had built a team culture that set us apart. We didn't think of ourselves as a collection of individual players, but as a cohesive group, each doing our part to achieve a goal. This spirit of camaraderie showed up in the inside jokes we'd share and the nicknames we'd give to one another. Davorin was known as "the Goran," and we called Anatoly "the Rocket." For a while Istvan Sipos went by "Steve the Magnificent."

Those few months leading up to the Pan-American reminded me of training for my first Olympiad with my sisters, trying to make history by unseating another seemingly unbeatable team, each of us galvanized by a sense that it was "us against the world." The Pan-American starts just after Christmas, when students are usually cycling down for a long vacation after their exams. It's a difficult time to get college kids motivated. But not this year. Our group of players had something to prove. I could see it in the energy they brought to our training sessions in the run-up to the tournament. The ethos that governed everything I did as a coach was that if you outwork your opponent, amazing things can happen— that luck comes to those who are prepared. And our players took this to heart.

It was freezing cold when we arrived in Milwaukee that December for the big event. I could feel something was about to happen. We weren't seeded in the top four going in. And we brought only four A-team players to the event: Davorin Kuljasevic, Andre Diamant, Anatoly Bykhovsky, Istvan Sipos. UMBC and UTD would often bring six per team, which enabled them to rest certain players and deploy last-minute line-up changes to surprise their opponents. We also had to beat out schools like Stanford, Yale, and the University of Chicago, as well as University of Texas at Brownsville (UTB), which had just then emerged as a strong presence in Division 1 chess. But we weren't discouraged. If anything, the sheer immensity of the task before us served as fuel. We had every intention of leaving there with a ticket to the Final Four.

That's exactly what happened—although just barely. Our team finished the Pan-American in fourth place, squeaking by the B teams from the other top schools. Our improbable performance got people's attention. "A couple of years ago, college chess could be divided into two tiers," *The New York Times* wrote shortly after the tournament. "The elite included the University of Maryland, Baltimore County, and the University of Texas at Dallas. The second tier was made up of everyone else. No more."

We got another boost in early April, when Georg emailed to tell us he would join the team the following semester. It was April 1—right on schedule—a sign of the German precision that we'd come to expect from Georg over the next few years. Texas Tech was about to have its first world-top-100 player. Everything seemed to be coming together at exactly the right time. And when play got underway in Herndon, Virginia, at that spring's Final Four, our players were all brimming with confidence and motivation.

My role on the team was always mainly as a trainer and mentor. It was Paul's job to think about strategy—to research the teams we were up against and help come up with opening strategies and player matchups that gave us the best chance to win in competition. Honestly, I would have chosen Paul for this job even if we weren't married. He had played exactly this role as captain of our 2004 Olympiad team, and his decisions throughout that event were critical to our historic silver-medal finish. What I knew and most didn't was that his feel for strategy—especially in team competition—was among the best in the game, as he demonstrated time and again that season.

For the Final Four, Paul made two interesting decisions. Instead of fielding our four players in order of rating, with the highest-rated player on board 1, he switched things up. Sipos was still the lowest-rated player on the team. But for that tournament, we tried him out on board 3—while letting Andre play on the bottom board. Our thinking was that forcing Sipos to upset expectations might give him a psychological edge. Moving Andre down a board, mean-while, would increase his chances of winning his games. To add an extra element of surprise, Paul also swapped the top two boards, creating a line-up that our opponents weren't expecting.

The first big test of our mettle came in round 1, when Anatoly was paired against UTB's Timur Gareyev, one of the few players in the event with a rating over 2600. Anatoly had yet to beat someone with a rating that high, and he desperately wanted to do so here. By the middlegame, however, the game had drifted into some murky waters, and Gareyev offered a draw in a very sharp position. Back then, a player had to consult with the team's captain (in our case, Paul) before accepting a draw. The safe move would have been to just say yes, take the half point, and let the rest of his teammates fight for the round. But Anatoly was on a mission. He asked for Paul's go-ahead to play Gareyev to a win. Paul didn't take the decision lightly. Were the circumstances different, Paul might very well have asked Anatoly to swallow his pride and take the draw. But he could tell Anatoly was playing with confidence and that the best thing to do was to affirm that confidence by letting him fight. "Go have fun," Paul said.

It was a complicated position, the kind that Gareyev usually excelled in. But Anatoly pulled it off, beating a path to victory against some truly long odds. That win decided the round in our favor and set the tone for the rest of the tournament.

Sipos had his chance to shine in the penultimate round the following day, when he played the much higher-rated Julio Sadorra of UTB to a win—exactly the kind of head-turning victory we had hoped would occur. But it was the final round that put us over the edge, and specifically Davorin's game over UMBC's Leonid Kritz. Davorin had had his eye on Kritz since we first started preparing for the Pan-American a year before. And, as with Anatoly's game the previous day, he got a decent enough position to induce a draw offer. Also like Anatoly, Davorin wasn't too interested in settling for the draw when he walked over to Paul for a consult. He wanted to roll the dice on a win. Paul responded the same as he had a day earlier: "Go have fun." Davorin went to work. Playing with the black pieces against the winningest team in college chess history, Davorin did what he came to do. He won. And he gave our team just enough points to go home as champions.

The moment the final game ended, our team exploded in celebration, discharging months of suppressed nervous energy in a single instant of exhausted, vindicating joy. Everyone was dancing and jumping and hugging as if we had just won the Super Bowl which, as far as we were concerned, we had. Paul and I had promised to bring home a championship within five years—something that, just a year earlier, had seemed impossible. We did it in four.

⋅•◦•⋅

In the eyes of the new administration, SPICE had been seen as the ugly stepchild of Texas Tech sports, a status I had reluctantly grown used to over the years. But I assumed a national championship would make a difference to them. We had built this team on what might generously be called a shoestring budget and taken them to the very top in record time. It was the stuff of college sports legend. Unfortunately, few in the administration seemed to care.

There was some formal recognition for the achievement, like a small ceremony with a few dozen people from the university, during which the team performed a classic Texas Tech sports ritual of ringing cowbells. Our players had their own float in a school parade, right up there with the basketball and football teams, which they absolutely deserved. But once all the fanfare had died down, the team found itself in an even more dire financial position than we had been a year before.

We put together another strong team for the following year, adding the GM Denes Boros from Hungary and, from Israel, the IM Vitaly Neimer. Elshan Moradiabadi, an Iranian grandmaster, joined the team in the spring of 2012. But the air of uncertainty surrounding the SPICE's future was getting difficult to ignore.

As ever, the university adamantly refused to guarantee any money for scholarships, even though high-quality young players from all over the world were now knocking on our door. That same donor had given us his business card and encouraged us to call him if the program needed more funding. Nevertheless, the administration warned us that if we tried to contact this person to ask for more money, Paul and I would lose our jobs.

The administration's top priority at that time was earning Tier 1 status for the university. And, until they achieved that goal, any conversation about future funding for chess would have to wait. It was their position that Paul and I should be happy with what we had, namely a paycheck and benefits for as long as we wanted.

Paul and I had started looking for the exit. We let the upper administration know that if they weren't interested in supporting SPICE, we owed it to our team—not to mention ourselves—to find another home. At first, the administration saw this as an empty threat, a negotiating tactic intended to extract more money for the program. And they pretty much dared us to find another school, fully confident that we'd never actually leave Texas Tech. But we weren't negotiating, and we definitely weren't bluffing.

Quietly, we got the word out that SPICE was looking to relocate. It didn't take long for the phone to ring. By the fall of 2011, Paul and I were in talks with seven different universities, several of which were eager to give our program a home. On our way to a campus visit, Paul and I made a stop in Dallas to visit our old friend, the grandmaster Babakuli Annakov. When Babakuli heard we were shopping around for a new home, he was shocked we hadn't been in touch with Julian Schuster, a serious chess player who happened to also be a college administrator. Paul had gotten to know Julian years earlier, through Babakuli. And they had met a few times since then. What we didn't know was that Julian was now provost at Webster University in St. Louis—and that he was in the process of starting a chess program.

Paul got on the phone with Julian a few days later—just hours before we were scheduled to sign a deal with a big state university. That signing never came to pass, because by the end of Paul's call with Julian, we had a tentative agreement to move SPICE to Webster.

The decision had less to do with strategy than with pure intuition. And the more we considered the details, the more we were convinced that Webster was the only place for SPICE. For starters, Julian was a veteran of the chess world with a deep love and appreciation of the game. His plans to build a chess program already had the strong backing of Webster's president at the time, Elizabeth Stroble. We also liked that Webster was a private college, and that we'd be spared a lot of the bureaucratic runaround that comes with working at a public university. Missouri's central geographic location would make it easier to travel to tournaments all over the country—especially compared to West Texas. And as an added gift from the universe, the nearby St. Louis Chess Club in the city's Central West End had recently established itself as one of the nation's biggest chess hubs. Having learned our lesson, we made sure to demand scholarship guarantees spelled out clearly in writing, which the university gladly agreed to provide. Most important of all, Julian was someone we could trust to keep his word.

That the whole deal came about through a casual conversation with an old friend—and at the last possible moment—made the whole situation feel preordained.

Paul and I headed to St. Louis not long after that first conversation with Julian to do some unofficial reconnaissance—scoping out the neighborhood and spending some time on campus, all without the administration's knowledge. What we saw positively charmed us: an idyllic tree-lined campus in a quiet suburban neighborhood just outside the city. This was the place—and there was no doubt about it.

We were still hashing out the details of the move to Webster when we heard from the family of the American grandmaster Ray Robson. I first met Ray at the 2009 SPICE Spring Invitational. He was just fourteen at that time and would soon go on to a first-place finish in the US Junior Championship. He was also racing to become the youngest grandmaster in US history—a distinction he attained not long after that, surpassing the reigning record holder, Fabiano Caruana, by just four days. Ray's talent was undeniable even back then. And over the years, I had watched him mature into a professional-level player. Paul and I had also become close with his parents since then. In fact, it was Ray's father, Gary, who called us that December to tell us his son planned to join the Texas Tech Knight Raiders. Both Gary and his wife, Yee-Chen, had accepted jobs running a school in Myanmar the following school year. They liked the idea that Ray might find a community at SPICE, and maybe even two parent figures in me and Paul, while they were so far away.

I had been following another generational talent, the young grandmaster and three-time Philippine chess champion Wesley

So, since we were first introduced by my old friend—and fellow Filipino grandmaster—Eugene Torre at the 2008 Olympiad in Dresden. Wesley and his father even visited Texas Tech in 2010 for that year's SPICE Cup. And we were pleasantly surprised when his parents contacted us late in 2011 asking if Wesley could join the team the following academic year.

Having these two young men on the team would propel us to number one in the nation. So there was no way I was going to pass up that opportunity. The Webster move was still under wraps. But if Ray's and Wesley's families were going to entrust me as their child's coach over the next four years, I would need to show them some trust as well. I explained to both families that we'd love to make them part of SPICE, but that if they wanted in, they'd need to come to Webster. They just couldn't tell anybody until we officially announced the move in a few months. Both families gave us the same answer. It wasn't Lubbock they were interested in; it was what I had built with SPICE. And if I was headed to St. Louis, then so were they.

I could only hope that the rest of the team felt the same way. Asking these young people to leave behind their lives in Lubbock and to start fresh at an obscure Missouri school they had no say in choosing—it wasn't a small request. I was expecting that at least one or two of them would say no. Paul and I broke the news to the team just hours after the close of that year's Pan-Am. Calling each player into our hotel room, we explained the situation—the lack of support in Lubbock, the benefits of moving to Webster, all of it. They were under no obligation to join us, we told them. But if they wanted to come with us, there would be a place for them in St. Louis.

The response I got bowled me over. Without exception, every titled player on the team wanted to come to Webster and said so right there in the room and without an instant of hesitation. It was a demonstration of trust—but also affection. Texas Tech was where they went to school, but SPICE was their family. It was as simple as that.

Early in 2012, when we officially informed Texas Tech's upper administration that this would be our last semester, the news caught them by surprise. They really didn't believe another school would want a program like SPICE. When they heard we were leaving, they changed their tune in a hurry. First they offered Paul and me generous raises. As for those scholarships we had been clamoring for, they assured us they would find the money. Even if we had wanted to consider this offer, we couldn't. It was too late. We had signed with Webster, and we weren't going back on our word no matter how much money they put on the table.

When the whole team visited Webster in February 2012, we were welcomed as the school's new celebrities. There was a huge reception with the provost and president. Since our relocation to Webster wasn't official yet, the visit was kept a secret. But that didn't stop our hosts from putting on a show for us. To commemorate our arrival, each player was awarded a baseball jersey with his name and a number on the back—like at a professional sports draft. Julian hung around for a while, playing blitz with the team, analyzing games, and telling stories. It was such a stark change from what we were used to. Back at Texas Tech, our players couldn't have gotten an audience with the university's top brass if they tried. Here, they were palling around with a high-level administrator on their first day on campus.

As a parting gift to Texas Tech, the Knight Raiders successfully defended their title at the Final Four that year and left Lubbock as the first new dynasty college chess had seen in a generation. Now it was off to St. Louis.

THIRTY

There are rare stretches in life when everything seems to line
up, when all of your experience and preparation collides
with the right people, the right opportunities, and the right
circumstances. You can never count on these happy coincidences.
But sometimes, for just a moment, the universe cooperates. That
first year at Webster University was one of those moments. For
the first time in my college coaching career, I wasn't fighting some
battle or trying to defy the odds. Each part of my life—my family,
my job, my team—seemed to complement and strengthen the
others. And, most important, I had found myself enmeshed in a
community built on mutual respect and shared goals, a community that I had played a part in shaping and nurturing, and that
had shaped me in turn.

Texas Tech's top administration had treated SPICE mostly as an
afterthought, forever shuffling the team's office from one campus
building to another, and rarely interacting with me or Paul directly.
Webster was different. From day one, the school installed us in
our own dedicated space, and soon after moved us to a beautiful,
nearly eleven-thousand-square-foot brick-walled facility with a
large area for chess training, a private office for me, and a massive

hall for hosting tournaments and receptions and other activities. If the team ever needed anything, Paul or I could just pick up the phone to the provost's office and arrange a meeting, often the very same day.

What was most touching for me was how Webster gave its star chess players the sort of recognition and glory most other schools reserved for football or basketball stars. The greatest example of this involved a billboard the university put up on Interstate 70 between St. Louis and Columbus. It was a strip of road well known for giant advertisements celebrating the University of Missouri–Columbia, or Mizzou, football team. Playing off of this idea, Webster put up its own billboard, which included a photograph of Wesley So sporting a bright yellow tennis sweatband and another SPICE player, Mara Kamphorst, with "eye black" smeared across her cheeks like a football player. Next to them, in big bold letters, was OUR TOP RECRUITS ARE CHESS PLAYERS above Webster's logo. Mara was one of several young women I had the pleasure of working with at SPICE. She had come to Webster with her husband, Andre Diamant, and their young child. And her tenure happened to overlap with that of a number of other talented female players at Webster—namely, the woman grandmasters Anna Sharevich from Belarus, Irene Sukandar from Indonesia, the Czech Katerina Nemcova, as well as woman FIDE master Luisa Mercado. The four of them would make up one of the few all-female teams in college chess. And in 2015, they would do Webster proud by winning that year's Pan American Intercollegiate Women's Championship.

The billboard garnered some significant national media attention for the team, thanks to an AP story that was picked up by papers across the country. And while the idea that chess players are college athletes on par with those in any other sport was played for laughs, it wasn't a joke, not at Webster. In fact, physical fitness was a major part of SPICE's identity in those years. We'd often use the large hall outside our training area as a kind of gym. For a while, we even had sponsorship from the founder of CrossFit, Greg Glassman, who happened to be a great lover of chess. We'd incorporate CrossFit into our regular chess training sessions, using the big room as a makeshift gym. This regimen became the basis for a Chess/Fitness challenge, the first of which was held at a CrossFit gym in St. Louis. Players would have to make a single move in a speed chess game played on a giant chess board before completing one in a circuit of CrossFit exercises, which included push-ups, squats, row rings, and sit-ups. Only then, could they rush back to the board to make their next move.

Our new home, the picturesque suburb of Des Peres, minutes away from the university in Webster Groves, felt like the kind of place my family and I could set down roots, with its tree-lined streets, charming nineteenth-century homes, and good public schools. We deliberately settled on a spacious house, knowing that we would use it as a kind of informal social headquarters for the team. To that end, we furnished the new place with a pool table, in addition to the Ping-Pong table we already had in Texas. Especially after living in a sprawling agricultural town like Lubbock, Webster Groves felt intimate and cozy. We also hadn't realized how much we missed trees, which were all but nonexistent in Lubbock.

What really made those years special, though, were our students. We had always been a tight-knit group at SPICE. But the move to St. Louis made our bond even stronger. That so many players uprooted their lives in service of the team reaffirmed for everyone that we were, in a very real sense, a family. In addition to Wesley and Ray, the former Mexican champion Manuel Leon Hoyos also joined our crew that fall.

We now had enough high-quality players to field multiple teams—while boasting the strongest A-team lineup of any school in the nation. This influx of elite talent was certainly welcome, but it also created some fresh challenges for me as a coach. I was no longer leading an upstart team of underestimated strivers. Many of our players were years into their own successful chess careers by the time they arrived at Webster. And, as is often the case in an individual sport like chess, big talent often breeds a healthy degree of self-regard.

Several of our newer recruits were minor celebrities where they came from. In fact, five of our players that year—Wesley, Ray, Manuel, Georg, and Inna Agrest from Sweden—would represent their respective home nations in the Olympiad that fall. Some of these players had spent years putting their own goals and achievements before everything else—and everybody else—in their lives. Along the way, they had come to see themselves as special, which, in many ways, they were. But now they were part of a team. And if we were going to succeed as a team, we needed to work as a unit. That meant embracing their status as one among equals.

The message that Paul and I sent from our very first Webster training session was clear and unequivocal: Check your ego at the door! Certain of our players were clearly more skilled and knowledgeable than others, but nobody would get special treatment.

This kind of team-spiritedness came more naturally to some than others. For instance, not long after accepting our offer to come to Webster, Manuel encouraged us to recruit a friend of his, the Cuban grandmaster and Olympian Fidel Corrales Jimenez—a suggestion that took Paul and me by surprise. We agreed with Manuel that Fidel would make a tremendous addition to the team. But Fidel was also higher rated than Manuel. Should Fidel come on board, Manuel would likely be moved from the A team to the B team. Manuel knew this, and yet he still pushed us to pursue Fidel anyway—for the good of the team. This was exactly the kind of unselfishness we were looking for.

Unfortunately, not all of our players shared Manuel's willingness to put the team first. And near the end of the Pan-American that year, a serious clash of egos flared up between several of our team members. We happened to field two very strong teams in that event, both of which found themselves competing for first place late in the tournament. It had always seemed questionable to me that two teams from the same school should have to play against each other in such an important tournament. But those were the rules. And, at least this year, the Webster vs. Webster face-off in the next-to-last round brought out a side of our players we hadn't known was there.

It started when a member of our A team decided to break one of Paul's cardinal rules. The player was a grandmaster, and he was paired against a Webster teammate who happened to be an international master. After the lower-rated player offered a draw, this GM rejected it on the spot instead of consulting Paul, as was mandatory in our organization. Had Paul been advised, he would have almost certainly told this player to take the draw. Paul and I knew that the B-team opponent was not only underrated but very comfortable in the sorts of positions this game was likely to produce if it moved forward. The A-team player took it upon himself to refuse the draw and play on—and ended up losing the game, and putting the A team in a 2–1 deficit with just one game still underway.

That final game sparked its own controversy, one also hinging on a draw offer. Once again, the B-team player offered a draw. Only this time, the A-team opponent consulted Paul—who advised him to play on, which he did, eventually winning the game. Now, ideally, this result should have suited our players just fine. Our A team and B team finished the Pan-American tied for first place. But by that point, each side had come to see the other not as a group of fellow teammates, but as their rivals. It wasn't enough for Webster to tie for first and move on to the final four. Each of our two groups wanted to beat the other—mostly out of pride and ego.

At the team meeting following the event, the B-team player who lost in that late game was absolutely furious. "Why would you play on in such a position—it's a dead draw!" At first, Paul and I didn't know what to think. Why were these kids getting so fired up about an outcome that, all in all, everybody should be happy about? But the argument just kept escalating until, worried that things were about to get physical, Paul stepped in to break up the squabble.

Before dinner that night, the entire team sat down for a meeting. Most of the players were expecting a firm reprimand from Paul and me. But Paul took a different tack. He didn't scream or bang his fist; he didn't shoot stern looks or cast blame. He apologized—calmly and earnestly. It was his job as captain to make the rules clear and to set the tone for how we compete, he said. More than anything, the outburst that day was evidence that he hadn't done his job.

It was exactly what the team needed to hear. Not only was Paul speaking from the heart, but he was modeling the kind of integrity, personal responsibility, and selflessness that we expected from our players. From that point on, every person at SPICE understood that their behavior and attitude—as a team, but also individually—mattered to Paul and me as much as anything they did over a chess board. When our students displayed bad form or poor character, in any part of their lives, we took it personally.

Of course we wanted them to be fierce competitors. In fact, we had made it clear to the group early on in that season that with this much talent in our locker room, anything less than first place would be a disappointment. It was never going to be easy balancing this win-at-all-costs mentality with the spirit of fellowship and solidarity that had been so central to SPICE's philosophy up until then. Nevertheless, as coaches, it was our job to strike this balance, and we hadn't.

Paul showed a level of leadership that night I didn't know he had in him. It impressed me deeply. If I'm honest, I don't really think he had anything to apologize for, and I suspect he didn't think so, either. But that wasn't the point. He knew he needed to defuse this tense situation before it got out of hand. And if that meant taking the blame, then so be it. Maybe it was all of years running a business, but he knew exactly what was required of him at that moment, and he rose to the occasion in a way that made everybody there take notice, even me.

We got a big boost our second year with the arrival of the Vietnamese GM Liem Le, the first player in SPICE history rated above 2700. Like many of our recruits, we had gotten to know Liem as a participant in several SPICE Cups. As a Vietnam native, Paul sparked up a fast friendship with Liem and his mom during those events. Even then, we were impressed with his maturity and diligence. Although a somewhat soft-spoken young man, he commanded a lot of respect from our players, not just because of his chess ability, but for his own high personal standards and his generosity of spirit.

One thing that remained constant after the move to Webster was my approach to training. It didn't matter that my team now consisted of anywhere from eight to ten grandmasters; my methods didn't change. We'd study as a group several times a week, solving puzzles, working on tactics and strategy, going over opening and endgame ideas. Then, I'd sit down with the players one at a time in the office for private sessions, which I would tailor to their specific needs and problem areas. I'd prepare exercises devised for each student, and we'd go over their games and work on their opening repertoires. Sometimes, if a player was dealing with a psychological hang-up—a lack of confidence, say, or difficulty managing their time—we'd just talk it out.

It wasn't a terribly complicated system. All I was really asking from my players was discipline and seriousness—a willingness to show up and work. I didn't expect them to be perfect, just as my father hadn't expected perfection from me during our early training sessions back in Budapest. The only unforgivable sin, as my father had taught me, was to lack focus and professionalism.

The approach worked almost without fail. One of the things I'm most proud of from those years, in fact, is that nearly every

player I coached reached their peak rating while at SPICE. Wesley
So's progress was perhaps the most dramatic of any player. He
was an extraordinary talent long before he started working with
me, of course. But I could tell that his aversion to discipline and
structure, as well as his indecisiveness and lack of killer instinct,
was holding him back. When he arrived at Webster, he was barely
among the world's top 100 active players; in fact, he was ranked
number 99. Once he bought into our training process, and started
to put in the work, his play took off. By the spring of 2013, he had
broken the 2700 mark for the first time in his career, and by the
beginning of the fall 2014 semester, he made it to number 14 on
the world rankings.

That October, we took several of our players, including Ray and
Wesley, to the Millionaire Chess Open in Las Vegas. The event still
holds the record for the most lucrative open tournament in history,
with a total purse of $1 million, $100,000 of which would go to the
winner. It took some cajoling to get Wesley to come along. Paul and
I tried to persuade him for weeks, explaining how big a lift it would
give to his career to win on such a big stage and to walk away with
so much money. To demonstrate our confidence in him, on behalf
of SPICE we even offered to cover all his travel expenses and tournament fees, with the understanding that he would pay us back if
he actually won. But he wouldn't budge. We thought it might be
nerves or modesty that was making him reluctant. During our last
big pitch to him, though, he revealed his real motive. He would
turn twenty-one during the tournament, and he was superstitious
about playing on his birthday.

"Is that all this is?" Paul responded. We told him we understood
his hesitation—and that we didn't take it lightly. Plenty of athletes
and competitors are superstitious. But we also explained that this
wouldn't be his last time playing on his birthday. And that, the next
time, he might not have a choice in the matter. Why not use this
as a chance to move past his hang-up once and for all? He thought

about it a little more after that and eventually came around. I'm sure he doesn't regret it.

There was a lot of buzz surrounding our group going into the Vegas tournament. We had already become the country's undisputed number one college team and had notched two consecutive national championships in the previous two years. As we filed into the playing hall before the first round, joining nearly six hundred players who had entered the event, a hush went over the room. Everyone seemed to be watching us, with many whispering to each other and pointing furtively in our direction. "Those are the SPICE guys," they seemed to be saying. "Look out."

Just about anything can happen in big open tournaments like this one, especially when there's a lot of money at stake. Unknown players can come out of nowhere to upset the field, and relatively low-rated players can have the performance of their lives, with no warning or explanation (as Sofia had years before in Rome). This tournament, however, belonged to Wesley and Ray. By the last round of the knockout tournament, they were the only two players standing. In the end, Wesley came out on top. He entered his twenty-first year with the wind at his back, money in his pocket, and one less superstition to worry over.

Unfortunately, Wesley's time at Webster was about to end. The speed with which his game had improved and the opportunities that were now open to him as a professional player had left him unsure whether college was the right place for him. Even before the trip to Las Vegas, Paul and I could both sense that Wesley was conflicted about how to move forward and no longer completely committed to the SPICE project. All I could do was let him know that whatever he decided, I would support him—but with one caveat. As long as he remained a member of our team, he'd have to make chess a top priority, and he'd have to continue to keep up his academic grades, just like everyone else in the group. Anything less would be unfair to his teammates.

As we got deeper into the fall semester, however, Wesley remained on the fence about his future with SPICE, and his ambivalence was starting to take a toll on the team's morale. Wesley was our superstar and a beloved member of the team. And his sharp sense of humor—a kind teasing one-upmanship with his fellow teammates—brought energy and fun to the team. But as much as we appreciated Wesley and wanted him to stay, we needed to know right away whether he was in or out. Paul explained all of this to him at the 2014 SPICE Cup and gave him a hard deadline of October 27 for his final decision. We were well aware of how indecisive Wesley could be when facing even minor choices. At restaurants, he'd often examine the menu far longer than anybody else before turning to Paul and saying, "I'll just have what you're having." The deadline was meant to force him to choose soon, before the team began preparing for that year's Pan-Am. That date passed with no word from Wesley. And at 12:01 a.m. on October 28, 2014, Paul sent out two emails. The first one was to Wesley, thanking him for his extraordinary contributions to our team, wishing him well, and, most of all, expressing how proud he and I were of Wesley and that no matter what, we would always be in his corner. The other email, which went out to the rest of our team, announced that Wesley So was no longer a part of SPICE.

We saw this as not only the right decision for the team but clear proof to all of our players that nobody gets special treatment—not even Wesley, who, by that time, was ranked tenth in the world. Unfortunately, that's not how everybody saw the situation, not at first. Most on the team were devastated. Even Ray—who had been Wesley's roommate for years, and who rarely displayed strong emotions, was noticeably hurt by Wesley's exit. Wesley was a part of the family. And now, just two months away from the Pan-Am, he was gone. The question that hung in the minds of most of the team, not to mention our rivals, was, What will SPICE do without him?

For my part, I knew we had enough talent to defend our title without Wesley. The rest of the team, however, wasn't so sure. And those doubts cast a dark shadow for weeks after Wesley's exit. As the semester wound down and we approached the Pan-Am—which, as in every year, took place between Christmas and New Year's— Paul and I struggled to pull the team out of their funk. Normally, we'd devote the short period between the end of final exams and the beginning of the Pan-Am to an intensive training program. It was Paul who recognized that this crisis in morale couldn't be helped with more study—that what our players needed was a shift in perspective. So that year, we gave our A Team a break for a few days and took the whole group to Branson, Missouri, for some R&R. Really, though, it was an exercise in team-building.

I'd like to say that Paul and I knew our strategy would work, but really, we were just hoping. There was a chance that breaking our normal training routine would only add to the players' self-doubt, that they'd take the Branson retreat as a sign that the old way of doing things—the way that had earned them multiple national titles—wasn't going to work this time around. But we couldn't do anything. And giving our kids a break, taking in some theater, playing some miniature golf, and sharing a few meals in a new environment seemed like as good an idea as any.

It also gave us a chance to check in with the team and work through their concerns with them. Our message on that trip wasn't anything our students hadn't heard before. We simply reminded them that our team has always been bigger than any single player, no matter how talented that player might be. The difference this time was that, with Wesley out of the picture, this guiding principle was about to be put to the test in a way it hadn't before. It's one thing to pay lip service to a "one for all, all for one" ethos when you've got the highest-rated team in the league, and a world top 20 player on your side. Now we needed to live by that creed.

When we arrived back in St. Louis, the group's whole outlook had shifted. They were no longer dreading the next few months of competition—they were hunting for a win. And goodness, did they win. Our A team swept the Pan-Am 6–0 that December. And they continued the streak at the championship in April, taking home another national title after a perfect 3–0 performance. What really made that year special, though, was our final score of 10 points out of 12 games. That dominant performance gave Webster an unprecedented 5½-point margin over the second-place finisher.

By the beginning of the 2017 school year, Webster was riding high, having just become the first team in college chess history to win five consecutive national titles. We headed into December's Pan-American tournament in Columbus, Ohio, as clear favorites, and fully convinced that our winning streak was just getting started. Our most stubborn opponent that season turned out to be our own bad luck.

Not long before we left for the tournament, several of our players developed flu-like symptoms. Most were well enough to play, but one of the pillars of our A team, Illia Nyzhnyk, was badly ill, forcing us to make some last-minute changes to the lineup. Illia eventually rallied, agreeing to make the trip with us so long as he could spend most of his down time recuperating in bed, which we allowed.

The next stroke of bad luck came during the trip to Columbus, when the bus we had chartered broke down on the side of the highway—in subfreezing temperatures.

Despite all of this, we found a way to finish the tournament in clear first place, giving us our sixth consecutive Pan-Am win and setting us up for yet another Final Four appearance the following April at the Marshall Chess Club in New York. To say we had confidence going into that tournament would be an understatement.

Not only were we the defending champions; we had just fought through a snowstorm, a flu outbreak, an eleven-hour bus trip, and a hotel mix-up to win the Pan-Am. If we could overcome those kinds of "acts of nature," then surely we could triumph in my former hometown—and at one of the most legendary chess clubs in America. At least, that's how I saw the situation.

As we all soon learned, however, our streak of misfortune hadn't yet run its course. After a come-from-behind win in round 2, our A team was set to take on a local rival, St. Louis University, in the third and final matchup.

That round would be decided by a single game between our co-captain, Ray Robson, and SLU's Dariusz Swiercz. Only a win would have secured us the title—a result that Ray seemed poised to provide. In fact, he played absolutely wonderfully for most of that game and achieved a clearly winning position going into the final stretch. All he needed to do was play soundly and keep squeezing his opponent, and another title would be ours.

With just thirty seconds on his clock, Ray was faced with a seemingly innocent choice between two different rook moves in an endgame clearly tilted in his favor. Both moves looked winning at first glance. What Ray didn't realize was that one of those two moves opened a path for the other player to force a draw—and deny Webster the championship. Admittedly, this was incredibly difficult to see under time pressure.

Forced to make a split-second decision, Ray chose the wrong move. Within seconds, his opponent replied with the only move on the board that didn't lose. The game ended in a draw soon after. For the first time in Webster chess history, we had failed to take home the national championship.

What made that result so painful wasn't just that we lost—but the way we lost. Ray was in complete control until the very final moves. All it took was a slight inaccuracy under intense time pressure—as well as a perfect reply from his opponent—to turn the tide of the game and obliterate our chance at another title. We had fallen victim to astoundingly bad luck.

Eating lunch with the team after that last game, I made sure to tell them how proud I was of what they had done, and that the result was no reflection on them as players. We had benefited from our fair share of lucky breaks along the way, I said. It was just somebody else's turn this time. With that, I broke down crying.

It was the first and only time my team had seen me shed a tear. And what happened next still stirs me to think about. Each of the players took turns comforting me, being strong for me—just as I had for them all of those years. They did it instinctively, the way one might comfort a sibling or a parent during a difficult time. Had we not been so close, they might have interpreted my storm of emotion as disappointment, but they knew what this was. I wanted this win for them, and I was devastated—with myself more than anyone—for depriving them of one more moment of glory.

———— ⋆•⋆•⋆ ————

It was the spring of 2020 when I hung up the phone on the second floor of our home and headed for the stairs to share some news with Paul. I can't remember what I needed to tell him, but it must have seemed important. What I do remember is that, somewhere near the top of the staircase, my sock lost its grip, and I went bouncing feet-first down the stairs, each step taking turns jabbing my back. I was lying at the bottom of the staircase when Paul rushed over. I knew it was a mistake to move. And after a few minutes of lying still, I wasn't sure that I could move.

Everything happened very slowly after that. The shock of the fall started to subside, only to be replaced by intense pain in my lower back—pain I took as a welcome sign that I wasn't paralyzed. When I finally made it to my feet with Paul's help, the pain became sharper and harder to endure.

I had already struggled with back problems from time to time, but this was something different. The pain eased up slowly over the next few months, although some days it was a lot worse than others. Walking even short distances could be laborious. And on bad days, the pain made it difficult to concentrate, taking precedence over every other thought and intention. But it was only after I was forced to abandon my love affair with high heels just to get around that I really understood something big had shifted in my life, and maybe for good. I held out hope that I'd eventually heal, but my progress was maddeningly slow. I felt happy to still be alive. But I also knew that my life as I had come to know it would have to change.

Paul and I sat down with Julian the following January and broke the news that this, my ninth year coaching Webster's chess team, would also be my last. "Please don't tell me you're going to another university," Julian shot back, trying to lighten the mood a little.

My injury had made it impossible for me to do my job at the level that I expected from myself and that my players deserved. And I refused to let my team down by staying on in my condition. Julian accepted the news like the great friend that he is. He asked that SPICE remain at Webster even after I left. Really, he didn't even need to ask. Webster was where SPICE belonged.

Still, Julian was caught off guard when I asked to name my successor. As a serious chess enthusiast, he had a few names in mind for who might helm the program, including some very well-regarded chess coaches from outside the United States. But Paul and I both agreed that only one person was right for the job: Liem Le.

Liem had been named team captain in his third year at Webster—a job he performed with a level of poise, steadiness, and moral integrity that one rarely sees in adults twice his age. An exemplary student, he had stayed in St. Louis after graduating summa cum laude with dual degrees in finance and management in

2017, and remained a familiar face around the SPICE building. Not to mention, he was a top 30 player, a former world blitz champion, and the highest-rated Vietnamese chess player in the world—all before he graduated. During my decade as a college coach, I hadn't met anybody I would trust with this job more than Liem. And that's exactly what I explained to Julian. It was all he needed to hear.

What I didn't realize, however, is that Liem had been seriously considering leaving St. Louis not long before we sat down with him to offer him the head coaching position. He had been waiting for his wife to join him in St. Louis from Vietnam. But the COVID-19 pandemic had delayed their reunion. As they waited for the lockdowns to lift, they had debated either moving to California or returning to Vietnam. Ultimately, they decided to settle down in St. Louis and buy a house. So when I asked him to take over for me at Webster, he couldn't believe his ears. Of course he'd do it, he said. It would be an honor.

By the end of my final year as a Division 1 college chess coach, our teams had won more world championships, national titles, other major titles, and Olympiad medals than all other US collegiate chess programs combined. We had spent ten straight years as the nation's number one ranked chess program and won seven consecutive Final Four championships. I didn't want it to be over. But if it did have to end, now felt like the time.

EPILOGUE

O n November 13, 2023, in the chess facility at Webster University, I was inducted into the World Chess Hall of Fame. It had been almost fifty years exactly since my very first tournament as a four-year-old in Budapest. Who could have known that little girl who had to sit on telephone books to reach the board would one day be immortalized as one of the game's greatest players? Well, my parents, maybe.

They had set out to make me exceptional, and it was because of their support, their strength, and their wisdom that I had achieved anything at all. The truth is, the award belonged just as much to them as it did to me.

Less than a year later, at a celebration of FIDE's one-hundredth anniversary at the 2024 Chess Olympiad, I received another lifetime honor—the award for greatest female chess trainer of all time. There to present me with my trophy was my old friend Vishy Anand. And, wouldn't you know it, the event just happened to take place in my hometown of Budapest.

My father always taught me that hard work is a necessary ingredient for greatness. But it isn't the only one. Luck is just as crucial.

And looking back on my long career as a player, coach, organizer, and teacher, I can't imagine being luckier than I have.

I was lucky to have a family that was as committed to my success as I was; to have friends and colleagues who filled my life with joy and wisdom and affection; to have a husband, Paul, who has never failed to be a dedicated and adoring partner, in life as well as in chess. I am lucky to be the mother of two extraordinary young men, Tom and Leeam. And I was lucky to have spent a career doing something I loved, a career that showed me the world and filled my life with people I love and respect.

It was so deeply meaningful to receive official recognition from the biggest organizations in chess, especially with so many of my loved ones there with me. I had spent so much time battling the establishment, trying to change the norms of the game. Now, at long last, I was being accepted. It was clear proof that what I had worked so hard to achieve hadn't gone unnoticed.

Of course, I didn't set out to be an activist, or a political dissident, or a symbol of gender equality. I just wanted to be great at chess. Yet, from as early as I can remember, I was surrounded by people who told me I wasn't allowed or not capable, and that my gender, my religion, even my nationality made me ineligible for greatness in anything, including this game that I love. A lot of people would have accepted these backward ideas, or at least learned to live with them. And my life may have been far easier had I done exactly that. I just refused.

My rebellion put me at war with a powerful regime bent on oppression and discrimination and made me an enemy of the state and a "prisoner" in my own country. But it also gave my life a purpose. What had started as a childhood passion for a beautiful game became something far larger: a battle for equality and recognition—not just for myself, but for millions of others who had been pushed to the margins of society and made to feel unworthy, incapable, broken.

It's a battle that still needs fighting.

The last few years have revealed a saddening number of instances in which female players have been harassed, belittled, and even assaulted by bad actors in the chess community, all of them men. My heart goes out to all of those victims, and to the countless more whose stories have yet to be acknowledged. Every one of those episodes is shameful evidence of how much work remains to be done.

I have shared my story in these pages to demonstrate that the ignorant hatreds and toxic ideologies that still pervade our world aren't as insurmountable as they seem. That if you want it badly enough, and are willing to work for it, they can be defeated. I'm living proof.

ACKNOWLEDGMENTS

I have written or co-written many books in my life, most of them technical treatises aimed at serious chess players. This book is different. It was written with the aim of inspiring anyone who has a goal to do what it takes to achieve it, no matter how impossible that goal might seem. And it came about because of the encouragement of a long list of friends and fans whose names are too numerous to mention.

A special thanks goes to Robert Herritt, who helped me with the writing, along with Suzanne O'Neill, who was essential help during the editing process. I'm also deeply grateful to Yasser Seirawan for his generous and thoughtful foreword to this book.

Naturally, the biggest thanks go to my family, and especially my mom, dad, grandparents, my sisters Sofia and Judit, my husband Paul, and my kids. They have been there with me through the triumphs, challenges, setbacks, and successes that have made my life a story worth telling.

I also would like to thank all my chess coaches and sparring partners who worked with me throughout my playing career, and who helped me understand the beauty and depth of our sport better.

I owe a huge debt of gratitude to my students, who were willing to work hard and make enormous sacrifices for the success of our teams. I am equally thankful to the administrators and colleagues who supported me at both Texas Tech and Webster University and who contributed immensely to the success of the SPICE program.

Finally, I would like to thank the supporters of the Susan Polgar Foundation, without whose help a lot of my work over the past two decades benefiting thousands of young people around the country would not have been possible.

APPENDIX

B obby Fischer and I played countless games of Fischer Random during the time we spent together, typically over dinner while waiting on our orders. Today, the variant is played with a symmetrical setup, in which the back rank of pieces is arranged in the same random way for both players before the game begins. That's not how we played, though—at least not early on.

Instead, we would begin each game with an empty back rank. Then, we would use our first eight moves to choose for ourselves where on the back rank each piece would start the game. In the end, each player would have a different, nonsymmetrical arrangement of pieces. Without the restriction of symmetry, there can be millions and millions of different starting positions. Bobby used to say with a characteristic chuckle, "I wonder how anyone will be able to analyze and remember all of those openings?"

Bobby asked me never to publish the games we played. Out of respect for him, I turned down multiple offers over the years to compile a book of our games. However, I feel that it is important to give chess fans a glimpse at a few of those games, so that they can get a sense of the process Bobby and I went through in developing the final rules of Fischer Random.

Here is the position from one of our nonsymmetrical games. I was playing white, and Bobby had the black pieces.

Here Bobby played 1...Nd7, which looks tempting, as it targets my pawn on b6.

However, that turned out to be a mistake as I did not have to waste time defending it. Instead, I sacrificed my rook with 2.Rxa6! Seeing that, he resigned, understanding that if he captures my rook with 2...bxa6 I can force checkmate after 3. Rxc6+ Kb7 4. Rc7+ Kxb6 5.Qd6+ Ka5 6.b4+ Kb5 7. c4+ dxc4 8. Bc6+ Kb6 9. Bxd7. This was one of my favorite chess memories from our games.

Eventually, after months of experimenting with different ideas together, we learned from a mathematician we consulted that even if we keep the pieces on the back rank symmetrical, there can still be 960 different starting positions. Bobby decided that 960 is a big enough number to prevent players from relying on memorized openings. From then on, that's how we would play.

We reached the following position in one of those games that began with a symmetrical position (which today is often called Chess 960). I was playing with the black pieces, and I had just moved my queen from b8 to d6.

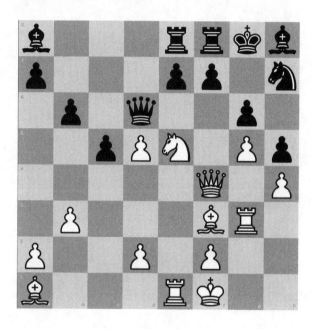

Bobby found a brilliant queen sacrifice with 1.Nxf7! which decided the game in his favor. If I capture the queen on f4, he check-mates me elegantly with 2.Nh6. Or if I capture the knight with 1... Rxf7, I would lose substantial material after 2.Qxd6. Recognizing this, I resigned.

ABOUT THE AUTHOR

Hungarian-born **SUSAN POLGAR** is one of the most decorated female chess players ever. She was discovered as a child prodigy, when at age four, she won the Budapest elementary school championship for girls with a perfect 10–0 score. In 1984, at age fifteen, she became the youngest ever to earn the world number one ranking. In 1986, she made history by qualifying for the Men's World Championship but was not allowed to play due to her gender. In 1991, she broke the gender barrier again by being the first female in history to earn the men's grandmaster title by norms and rating. She is the only player in history to earn all six of the world's most prestigious chess crowns (world chess triple crown, individual and team Olympiad gold, and world number one ranking). She became the first player to ever play 1,131 consecutive games, winning 1,112 games while losing only 3! She also broke the record for 326 simultaneous games played with 309 wins, and the highest winning percentage (96.93%).

In addition to her storied career, Polgar founded the Susan Polgar Foundation, a nonprofit 501(c)(3) organization to promote chess, with all its educational, social, and competitive benefits throughout the US, for young people of all ages, especially girls. After her professional playing career, she became the only woman to coach a men's Division 1 collegiate team (Texas Tech 2007–2012 and Webster University 2012–2021). Her teams in the past ten years have won more world championships, national championships, major titles, and Olympiad medals than all other collegiate chess programs in the United States combined, including a record seven consecutive Final Four championships, and ten consecutive years as the number one ranked team in the nation. She was inducted to the US Chess Hall of Fame in 2019 and the World Chess Hall of Fame in 2023, becoming the only woman to be inducted in both. Susan was the subject of a National Geographic documentary titled *My Brilliant Brain.*